Foreword

This book has been long in the making. It was first conceived by those involved in establishing the Bayburn Historical Society in 1989 and intended for publication as a millennium project. For various reasons, it has – like fine wine – matured. This means that it has benefited from the input of a greater number of sources and authors.

'Twixt Bay and Burn' aims to set out the history of the two villages of Crawfordsburn and Helen's Bay. It does not aspire to be an academic tome, but rather an easily readable book that can as simply be dipped into, as read from cover to cover. The editor and the Historical Society trust that there are no glaring errors, and have taken considerable pains to avoid them, but some of the accounts are inevitably subjective, reflecting individual perceptions and understandings. This also entails an element of duplication, as the narrative permits each author their own take on events. The book has to cover the big houses and some of the leading personages, but we have also sought to include a rounded perspective, reflecting all sections of society over the years.

The production of the book has been a collaborative project, drawing in particular on material obtained by the Bayburn Historical Society since its formation. We have been fortunate to draw on memories and material from residents who have sadly passed on and those who are no longer living in the two villages, as well as current residents. Of particular note are the elements that borrow from the work of the late Margaret Garner, an eminent local historian. Where a section has been written by one individual, the attribution is made clear.

To all of the contributors, we acknowledge our debt and gratitude. The book also contains a range of illustrations, including pen and ink drawings of local architectural features by Stuart and Basil White, both former chairs of the Historical Society. We are very grateful to all those who have participated in sharing their reminiscences and their photographs and other records. For assistance in preparation for publication, we gladly record our debt to the North Down Museum, the Ulster Local History Trust and to the Ulster-Scots Agency.

The editor in particular is conscious that in researching for this book, several stones have been left as yet unturned. It would be possible to delve a good deal deeper into some recesses of the past, drawing for example more fully on what might be available at the Public Record Office. Additional local residents might have recollections. It is certainly not our intention feel they might have had a contribution to make. However the view has been taken that the account has reached a point where enough has been obtained to do some justice to the story of the two villages. Indeed it may be politic to leave scope for future historians.

Perhaps three words sum up the picture captured in this book – community, characters and continuity. The change has been vast, yet the two villages retain their essential spirit. Who knows what the future will bring? As John Masefield wrote:

'To most of us the future seems unsure – but then it has always been so and we who have seen great changes must have great hopes.'

We hope that you will enjoy this book and that it may stimulate further interest in the history of our area. The Bayburn Historical Society would be delighted to respond to any enquiries, and to hear from readers who may wish to contribute their reminiscences and perspectives. Enquiries may be directed to the following e-mail address bayburnhistoricalsociety@hotmail.co.uk

Acknowledgements

As shown in the text, extracts from the Thomas Raven maps and a number of photographs are published with the agreement of North Down Museum. The portrait of Sir James Hamilton is courtesy of the National Trust, Castleward. The Dufferin illustrations are by kind permission of the Dufferin and Ava Archive. The Sharman Crawford portraits are reproduced courtesy of the Trustees of National Museums Northern Ireland. Thanks are also due to many local residents and others who have kindly provided photographs, postcards, sketches and other material that add to the pictorial illustration of our past. A full list of acknowledgements is at page 151.

Compiled and edited by Robin Masefield, on behalf of the Bayburn Historical Society, autumn 2011.

Chapter 1

The Beginnings

Introduction

'*Twixt Bay and Burn*' sets out the history of the two villages of Crawfordsburn and Helen's Bay. While of very different origin, both are attractive, largely semi-rural settings, rich in historical interest. This book, primarily compiled by local residents involved in the Bayburn Historical Society, also drawing on the recollections of former residents, aims to be of interest to all those who wish to know more about the area.

As in much of Ireland, our local history has been significantly shaped by the principal landowners and church activities. The two main estates are at Clandeboye House, the home of the Blackwood family (currently headed by the Marchioness of Dufferin and Ava), and the former Crawfordsburn House, previously the home of the Sharman Crawfords. The development of Crawfordsburn owed a good deal to its location on the route initially to Bangor Abbey and later to the port at Donaghadee, while the development of Helen's Bay followed the coming of the railway in the 1860s.

Crawfordsburn (from Ulster Scots: Crawford's burn meaning *Crawford's stream* – Irish: *Sruth Chráfard*) is a small picturesque village in County Down, Northern Ireland. The village lies between Holywood and Bangor to the north of the A2 road, about 4 kilometres west of Bangor town centre. Bounded to the north and north-east by Crawfordsburn Country Park, the village attracts many visitors. It had a population of just 127 in 1911, which had risen to 531 by the 2001 Census. Both it and neighbouring Helen's Bay are in the Borough of North Down; they are designated as proposed areas of village character in the draft Belfast Metropolitan Area Plan.

Before the Plantation of Ulster (*the land of the Ulaid* in Norse), the area of Crawfordsburn was known as Ballymullan (Irish: *Baile Ui Mhaoleín*). Crawfordsburn originated in the 17th century as a small settlement on an important route along North Down. It was named after a stream, which flows through the village. Although not as large as the neighbouring towns of Bangor, Holywood and Newtownards, Crawfordsburn was nevertheless an important element in the settlement of North Down by the Ulster Scots. It has retained aspects of its 17th century history along its Main Street including the coaching inn. The Sharman Crawford family developed the village in the 18th and 19th centuries. Crawfordsburn was promoted as a Victorian tourist attraction, particularly for those visitors using the railway to nearby Helen's Bay.

Helen's Bay is named after Helen, Lady Dufferin (née Sheridan), mother of Frederick Hamilton-Temple-Blackwood, First Marquess of Dufferin and Ava and the owner of the Clandeboye Estate. Helen's Bay was a planned village, which derived from the building of the Belfast and County Down Railway (BCDR) in the mid-19th century, and the aspirations of the local landlord, the Marquess of Dufferin and Ava, who wanted to develop the area as a luxury holiday resort to rival Portstewart and Portrush. The granting of 'villa' or 'house-free' tickets by the BCDR Company, which entitled the holders to free travel for a period of time if they constructed houses within one mile of the station, encouraged further development of the settlement. It had a population of 1,362 according to the 2001 Census.

Geology and Pre-History

The geology of the area is quite complex. We know that it reflects tectonic activity over hundreds of millions of years. Horse Rock at the south-western end of Helen's Bay beach was formed by lava from underwater volcanoes some 450 million years ago in the Ordovician period. But the dominant rock types are sedimentary including mudstone and greywacke (a muddy sandstone). The sedimentary rocks found at the headland between the two beaches are mudstones, which were deposited in a deep ocean basin. Much of this stretch of coast is dominated by greywackes, beds of muddy sandstone formed when earthquakes caused submarine landslides to sweep sand and mud from the continental shelf into the deep ocean basin. All of these rocks later underwent intense deformation caused by tectonic mountain-building processes associated with the collision between continental plates. This has steeply tilted the once horizontal layers and caused them to bend or break in many places, evidence for the type of plastic rock deformation which is to be found in the prehistoric roots of many mountain ranges and altered the mudstones into a slate-like metamorphic appearance.

A little closer to Belfast, at Craigavad (*rock of the boat*) and Cultra (*back of the beach* or the *corner of the strand*) there is clearer evidence of the different developments, from as long ago as about 350 down to only 60 million years ago. There we know that for millions of years a thin limestone band embedded with dark mudstones existed before it was crushed and eroded between adjacent harder rocks. It also suffered from the depredations of some 30 members of the Belfast Naturalists Field Club, the record of whose excursion to this part of the shore on 2 June 1883 is worth quoting:

> *'A short distance west of the pier thin bands of Carboniferous limestone are noticeable, beneath which is a grey shaley band rich in fish remains. The members who were fortunate enough to be possessed of hammers and chisels attacked this vigorously, and were soon handing round slabs showing scales and spines of Holoptychius, one of the ancient race of armour-plated fishes, which attained its highest period of development in the old red sandstone or Devonian seas…. A few yards further west of this outcrop, the Triassic beds are brought in by a fault, the line of which, like most of the fault lines here, is occupied by a basaltic dyke. After the excitement of the search for fish remains had in some measure abated, a brief notice of the geology of the neighbourhood was read by one of the party…. (Moving eastwards) the boulder clay which covers the beach here is excessively compact, and may in all truth be termed a conglomeritic rock. The geologist of the distant future will surely be delighted with the varied contents of this deposit… latest among the rock groups… it yields generously to the labours of the agriculturalist, and rewards his toil…. Fossils have also been recorded from these beds, they are however exceedingly rare.'*

The party noted that many of the ancient buildings in the neighbourhood have derived part of their material from these beds including Carrickfergus Castle and church. After a short halt at the sheltered little pier at Rockport, the party adjourned to the home of Thomas Workman at Craigdarragh House, where they examined many objects of interest including the large collection of Arachnidae. As the four hours ramble along the shore had given them 'a keen edge to appetite, ample justice was done to the good things so hospitably provided.'

Returning to our current geological assessment, while one can discern in local faults some evidence of the huge pressures on the landmass caused by continental drift in former ages, there is little to confirm that Northern Ireland, as part of Pangaea, was once in the equatorial region. The area is also short of fossil material, although we are blessed with some of the most beautiful beaches in Northern Ireland, adorned with child-friendly sand.

Drumlins (*small ridge* in Gaelic) are of course a feature of the County Down landscape. They were formed by the movement of the receding Ice Age some 15,000 years ago. They have had effects on subsequent development, such as field patterns and the routes of minor roads. Raths (round forts) were usually built for defensive purposes on

Above: Sunset behind the rath on Irish Hill, Helen's Bay.

the top of drumlins. In recorded times, tree cover in Northern Ireland has been much below that in the rest of the United Kingdom, even though at the start of the 19th century grants were offered to those willing to plant trees to improve the position.

One feature of which many local residents will be well aware is the thick layer of clay that underpins so many of our gardens. An article in a local paper (*The Downpatrick Recorder*), dated 4 October 1856, bemoaned the fact that 'the soil of the home farm at Clandeboye is naturally a heavy clay, of a cold, retentive nature.' (The same article later recorded that Lord Dufferin was awarded a gold medal and the Purcell Cup 'for the greatest quantity of land in Ireland drained in the most efficient manner'.) While this may not hinder the growth of certain plants such as roses, it can also lead in rainy periods to lying water - creating areas similar to the 'mosses' identified in Thomas Raven's 17th century maps. The two villages do however benefit from their proximity to the sea and indeed to the Gulf Stream. Plants such as palms and *Griselinia* thrive here when they would not elsewhere. (Incidentally, when Helen's Bay Golf Club undertook work during the war, some of the clay they excavated was used by local residents to make coarse pottery.)

The last great ice sheet which had spread here from Scotland (Ailsa Craig microgranite pebbles can still be found on the beach), and could have been 2000 metres thick, commenced its recession around 12,000 BC, and by 8,000 BC the climate had warmed sufficiently to provide habitable conditions over the whole of Ireland. However, by this time the last land bridges between Great Britain and Ireland had been severed, and early people must have arrived by boat, crossing the narrow waters from Scotland and Wales. They would have found a land with spreading thick oak and elm forests through which transport was becoming difficult or impossible, so they lived around the coastline, and so it is that the first evidence of human presence in this area is in the form of flint arrow heads, found by local resident John Murphy. While some were found a few fields inland from the shore (as the sea level was higher then), it does appear also that there was an actual settlement at Grey Point; it is marked as an occupation site in the *Archaeological Survey of County Down*.

The illustration is a sketch of Mesolithic flint tools found around Irish Hill in Helen's Bay. (Top left is a harpoon, in the middle is a concave scraper, while the bottom row contains a hand-axe.) The finding of hammer stones would indicate that the flints were knapped on site, while a harpoon would suggest that fish were caught locally. The implements date from around 6500 to 5000 BC. These were Mesolithic or Larnian

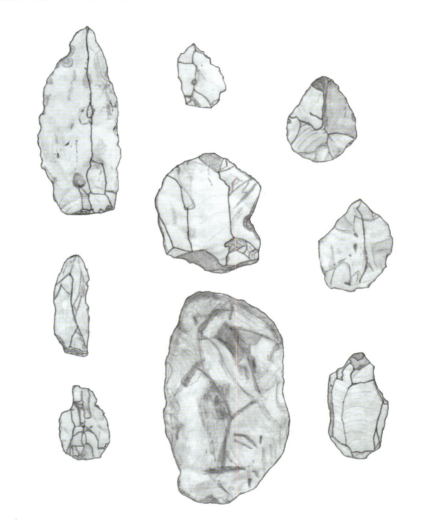

Above: Pencil drawings of Mesolithic flint tools found around Irish Hill, Helen's Bay.

people, hunter-gatherers, who lived by fishing, hunting and gathering fruit and berries. They would have hunted the Irish 'elk' *crevus giganteus* and wild boar, and had to deal with wolves and bears. They had no agriculture or permanent dwellings, so left few traces behind them. About 3000 BC a fresh wave of people (Neolithic) arrived, bringing with them agriculture and religion which moved them to erect megalithic tombs. They had polished stone axes, which enabled them to clear some of the trees, so beginning the transformation of the landscape to what we know today. These ancient people soon became the dominant population of Ireland, and have remained so to this day. They are the principal ancestors of the present day population.

Around 500 BC there were arrivals of Celtic-speaking people (Q Celts) whose superior Bronze and Iron Age culture and Celtic language replaced earlier forms throughout Ireland, although their influence was out of proportion to their relatively small numbers. Their Celtic language would have been spoken in North Down, as elsewhere in Ireland, until the coming of the English (Norman) and Scottish (Plantation) settlers, but before that, there was the arrival of Christianity in the 5th century, the foundation of Bangor Abbey and Holywood Priory, and the Norse raids from the end of the 8th century. No Norse remains have been found in Helen's Bay or Crawfordsburn, though a Viking burial has been unearthed at Ballyholme. The Norsemen came south from the Scottish islands, landing first on Rathlin Island and then raiding Bangor (believed to be from *Beannchair*, place of cow horns) and continuing on to Lough *Cuan* (Strangford Lough) and beyond. They must have had a significant presence on the shores of Belfast Lough, having established a trading depot on the Copeland Islands (*Kaupmanneyjar = Merchant Island* in old Norse, from the *Saga of Hakon the Old*), and Grey Point, in clear sight from there, would have given excellent shelter from the prevailing winds as it does to today's yachtsmen. These warlike pagans destroyed the monastic settlement they found at Nendrum and fought battles at Downpatrick, leaving their king, Harald Barelegs (because he wore a kilt), dead at Ballydugan where his alleged burial mound may still be seen.

At this time, while Crawfordsburn was on the main route from the ecclesiastical capital at Armagh to Bangor Abbey established in 558 AD (where at one time no less than 3,000 students trained), the area which is now Helen's Bay was an undrained marshy triangle between this route and the coast, unattractive and off the beaten track. So it was that Crawfordsburn developed into a village while Helen's Bay remained an inaccessible wilderness until much later. The name, Clandeboye, is also of later origin, deriving from the *Clann Aodha Buidhe* (family of the blond-haired), a branch of the Northern Ui Neill, first recorded as a place name in 1590.

Sixteenth and Seventeenth Centuries

Helen's Bay and Crawfordsburn were in the possession of Bangor Abbey until the dissolution of the monasteries around 1540 in this area. In 1555, the Lord Deputy and Council of Ireland tacitly agreed to the assertion of the O'Neills of Claneboye that the land was theirs, with it going to Hugh mac Felim O'Neill. When Hugh was imprisoned, the land passed to his younger brother, Sir Brian mac Felim. Queen Elizabeth granted the land to Sir Thomas Smith, her Secretary of State, in 1571. Smith made an unsuccessful attempt to set up a major colony based on what became Newtownards, (as chronicled, for example, in the Ulster-Scots Agency booklet on *Sir Thomas Smith's Forgotten English Colony of the Ards and North Down in 1572*). Despite describing this area as 'a land that floweth with milke and hony… another Eutopia', Smith failed to oust the Clandeboye O'Neills from County Down. With the death of Sir Thomas's illegitimate son in 1573 (he was killed and his body was boiled and fed to the dogs), and the death of Sir Brian (beheaded by the English) in 1574, the land was claimed by his cousin, Con O'Neill whose seat was in Castle Reagh. On his death in 1589 the land went to Con mac Neill mac Brian O'Neill. This latter Con was imprisoned by the English, at Carrickfergus Castle. It is reputed that he came to an agreement with Sir Hugh Montgomery, a Scotsman, that if Hugh agreed to help him escape he would give him half his land. Con did escape in due course. In order to secure the land, Con and Hugh joined up with another Scotsman, Sir James Hamilton, who had been educated at St Andrew's and was for a while a schoolmaster in Dublin where he played an important part

Above: *Sir James Hamilton, Viscount Claneboye 1559-1644.*

in the early history of Trinity College, being its Bursar in 1598. One of Hamilton's students was James Ussher, later Archbishop of Armagh, who calculated from the Bible that the world began in October 4004 BC.

It was probably Sir Thomas Smith's nephew, Sir William Smith, who took over the grant to the original 'colony', and who whetted Hamilton's appetite; it was written later that he had been 'tricked out of it by the knavery of a Scot, one Hamilton.' Hamilton made application to James I for all the land, which was granted, the property then being split three ways. In a short time Con had lost his share apart from land at Castlereagh, with most of it ending up in the ownership of Hamilton (Bangor) or Montgomery (Newtownards and Donaghadee). (Sir Walter Scott referred to the loss of land by O'Neill and the beauty of Clandeboye in *Rokeby, canto v* – 'Ah, Clandeboye! Thy friendly floor Slieve Donard's oak shall light no more!')

Hamilton and Montgomery are seen as two of the founding fathers of the Ulster Scots. They advertised successfully for settlers in their native Ayrshire, with the initial arrival from Portpatrick at Donaghadee in May 1606 of the first boatload and then in greater numbers thereafter. It is believed that Andrew Crawford, who gave his name to the village of Crawfordsburn, came from Kilbirnie in North Ayrshire. Indeed, although they may not have settled in the village on their first arrival, some of the other family names which have been prominent in Crawfordsburn over the past 100 years or so, are those associated with early settlers such as Lindsay and McEwen.

The Montgomery Manuscripts record that the first settlers found little to help them as much of the land in North Down had been laid waste. The rent in those early days was about one shilling an acre, per year. However, within a few short years, the settlement had taken root.

Although they had been childhood neighbours, relations between the two founding Scots were never good – in his will Montgomery stipulated that any daughters of his should have no dowries if they married Hamilton men. In the same will he did however remember some of the native Irishmen who had helped him in his early days – James O Dornan, Manus O Hamill of Ballyholme and Towl Og O Gilmore of Ballysallagh were to pay little or no rent for good land.

Montgomery died in 1636, having on 8 September a huge funeral at the Newtownards Priory, presided over by Bishop Leslie who had the previous month deposed four Presbyterian Ministers who sailed the very next day with 136 other Ulster Scots settlers on the 'Eagle Wing' from Groomsport. One of the Ministers was Rev Robert Blair, who had subsequently married one of Montgomery's daughters, Catherine, and was the founding Minister of First Bangor Presbyterian Church in 1623. (Blair had been brought to Bangor by Hamilton. His first wife was Beatrix Hamilton, a sister of Jenny Geddes who famously threw her stool at the Dean of Edinburgh in July 1637 when he read from the *Anglican Book of Common Prayer* in St Giles.) By coincidence the first three of First Bangor's Ministers married descendants of Montgomery. The wife of the 2nd Earl of Clanbrassil (Viscount Claneboye) pulled down the original Bangor church, obliging the congregation to use 'a green hill overlooking the sea' as their meeting place for several years.

Hamilton lived on until 1644, having been created Viscount Claneboye in 1622.

Although John Blackwood bought Ballyleidy (now Clandeboye) in July 1674 from the 2nd Earl of Clanbrassil who died the following year, much of the land passed to James Hamilton of Neilsbrook in County Antrim in 1676 on the death of the third Viscount, this Hamilton being the nephew of the first Viscount. His daughter, Anne, married Colonel Hans Stevenson of Ballygrot. In the 1740s we find both Robert Blackwood of Ballyleidy and John Crawford of Crawfordsburn as 'Gents of this part' and leading members of First Bangor Presbyterian Church which achieved a new site for the church by the shore. The full lands finally came into the possession of the Blackwood family, when the Stevensons' granddaughter, Dorcas (created Baroness Dufferin and Claneboye in 1800) married Sir John Blackwood of Ballyleidy. (In 1798, the Blackwood family which had originated in Fife was itself a house divided; Sir John Blackwood was described as 'a friend to the United Irishmen', while his second son Sir James Stevenson Blackwood was in the Army which defeated them at Ballynahinch.)

Maps, Rent Rolls and Other Sources

Maps over the centuries tell us a good deal about the development of the two villages, though they also provide for further speculation. (In this section the original townland names are used as they appear in the records.)

In 1625, partly as a result of disputes over the land with Montgomery, James Hamilton commissioned an English map-maker and surveyor, Thomas Raven, to produce maps for all his lands which ran from Orlock through Bangor to Holywood and extended to Comber and Ringdufferin. The superb original *Raven Maps* can be seen in the North Down Museum (having come from the Dufferin family through the Wards of Bangor Castle). Many of the townlands which now make up the villages of Helen's Bay and Crawfordsburn are shown - Balle Skalle, Balle Grott, Balle Robert and Balle Gilbarte – today's Ballyskelly, Ballygrot, Ballyrobert and Ballygilbert. (Ballydavey is shown as Balle Deved.)

The Ulster Scots mostly kept the traditional townland names; each townland usually covers about two or three hundred acres. Where the townlands are not named, the maps instead show the names of local landowners, for example around Crawfordsburn, Andrew Craford,

Top right: The compass and dividers motifs from the Raven maps. Above: The Raven Map of the Helen's Bay area.

William MaGee and Quintin Hamelton (and the size of their holding – 117 acres in Craford's case). Reliable information about boundaries, acreage, mills and tenants was at a premium for the early settlers. At the boundary between Ballyskelly and Craford's land is shown a 'myll' – the only building depicted in Crawfordsburn, while a striking triangular fort is shown on the shore at the boundary between Ballyrobert and Ballygrot, (close to a word that might be read as 'tombs'). The map however does not do full justice to the promontory of Grey Point. (One suggestion is the name derives from a Mr Grey who was shown as owning the land on a 1570 chart of Belfast Lough, although this may be doubtful given this was about the time of the original Smith plantation.) Although Raven was not greatly interested in topography, two raths or round hill-top forts are marked within Ballygrot – one close to the summit of what is no doubt Irish Hill, and another at the south end of the Ballyrobert/ Ballygrot boundary. (This could well be at what is now the Cheatley's farm at Brookmount.) The latter rath is marked as fairly close to a cross which might perhaps indicate some form of a chapel in that locality, closer to the boundary with Ballydavey. (Incidentally Raven's mapping of Bangor is enlivened with some charming if primitive depictions of rabbits in the Cuney Borrow.) It is understood that a project is beginning on making the *Raven Maps* more accessible which is likely to help our future understanding of the rich, indeed unique, information they provide.

From Seamus Pender's edition published in 1939 of the 1659 *Census of Ireland* commissioned by Sir William Petty, we have some population figures. This shows the princely total of 36 inhabitants at Ballemullen, 20 in Ballygrott and Ballyskelly combined, and just 7 in Ballygilbert; divided between the 'English and Scotts' and 'Irish', the respective sub-totals for the three areas are 27 and 9; 14 and 6; and 6 and 1. This suggests a very limited settlement of this particular locality at this time (though note the impact of the Ballydavey massacre in 1642, as set out in the account below).

We next have the original *Rent Rolls* of Bangor and the surrounding area, on the Estate of Viscount Claneboye who was also the Earl of Clanbrassil. The full title of this historic book, again held by the North Down Museum, is the *Rent-Roll and Tenures of the Estate of Henry the Viscount Claneboye and 2nd Earl of Clanbrassil, 1670*. The distinguished local historian Margaret Garner analysed the document in an article for the Belfast Natural History and Philosophical Society (which she discussed with the editor subsequently).

The tenures, with leases dating from as early as 1623, give a unique glimpse into life in North Down as it was then lived by the settlers. The first requirement for agriculture was fencing or at least enclosure which features prominently in the leases, accompanied by hedging and ditching. When it came to ploughing, the settlers were assisted by the local cottiers who had previously done both this and herding for the Irish lords – one account recorded that the settlers found them 'quick and clever at their work'. The crops sown by the planters were almost entirely oats and barley (often of the kind called *bere*, found in Ayrshire, which was less likely to be flattened in wet weather) – wheat is only mentioned once. (Current gardeners who find that peas and beans can be grown well on the clay soil of North Down may be interested to know that a Pea Hill is recorded on a *Raven Map*.) Kelp, as well as manure, was spread on the fields. They reared cattle and sheep, hens and cocks.

When the corn was harvested, it had to be ground; the mill

Above: The Raven Map of the Crawfordsburn area.

plays an important part in the *Rent Book*. The mills all belonged to the Earl who would lease them to his chief tenants. Practically every lease includes the requirement on the tenant to take his grain to be ground at the landlord's mill, usually paying a portion both to the landlord and to the miller. Another requirement was to take any small legal cases to the Manor Court. In a lease of 1674,

'.. the Toole and Moulter of ye succan of ye sd mill, except B Robert and B Davy, which after ye exploration of ye lease granted to sd W Crafford and his mortgage paid is to be of ye succan of Holywood Mill.'

Some explanation is required. The miller made his profit from the toole and moulter which were terms for payments to him, while the succan is the acreage of the area from which a miller could expect to draw his customers. There was a stiff fine for every bushel of corn which a tenant had ground at any mill other than his lord's. (Although an Act of Charles II made the hand mill or quern illegal, the Irish continued to use them, even despite bailiffs breaking querns up wherever they could be found. Nor were millers popular – in 1641 the miller of Balloo near Killinchy was mutilated and left to die.)

As there were few trees, the settlers had to turn to bogs or mosses for their fuel; though there were plenty, these too belonged to the Earl or his chief tenants. In the 1674 lease to William Crafford the reference to 'all royalties especially the waies leading to the mosses of B. Leidy and Bangor' shows the importance of keeping the tracks to the bogs open; again individual tenants had no choice over their source of peat. 4d was the going rate payable by each man for a day's cutting – it was also the value of an individual hen.

The rent was to be paid in a variety of ways, usually including cash, livestock (beef, mutton and/or hens and capons – though not pigs), cereal, and often days work. Interestingly there are two early references, (though as it happens not in relation to Crawfordsburn), to tenant right – its importance in subsequent centuries is described in Chapter 9 on the Sharman Crawfords.

Turning to the local detail in the *Rent Roll*, unlike the *Raven Maps*, it now uses the term Bally Mullin. The records show that William Crafford was renting from 1674 part of Bally Killare and 80 acres of Bally Mullin which included a (mortgaged) corn mill; his rent included eight pounds, one bole of oats to the bailiff and 4 pence for each day's cutting in the Earl's 'mosses' (peat bogs – Raven also called them mosses) of Bangor and Ballyleidy. The heiress of Archiboll Hamilton of Ballygroat had had the deed to Ballyskelly since 1626, for which including the mill 'then built on the premises' the rent was no more than 10 shillings, a proportion of King's rent – five shillings, one choice fat beefe and six days work of man and horse. The rent for Ballygroat was however as much as three pounds. In both cases an additional stipulation was that the 'mortuarys were not to be aliened without license'. The *Rent Roll* then lists individuals holding half, two-thirds or all of single tenements in Bangor, for which the rent was usually around 10 shillings, but here too in addition the holder must pay the Earl a prescribed number of hens and perform so many days work. One lessee in the Church Quarter of Bangor is recorded as having to pay '1 peper corne if demanded'. There were 108 leases of property in Bangor by this time, although almost all the houses were made of mud still, and most were thatched 'in the manner of the Scots', albeit a few had slate roofs.

In 1681, following the death of Alice, Countess of Clanbrassil four years earlier, when in legal proceedings the extensive Clandeboye Estate was assessed for division between two members of the Hamilton family, the total annual rental in cash amounted to £2,156. Some of the familiar names are shown eg John Blackwood at Ballyleedy and in Belfast Thomas Pottinger in Ballymacarett. William Crafford is again shown as renting parts of Bally Killare and Ballyornon etc. The Kennedys had considerable holdings in Bally-Robert, Bally-davy and Cregivad, (forming the basis for the future Cultra House Estate) and further afield; Hugh Kennedy of Bally Cultra was a 'Doctor of Physiche' with land as far as Ballybeen and Dundonald. He is also recorded in the *Montgomery Manuscripts* as having cured the Second Earl of Mount Alexander of a dangerous surfeit of fruit. Ballyskelly is held by William Hogg and Ballygrott by John Stevenson (who also shared Bally Killare with William Crafford) for annual rents of £18 pounds and 14 shillings each which would suggest a significantly higher valuation on the land by this time.

In a 1740 land register, an account of several seats in the manor of Bangor recognises 'Crawford's Burne of John Crawford Gent'. In 1744 a book by Harris on *The ancient and present state of County Down* noted that

'Gray Point shoots itself a good way into the Bay of Carrickfergus, forming a safe little harbour for boats, and is reckoned the extreme point of land in this county to the north'. In 1765 James Crawford of Crawfordsburn as a First Bangor elder is the representative at the Synod.

Skinner's 1777 *Maps of the Roads of Ireland* shows blank countryside between Mrs Pottinger at Craigavade and Crawford at Crawfordsburn. In later years it is recorded that land between Crawfordsburn and the Bangor Bog was farmed by the Cargo family (recorded in the street name today).

There are few accounts of the 1798 Rising that bear directly on the area. Kenneth Robinson's book records that

'Patrick Wightman of Crawfordsburn hurried to Bangor sometime on the 10th June, probably to try and prevent the swivel guns being taken off his sloops in the bay. Finding them gone, he continued to Conlig to remonstrate with the rebel leaders and urge the people to return to their duty, persisting in his loyal talk even in the insurgent camp on Scrabo'.

(The account comes from his subsequent court martial where he is listed as a merchant of Bangor, honourably acquitted.)

Crawfordsburn does feature directly in a letter from Colonel Atherton to General Nugent in Newtownards dated 20 June 1798:

'I have had tolerable success today. We have burned Johnston's house at Crawfords-Bourne-Mills at Bangor, destroyed the furniture of Pat Agnew; James Francis and Gibbison and Campbells not finished yet.'

Separately John Crawford of Crawfords-Bourn is listed as one of the local magistrates who were not to be found at this time and who were believed to have sympathies with the United Irishmen's cause. The Colonel wrote:

'A gentleman of any kind, but more particularly a magistrate who deserts his post at such a time, ought to be – I will not say what'.

Crawford was considered to have pushed for parliamentary reform in the previous year, rather than quieting his tenantry, thus giving encouragement to the enemies of the establishment.

One snippet from the early 19th century that has survived is a notice on behalf of the administrators of the deceased, advertising the sale by auction on 26 June 1811, at the house of the late Jane Finlay of Ballygrott, of all the household furniture, horses, cows, pigs, farming utensils, etc. The terms were very clear – sale was for 'ready money' only.

An important source of historical material is the *Ordnance Survey* series of maps beginning in the 19th century. (Unfortunately the maps are not yet at least available on-line; they can be viewed at the Public Record Office in the Titanic Quarter.) The maps are accompanied by the 'memoirs' of those involved in the compilation of the maps. In the Bangor parish the map and memoirs were produced by a Lieutenant Tucker and colleagues in the Sappers who were measuring the terrain in the 1830s; they may be said to have put Helen's Bay and Crawfordsburn on the map in 1835. We are fortunate that the memoirs have been published by the Institute of Irish Studies at Queen's University, although what they leave out is also a source of frustration for a modern historian. In his notes, Tucker described Ballygrot as 'seven acres of uncultivated land and patches of rocks' – as shown graphically on his map. (This was a reasonable assessment of its translation as *place of hillocks*.) Ballymullan is noted in the accompanying fair sheet for the 21 acres of mill pond and the corn mill belonging to Sharman Crawford MP. It has a large undershot wheel of 15 feet in diameter and 5 feet in breadth, bigger than many other similar mill-wheels as recorded. Referring generally to Bangor parish, he states that;

'.. owing to the very peaceable character of the inhabitants, there are generally but two or three policemen stationed at Bangor and there are no others within the parish. Outrages are scarcely ever heard of. No illicit distillation is carried on.'

He does however note the incidence of 'scrofula which is attributed to proximity to and intercourse with Scotland'.

Above: Auction notice for Jane Finlay's farm in Ballygrott, 1811.

His colleague, Lieutenant Bordes, commenting on Holywood parish is rather more prolix. The population breakdown of each townland is recorded, along with their occupations. Thus Ballyrobert has five farmers employing labour, five labouring farmers and 17 labourers employed by farmers, as well as 17 servants (mostly female), one person employed in handicraft, and one 'capitalist'. It is not recorded if this was the Miss Sims who was living in the 'gentleman's seat' at Glencarrick in Ballyrobert. While there were not many lime kilns, lime was obtained from quarries on the opposite coast of Antrim; stable dung manure was drawn from Belfast. He also noted drily 'a great quantity of rain falls'. John O'Donovan, one of the surveyors whose job it was to translate place names from Gaelic to English, protested that 'the pronunciation is very bad, mainly Scottish English and Irish which is completely unintelligible.'

The townland names mostly become fixed. Ballyrobert is marked to the west of Ballygrot up to and including Rockport House (built around 1800 according to architectural historian Tony Merrick), adjacent to Craigavad; however Ballyskelly is not shown, coming within Ballygrot. Irish Hill is marked by name in Ballygrot. Ballymullan is shown, and Ballykillare comes right up to the edge of Crawfordsburn village. Grey Point is now accurately mapped and Swinely Point is marked, though what is now Quarry Port is marked as 'Garry Port'. The area round Crawfordsburn House has a good deal of forestation, whereas there is very little woodland shown elsewhere. Close to the shore are marked two wooden bridges over the stream and both a bathing and a boat-house. Apart from the two big houses no habitation is named in Helen's Bay, though it does appear that farm buildings at Skelly Hill, Glenholme and Glenside are marked. (Sadly the map does not show a property on what is now Golf Road, Ardseein, which is rumoured to date from the 18th century. According to one previous account it was thought to have been built to control brandy smuggling in the bay. A small room originally on the ground floor with a narrow peep-hole could have made a temporary lock-up, as the walls are 22 inches thick. There was also rumoured to have been a tunnel running down to the sea in former times, but no trace has been found; an old well did however exist.) There are two buildings shown on Bell's Hill, with a track marked leading to the high point of Grey Point, the significance of which is explored in chapter 10.

Apart from a schoolhouse on the Ballymullan Road and another on the Cootehall road (not far from the present primary school site), only a few dwellings are shown in Crawfordsburn. (They do however include what was later named The Square – houses built for workers on the Crawfordsburn Estate – now all demolished on Old Windmill Road. Alfie Mairs was later born in a cream cottage which he described as being 'in The Square, but not of it'; the Estate carpenter, and Billy Johnston both lived in cottages in the Square.) The next big houses are in Ballykillare with Belle Vue and on the other side of the road, Ballywooley House. Two forts are shown, as are two quarries on the Ballyrobert Road near to 'Turner's Farm' close to what is now the main Bangor-Belfast Road, though no ecclesiastical remains are identified. There is another fort on the south side of the main road, close to Carney Hill. The windmill, known by some as Paddy Wightman's, is marked as a stump showing that by this time at least it had become derelict. (One local resident asserted that it had never fully functioned, although other research suggests it did feature as intact on a map dated 1767.) Interestingly the only track shown branching off from the Holywood to Crawfordsburn road follows pretty well the route of part of what later became the Clandeboye Carriage Drive – Craigdarragh Road did not exist. A flax mill and pond are shown in Ballysallagh.

A valuable source of information about residents is contained in *Griffiths Valuation* of 1863 which records occupiers and their landlords by townland. For example, Andrew Patterson is listed as holding from Lord Dufferin the house, offices and land in regard to Rockfield House. Lord Dufferin received half the annual rent of the Coastguard Station house and land, valued at 27 pounds, 10 shillings. One can also observe that

Above: The ruined windmill known as Paddy Wightman's in the Crawfordsburn Estate.

while in Ballygrot Lord Dufferin is the major land-owner, John Crawford also has some property. In Ballymullan their holdings would appear to be split roughly half and half, whereas in Ballygilbert, there are a number of smaller 'immediate lessors' including Henry, William and George McWha, and Robert Burns, besides Lord Dufferin. Paddy Wightman is recorded, though not specifically in relation to the ruined windmill. In a separate account, a local resident is recorded as receiving the sum of £130 from John Sharman Crawford in 1862 'being compensation and interest for the land taken from me at Ballygrot in November 1860.'

The development of the two villages has progressed by the time of the 1860s revision of the *Ordnance Survey map*, not least as the railway has now arrived, as has Craigdarragh Road, perhaps in part needed for access to lay the track. Craigdarragh House has just been built, continuing a line of new large houses along the coastal strip from Craigavad through Glencraig. We now find a new label – The Seapark – attached to an area between the railway line and Grey Point. A quay is marked at the end of Helen's Bay beach at Quarry Port, to which a track leads directly across what is now the golf course. Crawfordsburn House has by now erected its flagstaff. (It also had more than that, for *The Downpatrick Recorder* of 10 November 1855 noted that during a Viceregal visit to the Belfast area, a Royal salute was fired at Crawfordsburn.) 'Clandeboye' station in Helen's Bay is recorded, (although of course the subsequently adjacent Crawfordsburn Hospital and Seahill stations were not created for another hundred years). Helen's Bay is beginning to take shape, as one can see the makings of Bridge Road and Coastguard Avenue leading down to the 'Coastguard Station'. In Crawfordsburn the school is now designated as 'Ballymullan National School'. There is a second school on the Cootehall Road, and the mill pond is now more clearly delineated. A corn mill is marked in the village just above the waterfall. One can see the beginnings of the tree clumps planted by the Marquess but they are not given names until the next map in the series appears. The Carriage Drive now extends to Clandeboye on the other side of the Ballyrobert Road, (the bridge over the Drive there is dated 1854). Enfield House, at the corner of Craigdarragh Road and the main road has now been built. A big house at the boundary of Ballygilbert and Ballyrobert, is now named Sarahfield, with its own gatelodge. The flax mill is no more.

By 1904 the modern lay-out of the map is clear and the roads are named; the golf course is shown. In the 1901 census, there were 330 inhabitants living in 74 houses. Larger houses and villas are named, including Eldon Lodge, Tordeevra and Rathwyre on Kathleen Avenue in Helen's Bay, and Red and Glendore Houses in Crawfordsburn, as well as the Home Farm. (Glen House in Crawfordsburn either just before or after this time housed James Craig for a while.)

This map is the first to show the site of a church at Carrig Gorm, off Bridge Road of which no physical trace now remains, and about the existence of which Margaret Garner was somewhat sceptical, although Con Auld has more recently commented that it might have been a chapel of ease in connection with Bangor Abbey. Some light may be shed by the entry by Rev James O'Laverty, in his account of the *Diocese of Down and Connor Ancient and Modern, volume 2*, 1880. He recorded that on an old map in the possession of Lord Dufferin, a cross, of the Irish pattern, was drawn suggesting a location near the site of the railway station. O'Laverty suggested that as the townland name for Crawfordsburn was Ballykillare 'which might signify the townland of the Western Church, it is probable some old cemetery may be discovered in that locality'. The list of sites and monuments recorded on the DOENI website does list the site of a church and holy well at Ballygrot, so the authorities have come down on the side of the believers.

Clandeboye station is now shown as having a goods shed, while Helen's Bay has acquired a post office and a manse; Church Road however does not extend formally much past

Above left: Quarry Port looking towards Grey Point, 1912. Above right: The storm-damaged boat-house on Helen's Bay Beach.

the Presbyterian Church. Quarry Port has a 'perch' and a slip as well as a boat-house (which was demolished in a great storm in December 1989). Skelly Hill now appears, but not as its own townland. The school on Cootehall Road is now described as a 'Sunday school', and Cargo's Hill is shown; a sluice and weir are now shown below the mill pond. The corn mill above the Glen has by now been converted into a saw-mill. Two bathing houses are now marked at the western end of Helen's Bay beach, though the Crawfordsburn beach has lost its bathing hut. Even so, bathing was not without its dangers; *The County Down Spectator* of August 1910 contained the following article:

> *'A Belfast visitor had a narrow escape from drowning at Helen's Bay on Wednesday afternoon. The man was bathing near the Horse Rock when he got into difficulties and had sunk twice and was about to go under again when a timely rescue was effected. A couple of gunners of the Royal Garrison Artillery belonging to the adjacent Fort had taken in the situation at a glance. Leaping over the wall, they ran along the rock, and plunged into the water. Swimming out strongly they clutched the bather, whom they succeeded in bringing ashore.'*

Above: Church Road in Helen's Bay, before the First World War.

Helen's Bay was clearly attracting significant numbers of visitors from Belfast lured by accounts such as this one from the *Belfast and County Down Railway Guide* 1898:

> 'The water is delightfully pure. The beautiful sylvan and coast scenery, the bathing facilities, the shortness of the railway journey (about 20 minutes) and the convenient refreshment-rooms near the station, combine to make Helen's Bay one of the favourites of the Belfast seeker of a day's enjoyment.'

A final comparison is with the map from the 1930s. St John's Church Hall is marked, as are Point House (briefly used for Golf Club meetings and sadly demolished in the last couple of years) and Vancouver (as Pam Gilmer's bungalow was officially called); Horse Rock is so named. Church Road is now complete, including no 26 where Brian Faulkner, Northern Ireland's last Prime Minister, was brought up. He was born in Helen's Bay in February 1921; his father James owned the vast Faulat shirt business which at its height is reputed to have employed 3,000 people. The family moved to Helen's Bay for some years, after selling their Glengall Street accommodation to the Ulster Unionist Party.

In Crawfordsburn, the Country Club has been built with its 'Tennis Ground'. Power supplies now feature – among others, an electricity line is shown leading to Crawfordsburn House, and a windpump is marked near to the current Rosevale Cottages.

Above: The Old Mill Dam, Crawfordsburn.

The Ballydavey Massacre – 26 January 1642

Although the townland of Ballydavey is strictly outside Helen's Bay or Crawfordsburn, the scale of the little-known massacre on a wild winter's night early in 1642 justifies its inclusion in this book; moreover some of the perpetrators came from Crawfordsburn. The massacre does need to be seen in the historical context of a violent time, which included the 1641 rebellion and province-wide atrocities.

The Holywood historian Con Auld skilfully tells the tale in his recent book *Holywood Co. Down, Then and Now*, but the following account includes more of the testimony of eyewitnesses who survived. (The language is not always easy to read, but the original has been used throughout.) A Government Commission led by Ambrose Bedell to enquire into the events took evidence some 11 years later. The facts of the tragedy are not in dispute as a result of the Commission's work. (The depositions are held in Trinity College, Dublin and have been published on-line.)

In summary, a large group of Scots settlers, mostly from Bangor but including one or more from Crawfordsburn, and a group of Montgomery's horsemen, went to the small settlement known as the Island Field in Ballydavey, on what was then an island surrounded by a river and boggy land, occupied by about a dozen O'Gilmore families, tenants of Lord Clandeboye. The location is between the Ballymoney and Ballygrainey Roads, above Carney (Carnage) Hill, though no substantial trace exists today and it is not easy to view the site. (Interestingly, the adjacent pasture is known as Fort Field.)

Some months before there had been a fracas involving the O'Gilmores and Scots settlers at Dundonald, though given the disturbed state of the country and indeed the Proclamation referred to below, this is unlikely to have been the sole motivating factor.
After

> '.. that party of Scotch men did abyde with them and supt with the said Irish and were very merry till about midnight, the party fell upon ye said Irish and stript them and a little aforeday fell a-killing of ye sd. Irish.'

At the end of this treachery, 73 Irish had been killed.

Katherine O'Gilmore, who subsequently moved to Ballynahinch, escaped by hiding in a ditch. She told the Commission, which appears to have involved the High Court of Justice sitting at Carrickfergus:

> '8 days before Candlemas next, after ye Rebellion, shee then living in ye townland of Ballydavy, in ye Barrony of Castlereagh, altogether with tenn familyes more, of all which 11 familyes there were (of men, women, and children) killed to her own knowledge, seaventy and three by a great company of people (being) to her estimacon in number about 200, who were brought thither by one Andrew Hamilton of the fforte, James Johnson the elder, and James Johnson the younger, both of Ballydavy, John Crafford of Craford's Burne; and further she saith that James Johnson the elder killed one Henry O Gilmore, brother to the examinat, at her own sight, and likewise she saw the sd. James with his sword slashing at one Edmond Neeson, who was killed but shee knoweth not whether he made an end of him or not, for on the recept of the first blow, the sd. Neeson rann to the lower end of the house, among the rest of his neighbours, the cause of her knowledge is that a short space before, the said Andrew Hamilton had putt her out of the door of the house in consideracon of her tartan, after which shee lay her down in a ditch which was right before the door where she was unespied of any as she supposeth, the night being very darke, rayny and windie. The Examt. Further saith, she saw one Abraham Adam kill

Above: The believed site of the Ballydavey Massacre.

James O Gilmore, her owne husband, and Daniell Crone O Gilmore, and Thurlagh O Gilmore; shee further saith, that at her going forth of the house, a sister of hers tooke houlde of her for to go out with her, and the sd. Abraham Adam strock of her sd. sister's arme from the elbowe, with a broade swoord, the sister's name was Owna O Gilmore.

Owen O'Gilmore escaped by hiding himself in a limekiln on Ballydavey Hill. He told the Commission:

'Andrew Hamilton, now of Crawfordsburn in Bangor parish came to them who was to bring order for that work, and came and shott off his pistoll before Bryan Boy's doore, whereupon ye sd. Scots party fell upon killinge ye sd. Irish, and so killed of men, women and children, three score and odd, and ye names of ye persons yt this examt. remembers yt were at ye place yt night were ye sd. Andrew Hamilton, John Crawford, James Johnson senior, and James Johnson junior, Captain Will Hamilton, Robert Morris, John Watt and Gabriell Adam, and did see ye sd. Watt and Morris kill seven of ye sd. persons. Also this examt. saith, yt he, escapeinge this danger by hydeing himself in ye kilne, did so soone as he could escape thence towards one Hen. M'Williams M'Gilmore's house to secure himself, and as this examt. came nere the sd. house, he heard the Scotchmen aboute the sd. house, and so durst not go thither, but perceived yt ye sd. persons were the two James Johnsons, aforesd., and the said Watt and, others not known to this examt.; but this examt. heard ye sd. James Johnson junior, say to ye sd. Gilmore, Open the door, but ye sd. Gilmore denyed, and then ye sd. Johnson said, You know me, to wch. Gilmore said, yes he did, but for all ye must not open ye door; then ye sd. Johnson desired ye sd. Gilmore to light some straw, ye wch. Gilmore did, whereby ye sd. Johnson put in his pistoll and shott and kild ye sd. Gilmore, whereupon they broke open ye doore, and went in and kild one of ye children of ye sd. Gilmore and did wound ye sd. Gilmore's wiffe and one child more, and left them for dead, but ye sd. wiffe recovered and tould this examt. the foresd relation.'

Thomas O'Gilmore survived the massacre but only for four days. Owen reported what happened:

'Ye constable one Robert Jackson of Hollywood, did bring with him one Thomas O'Gilmore, uncle to this examt.; whom ye sd. Jackson brought to ye sd. place with his hands bound behynd his back with match, ye sd. Jackson brought ye sd. prisoner to Bangnell to ye ….

And ye sd. Capt. would not receave him at all; so so sd. constable took ye sd. prisoner back, and this exampt., thinking yt they would cary him to Bangnell accordingly did follow them; but as ye constable (and another man) went up ye mountaine betwixt ye sd. Kirkdonnell and Hollywood, this exampt. did see ye sd. Jackson, constable, kill ye sd. prisoner, Thomas O'Gilmore with a sword, and this exampt. did goe to him after yt ye sd. constable was gone away and perceaved severall wounds yt ye sd. Tho: had, both cutts and stabbs.'

We also have information about the planning of the event, which was clearly premeditated. James Gourdon of Clandeboye was pressed to join in the attack:

'His mother told him that there were some of the town, two or three tymes looking for him, to speake with him, and that she heard it was to goe out with them to kill the Irish that lived neere and about the towne; therefore she advised him to put himselfe out of the way and not to have any hand in the busines; whereupon he tooke his bed clothees and went and stayed and lodged in his mault kilne, a pretty distance from the sayd towne of Bangor. And he furthermore sayth that within a night or two after most of the towne of Bangor and the parish together made a compact with those of Ballydavy about Holliwood to fall out in two partyes in the night upon the neighbouring Irish to kill and plunder them. And they went forth in the night and killed of men, women and children (poor labouring people and their familyes) a great number. His cause of knowledge is, for that the next morning after the sayd murder was comitted he saw those of the towne of Bangor that had beene acters in it come in with bloody brakans (a kind of tartan or plaid) and other goods, cattle and household stuffe; his further cause of knowledge is that there was a collection made through the whole towne of Bangor for burying those were killed, wherefore this witness played a part but cannot now remember how much.'

Local tradition has it that many of the bodies were buried in the Ballydavey limekiln. These tragic events are not perhaps as well remembered as they should be. It is some comfort however that many townsfolk of Bangor were so appalled at the events that they contributed to a collection for giving those killed a decent burial. The Rev James O'Laverty writing in the late 19th century links this massacre, along with one in Island Magee, to the Proclamation issued by the Lords Justices and Council in Dublin Castle in 1641/42, which in effect encouraged

> 'all his Majesties good and loving subjects to pursue and plague with fire and sword, apprehend, destroy and kill, by all means and ways they may, named rebel leaders and their partakers, aiders etc'.

In his *History of Holywood*, P McNamee records that one consequence seems to have been that it 'completely cleared the parish of Holywood of the old Irish Catholic race.' Harris wrote in his *History of the County of Down* published in 1744 'it is said that only one papist lives in the parish' and the return given to the House of Lords in 1764 shows only seven; when the Catholic Bishop of Down and Connor caused a census to be taken in 1831 of all the catholics 'belonging to the chapel of Holywood', which included Dundonald and Crawfordsburn, the figure had risen to 81. Other sources suggest that at least some of the remaining Gilmores were driven into the southern end of the Ards peninsula, where the land was not so fertile.

Peter Galbraith who farms up Carney Hill, had another local source, long since passed on, who maintained that in addition no less than three Irish chapels had also been destroyed at around this time; there does not appear to be any contemporary record of that, but it may be worth noting that the *Raven Maps* do have one and possibly two chapels in roughly the right area, indeed the one at Craigavad was next to a plot recorded by him as the 'Priest's Quarter'. It is also suggested that the Ballydavey settlement could have been a more linear one, along the route of what was then an important track, probably between Crawfordsburn and Dundonald, (crossing the Ballymoney Road at Pinch Hill). It is a photograph of the supposed site that is shown. While no trace of the kilns or bodies has been found, local farmers have found mediaeval potsherds in the area, and there is an unusually large quantity of large stones at the one location.

Above: The Old Inn from the bottom of the Ballymullan Road, 1900s.

The Old Inn, Crawfordsburn

The Old Inn is probably the oldest building in the two villages. The thatched portion is the most ancient and is said to date from the end of the reign of Queen Elizabeth 1. Records show it was standing in its present form in 1614, though substantial additions were made in the mid-18th century comprising of kitchen quarters and some bedrooms. In former times it was known as the Old Ship Inn. The east wing is modern though it is based on Irish Georgian designs. There was further redevelopment in 2010, which again underlined the interconnection between the Inn and village life. When Donaghadee was an important cross channel port in the 17th and 18th centuries, the Old Inn was conveniently situated for the mail coach from Belfast that connected with the sailing packet, and horses were changed here. There were clearly many challenges in the early days. The road was described in one 19th century account as 'very badly maintained and almost impassable at times', which may be why it took three and a half hours for the journey from Donaghadee to Belfast.

Before that, the Inn-Keepers (Ireland) Act of 1662 had been introduced on behalf of,

> '.. gentlemen and others (who) are many times disappointed of their horses, and often do lose them upon pretence of stealth and the like, whereas sometimes they are conveyed away by the practice and privity of those who are entrusted with the keeping of them.'

In consequence every 'hostler and inholder' was made 'henceforth answerable for such horses, geldings or mares which shall be delivered to them to be kept'. The penalty for failure was – perhaps just as well – not specified. In the first half of the 20th century one 'inholder' was brought before the authorities on a different charge, but one which led to his relinquishing the reins of the Old Inn.

The Inn came to be patronised by many notable persons, including, it is said, such literary figures as Swift, Trollope and Dickens. Field Marshal Earl Roberts of Kandahar VC (whose active service ranged from the Indian Mutiny to the Boer War) and the First Marquess of Dufferin and Ava stopped in the Inn, and, more recently, former US President George Bush. (The tale was told by Mrs Greeves that when Roberts was at the Inn, he looked such an elderly care-worn gent that the lady of the house took pity on him and gave him dinner. Next day she received a vast bouquet of flowers from Clandeboye. It is also said that, as he had Irish and latterly Ulster connections, Roberts had been asked by the UVF to take on an honorary role during the crisis over the Third Home Rule Bill, but had declined on grounds of his age.) The 1937 film *The Luck of the Irish* included shots at the Inn according to Viney Robinson, a pioneer member of the Historical Society, who recalled that the family's straw from their cottage across the road had been used to make the scene authentic.

Above: Crawfordsburn Main Street, from near the burn.

Above: The same view (as on page 19) some 20 years later.

In earlier times, the Inn had also been associated with some famous names of the 1798 Rising, including, it is suggested, Henry Joy McCracken and Robert Emmet. Less well authenticated are visits by Paul Jones, Dick Turpin during a period of hiding in Ireland, and Peter the Great, Czar of Russia whom some claim visited ship-builders at Donaghadee. A portion of King William's Army, under the Duke of Schomberg, marched through Crawfordsburn on their way from Groomsport to join the main body of the forces in Belfast – it is not known whether they had the chance to sample its hospitality.

Ralph Bossence, writing in the *News Letter* in 1971, recorded that earlier in the last century the Inn was a meeting place for young men from the Continent who came from Belfast especially for Sunday lunch, and who were all employed as foreign correspondents in the linen industry. 'Extremely well-behaved they were,' according to Mrs Reid, then the proprietress. The owner before her had been a Mrs Campbell whose husband, a sea captain, was drowned. Her niece, Miss Jane McConnell, lived with the widow. When she was 15, she asked her aunt to let her make tea for passers-by, in addition to the traditional serving of alcohol. She in due course married Mr RR Reid, a traveller with Dunville's Distillery. Postcards from that era survive, showing the splendid tea verandah and 'the Garden of Eden'. Mrs Reid lived to be 94, in her house on Ballymullan Road close to the school. She was a familiar figure walking up the road in long skirts, even in the height of summer, with her bag of sovereigns.

Top left: The Tea Verandah at the Crawfordsburn Inn, RR Reid, Proprietor, telephone No 7, Helen's Bay.
Bottom left: Crawfordsburn Inn, Arbours and Rose Gardens. Bottom right: The Inn's old kitchen, in Mrs Reid's time (note the spinning wheel hung from the ceiling).

In 1885, writing in *The Bangor Season*, WG Lyttle noted that 'Mrs Campbell's hotel is too well known to require a passing word of recommendation', but did go on to add:

'Everything possible is done for the comfort of visitors… the charming gardens are usually crowded every day in the summer.'

Some 20 years later, it was clearly strong on musical entertainment too, as in 1907 there were no less than seven pianos on the premises, as well as 'an organ and a great ballroom', according to one appreciative patron.

In more recent times, CS Lewis stayed there regularly, including a week on a belated honeymoon with his bride Joy Davidman in 1958. He was a great friend of Arthur Greeves, a boyhood companion from their time in East Belfast, who had moved in 1949 to Silver Hill in Ballymullan Road, Crawfordsburn. It is recorded that from that year Lewis would usually spend the first week of his summer holidays at the Old Inn, a short walk from Silver Hill. (Hundreds of letters from Lewis to Greeves were published by Walter Hooper in 1979, titled *They Stand Together*.) While in Crawfordsburn, Lewis would worship at St John's, Helen's Bay.

The Inn still offers shelter and food to weary travellers, but sadly not at the prices obtained in the 1930s. Then Bed and Breakfast was 12 shillings and 6 pence (62 and a half pence today), Breakfast 3 shillings and 6 pence, Luncheon Table d'hote 3 shillings and 6 pence, Afternoon Tea 1 shilling and 6 pence, and Dinner Table d'hote 5 shillings. Weekly En Pension was from 4 guineas.

The owner after Mrs Reid, up to the early 1930s, was Mr William Johnston. In relation to a restaurant in Bangor long since closed, he was described thus in a letter to the *Spectator* 'a jolly, rubicund man who whistled and sang all day long, wore a straw boater both winter and summer and bathed in the sea every day of the year – one of Bangor's loveable eccentrics'. (Besides the Inn, he set up the Burlington in Ann Street in Belfast; one of his sons was known as Burlington Bertie.)

He and his wife Annie had eight children in all, six of whom survived to adulthood. Two sons were in the Navy during the second war, and Billy became a well-known Crawfordsburn character, as recorded later. His daughter Peggy, born at the Inn itself in 1914, recounted how most of the villagers worked for Colonel Sharman Crawford on his Estate. Pay day was Friday and they would descend on the Inn that evening. Her mother Annie would take their wages from them, give them a shilling to pay for a Guinness and a whiskey, and keep the rest safely to be collected by their wives in the morning. Peggy remembered handing out the stirrup cup when the hunt came to the village – a tradition that continues to this day. She served in the tea-room, writing down customers' orders in pencil on her big white cuffs. There was a separate room in the Inn where local farmers could do deals on their livestock. Christmas was an especially busy time, with no opportunity of festivities for the Johnston family.

Until the 1930s, the current Inn car park had remained a little field of rough grass, although there had originally been a cottage, including it is understood a butcher's shop on the site; some tumbled down walls remained for many years. CG 'Paddy' Falloon took on the Inn's lease in 1935. He remained the proprietor until later in the 1950s. Initially it seems that his former secretary took on the Inn, but after her husband's untimely death she sold the premises to Mrs White. Mrs White ('Madam') lived for some time in Craiglands off Kathleen Avenue, in Helen's Bay. She encouraged Thomas Lindsay to cut fallen trees in the Glen below the Inn to provide the hotel with its winter fuel supply, in return for which he could take enough for his own house. Her daughter Heather had a pony, and a wee trap, and took over the hotel for a short while until Mr Rice acquired it in the 1980s. Miss Crilly was the manager for some years for Mrs White; she ensured no single ladies were allowed unescorted into the Inn. George Rooney's brother Dan, who was a cabinet-maker from Tyrone who had come to live in the village in the 1920s, repaired the furniture.

Today the hotel's general manager is Brendan McCann who has been 46 years in the hospitality business; he was recruited by the Inn's current proprietor, Danny Rice. The Inn's famous thatched roof succumbed some years ago to storm. Thatchers were found in Coleraine who did the job with reeds imported from Turkey. Now American

Above: Mr William and Mrs Annie Johnston, with from left David, Peggy, Wilhelmina and Billy.

ambassadors, Ministers of State and Van Morrison put up at the Inn. The AA's award of two rosettes to the restaurant is an honour achieved by only some 30 establishments in the entire Islands.

Part of a student's discipline at the ancient colleges of Bangor Abbey included the grinding of his own meal supply, and for this purpose he was given a quern grindstone carved with the sign of the cross. One of these is to be seen in the hall of the Inn. Times do change though – the monks of old might find it hard to conceive that the place is now a licensed venue for weddings.

Above: Crawfordsburn Old Inn., early 20th century.

Chapter 2

The Development of Helen's Bay and Crawfordsburn

The Clandeboye Contribution

In the 18th century there seems to have been little to commend the Helen's Bay area. One commentator, a land agent, wrote to a County Down landowner in 1752 about Ballygrot:

'Poverty of tenants Townland of Ballygrot….than which I never saw so bad a corn country, tenants move with the face of poverty as they are constantly flitting, being only from one year and at will'.

However by the end of the following century:

'The beautiful and sylvan coast scenery, the bathing facilities, the shortness of the railway journey (about 20 minutes) and the convenient refreshment rooms near the station, combine to make Helen's Bay one of the favourite resorts of the Belfast seeker of a day's enjoyment.'

Thus Robert Lloyd Praeger commended the growing little 'watering place' with the pretty name in 1898. The eminent Irish naturalist and librarian at the National Library in Dublin had been commissioned to compile the *Belfast and County Down Railway's Guide to County Down*, and was almost on home turf here, as he was a Holywood man.

But it was another eminent North Down figure to which Helen's Bay owes its name, and, largely, its existence. Frederick Hamilton-Temple-Blackwood, First Marquess of Dufferin and Ava (1826-1902), Governor-General of Canada, Viceroy of India, and variously Ambassador to Russia, Turkey, Italy and France, was the epitome of the Victorian diplomat. Yet his long absences abroad did not hinder his enthusiasm for improving his estates. Renaming Ballyleidy House and reconstructing it as Clandeboye House; building Helen's Tower on the highest point of his estate; re-routing the main road over Craigantlet to make a huge lake; planting copses of trees on top of many drumlins: in these and many other ways the First Marquess left a personal imprint on the landscape of North Down that is still very much apparent today.

The young man attained his majority in 1847. *The Downpatrick Recorder*, dated 21 August, devoted several pages to the occasion of a dinner given by the tenantry at Ballyleidy House, including all the speeches. No hyperbole was omitted by the correspondent:

'The remarkable fineness of the day, the singular beauty of the scenery, the exhilarating music, the respectable and independent appearance of the men, assembled in one of the most fertile and comfortable districts of intelligent and happy Ulster, to pay a well- deserved tribute of respect to their youthful Lord – the scion of an ancient, noble and time-honoured family, all calculated to make a deep and lasting impression upon a thoughtful mind.'

In concluding his remarks, Lord Dufferin said that it would be his tenants' fault and not his, 'if their farms were not the best cultivated in the county, their children the best educated in the county, and their firesides as happy as any in Ireland. His Lordship resumed his seat 'amidst a burst of rapturous and reiterated applause'.

Councillor Lowry said,

'.. in an assembly of Irishmen, especially in an assembly of County Down tenantry, he expected that that name would call forth enthusiastic plaudits; need you mention the name of Mr Sharman Crawford? It would not be right to expect that in an assembly composed of persons of different political and religious opinions, unqualified approbation would be given to all Mr Crawford's public acts. This much, however, he would say, that all his public acts flowed from honest, pure and disinterested motives. There was one question which Mr Crawford had made peculiarly his own – a question which he could not pass by – the question of tenant right'.

Above: The Earl of Dufferin, from a Punch cartoon.

There were loud cheers. The chairman thought it was wrong for Mr Lowry to introduce that topic; speaking next, Mr Sharman Crawford said that he was quite unprepared for the honour which had been done him, in conjunction with the resident landlords of Ireland. He was proud of being present at the meeting of such respectable tenantry. Tenants had confidence in their landlords. The County Down in particular was pre-eminently distinguished in its excellent landlords. He hoped the Lord Dufferin would be duly impressed with the saying of a distinguished man now no more – that

> '.. property has its duties as well as its rights. That was a maxim which required to be impressed upon all landlords.'

Dufferin achieved some prominence when he and fellow graduate George Frederick Boyle travelled 'from Oxford to Skibbereen' to see for themselves the effects of the potato blight and famine. Their account, under the full title *Narrative of a Journey from Oxford to Skibbereen during the year of the Irish Famine*, was one of those that did go some way to making the British authorities play a more interventionist role. It is recorded that in 1847 Lord Dufferin abated the rent of his tenants for five years.

When the young Marquess was only beginning to improve the 'misty mockery of a park' that he had inherited, thereby perhaps relieving unemployment and destitution caused by the Famine, he had Helen's

Tower designed by the Scottish architect William Burn (who also designed Bangor Castle, now the Town Hall, in 1852). Gavin Stamp in his article on Helen's Tower describes it as,

> '.. a product of twin mid-Victorian obsessions: with the revival of Romantic and historical building traditions and with the raising of towers.'

One story concerns the flagpole, which unusually at least in those times was placed horizontally, rather than vertically. Lord Dufferin arrived to inspect progress and observed the pole needed painting. He bet one of his Estate staff 20 guineas – a considerable sum in those days – that he couldn't slide out and paint the entire pole in situ. The man successfully completed the job, and got his reward, by dint of tying his feet together round the ankles to ensure he didn't fall off.

Above left: Helen's Tower. Above right: Helen, Lady Dufferin, from a drawing by Swinton.

The Tower (the final fitting out of which was not completed until October 1861) and, in due course, Helen's Bay, were named after Frederick's beloved mother – the young, vivacious grand-daughter of the playwright Richard Brinsley Sheridan. In *Helen's Tower* by Harold Nicolson, the nature of the relationship between the witty young widow and her son is discussed:

'She shared his every interest and his every pleasure, she shared his friendship and his adventures; they enhanced each other's merriment and inspired each other's wit.'

The topmost panelled, octagonal room in the Tower contains a number of poems, also commissioned by the young Marquess, as tributes to his mother. The best known is by Alfred Lord Tennyson which begins:

*'Helen's Tower here I stand,
Dominant over sea and land,
Son's love built me, and I hold,
Mother's love in lettered gold.'*

Although the others include contributions by Robert Browning and Richard Garnett, the Marquess thought so highly of Tennyson's poem that he wrote to say that 'you have made me supremely happy'.

From Clandeboye, the First Marquess constructed a long, curving, tree-lined Carriage Drive to the shores of Belfast Lough in the townland of Ballygrot, which also provided carriage access to the railway station for his distinguished house guests. Thus Helen's Bay was born.

In Clandeboye House today, the archivist can show visitors a remarkable illustration of what might have been at Helen's Bay, but wasn't. At first glance, it seems Brighton, Eastbourne or Clacton is being depicted. Long terraces of tall elegant villas front onto a promenade on which strollers pass. Extending out to sea is a long, elaborate pier for pleasure steamers. This, though, was Lord Dufferin's idea, or maybe it was not much more than a dream, for his seafront lands at Helen's Bay. It was the age of steam 'railway mania' – and not just trains, steam ships too. Belfast and Bangor were already linked several times a day in summer by paddle steamers; why not build an intermediate pier at Helen's Bay and populate the shoreline with villas (for the superior classes of course) and hotels? Dufferin did commence the project with the building of a battery wall and promenade at the head of the beach.

Artist's impression of the grand plan for Helen's Bay.

Ultimately, this never seems to have hardened from an idea even into a concept but the coming of the railway did transform Helen's Bay from the 1860s (see page 31 below for the fuller story), and Lord Dufferin was naturally very much involved. The showpiece of the new Belfast to Bangor line was a station, built at his expense, originally named Clandeboye. Legend has it that he himself designed it in Scottish

Above: An artist's impression of the grand plan for Helen's Bay.

Baronial style, all crow-stepped gables, arrow slits, coats of arms and turrets. The gables feature an inset panel bearing the Dufferin and Ava initials surmounted by a coronet. His nephew Harold Nicolson drily referring to 'Lord Dufferin's optimism regarding his own capacity as an architect', describes the station as 'one of the most fantastic in the United Kingdom'. According to Mark Bence-Jones writing in the *Country Life* in October 1970, it was Benjamin Ferrey who principally designed the entrance to the station for Lord Dufferin. All trains were required to stop there, even if no aristocratic passengers were waiting (and up to five years could pass with the Marquess away overseas) but the Belfast and County Down Railway had wished to go through his land, so he could, in Victorian style, make such a condition. Besides, the work provided valuable employment to the tenantry, who generally looked on the

Above: The Clandeboye Estate wall along Helen's Bay Beach. Bottom right: A sketch of Helen's Bay Station.

Dufferins as reasonable landlords. The Rev John Quartz of Ballygilbert Presbyterian Church in 1870 presented to Lord Dufferin an address on behalf of 86 tenants declaring their 'grateful esteem and affectionate regard' – he generally composed and read addresses on behalf of the tenantry gathered in the village square to the Marquess and his lady on their return from overseas trips, when they arrived home at the station.

In his splendid biography of his uncle, Harold Nicolson reflects on his boyhood memories of the station and its gloomy waiting room especially reserved for the Clandeboye family – 'Descending to a forecourt surrounded by feudal arches and then embarking on the Carriage Drive made progress on to the house'. All this, of course, is thankfully still there. (Harold Nicolson's mother was one of the Rowan-Hamiltons of Killyleagh Castle, and a sister of Lady Dufferin.) Nicolson also records that porridge at Clandeboye was eaten standing up – Lord Dufferin wrote that,

'I always think that breakfast is the pleasantest meal in the day; my illusions in regard to my fellow creatures have reshaped themselves during the night; and I again believe in the goodness of men and women.'

Dufferin also encouraged the associate of Charles Lanyon, William Henry Lynn, to draw up grandiose designs for Clandeboye, and – Mark Bence-Jones believes – Grey Point. The plan for the latter shows a huge

Above: Dawn of autumn, Helen's Bay.

building, variously described as a marine residence or a castle, somewhere between Belfast Castle and Versailles in appearance. In his last years the Marquess did recognise that such fancies were beyond his means, but had them bound in a handsome volume kept at Clandeboye in the hope that future generations might draw on the plans. At one time, the Marquess owned over 18,000 acres, though he was obliged to sell the majority off, to meet his debts.

Also still there, on the low hilltops (including on one potential fort site at Jan Mayen) around Helen's Bay, Ballygilbert and Crawfordsburn, are clumps of trees planted by Lord Dufferin. A moment's thought makes us realise that later generations like ourselves are having more benefit from the pleasant sight they make, because they took so long to come to maturity. Each has a name, which appear on large-scale maps, inspired by places Lord Dufferin visited in his large yacht, (about which he wrote in *Letters from High Latitudes*) such as Spitzbergen Clump, or by the novels of Sir Walter Scott, such as 'Talisman Clump' on Helen's Bay golf course. And his romantic impulse to name features on his Estate was not confined to trees: the road from Crawfordsburn which meets the main Belfast to Bangor road at Ballyrobert goes through Edith of Lorne's glen.

The First Marquess was greatly interested in the Irish land question, defining the problems as arising from overpopulation and the endless subdivision of a family's land. His belief resulted from his visit to Skibbereen in County Cork. His position may be compared with that of his neighbouring landlord in his early days, William Sharman Crawford (1781-1861), MP for Rochdale in Lancashire, at the time of the Famine, who was a prominent radical, campaigning for the rights of tenants.

The career of the Marquess is sufficiently recorded elsewhere, so we have chosen not to treat it more fully here. However the story of the Sharman Crawfords is not so accessible; Peter Stark's thorough researches on the latter are therefore included at chapter 9.

In summary, the Crawfords had first come to the area as millers on the stream that became known as 'Crawford's Burn' in the Hamilton plantation of Scots from 1606 onwards. When John Crawford died in 1826, his brother-in-law William Sharman of Moira Castle inherited the Estate and added Crawford to his existing surname. Crawfordsburn House then was a newish building with a walled garden, and access to pleasant walks by the stream where the first Crawford had built the mill.

The House had a delightful gate lodge on the Bangor road. Research has shown the architect was the very distinguished John Nash (1752-1835), most famous for the Brighton Pavilion and Regent Street, London. The Earl of Caledon was employing Nash to improve his seat in Co Tyrone. The Earl's mother Anne was a Crawford, and so this must have been the connection leading to the Crawfordsburn commission. The gate lodge is a gem of North Down.

The Crawfords around this time first planted the Crawfordsburn Glen that we know today, too. Many of the older trees such as beech, larch, Monterey Cypress and Californian Redwood are not native; (recent planting – the area opened to the public in 1971 as a Country Park – has been of native trees like oak, ash and hazel). The Sharman Crawfords owned a total of 6500 acres.

Above left: Lord Dufferin, First Marquess of Dufferin and Ava, Commodore of the Ulster Canoe Club 1894-96.
Above right: Crawfordsburn waterfall.

Bassett's County Down Guide and Directory summed up the delights of Crawfordsburn in 1886:

> 'Mr A Sharman-Crawford is the owner of the charming place known as Crawfordsburn. It is one of the many objective points in the drives made by summer visitors at Bangor. A glen, cascade and tastefully planted grounds are among the attractions. This year Mr Sharman-Crawford made use of the water of the burn to generate electricity for lighting purposes. Lamps are erected in the glen, and one beside the cascade, on dark nights, producing a beautiful effect. The workmen's cottages, and Mr Sharman-Crawford's own residence, are also supplied with the electric light'.

A little earlier, writing in the 1850s, Edward Sloan began his poem as follows:

> 'A lovely summer's evening sun
> With burnished gilding crowned the trees,
> And drooping hung the listless leaves,
> Scarce waken'd by the whisp'ring breeze,
> As, musing, forth I lonely strayed,
> My laggard steps were slowly turned
> To the sweet, winding walks within
> The lovely glens of Crawfordsburn.'

Another impressive feature of the glen, and one still imposing today, was the great sandstone viaduct carrying the Belfast to Bangor line built in the 1860s to the design of leading Ulster architect, Sir Charles Lanyon.

Crawfordsburn, without a station directly serving the village, never developed in the way its neighbour Helen's Bay did. As well as new villas, mostly still there today, on Bridge Road, Church Road and elsewhere, the coming of the railway also stimulated the foundation of Helen's Bay Golf Club in 1896. Belfast golfers could easily access the pleasant seaside course on Lord Dufferin's land, and more villas extended along Golf Road. The rise in population led to the need for new churches and Helen's Bay Presbyterian Church was established, following services conducted in the village's Temperance Hall in 1892. Most of the early worshippers there belonged to the nearby Ballygilbert congregation, but they became convinced of the need to build a new church. Lord and Lady Dufferin laid the memorial stones. The initial Minister was Rev Thomas Johnston. Early in the 20th century, St John Baptist Church of Ireland was also founded.

The Belfast and County Down Railway – 'Every creeping thing'

The railway deserves its own section in this book. It was a long time coming to Helen's Bay and Crawfordsburn. An Act of Parliament in 1846 gave approval for branch lines from Belfast to Holywood and Bangor. A line was completed from Belfast as far as Holywood two years later – the second to open in the north of Ireland – but no further progress was made towards Bangor. According to Robin Morton the original intention had been for a more inland route to be known as the Belfast, High Holywood and Bangor Railway, but sense prevailed. In 1860 the Belfast, Holywood and Bangor Railway (BHBR) was incorporated. The line to Bangor took five years to build, constructed by Messrs Edwards. The extension from Holywood through Helen's Bay but bypassing Crawfordsburn village was opened on 18 May 1865,

> '.. the first train leaving Belfast at eight o'clock. All the trains were despatched with the utmost punctuality, and the numerous passengers seemed greatly pleased with the excellent arrangements of the company.'

In the first timetable Morton states that eleven trains ran hourly in each direction, the first class fare being sixpence and the second class fourpence; (third class only became available on all trains in 1873). Nineteen years later this Railway, the BHBR, was taken over by the original Belfast and County Down Railway (BCDR). Traffic built up; in a report for the House of Commons in 1881, Joseph Nobel, General

Above: A sketch of the Crawfordsburn Viaduct, designed by Sir Charles Lanyon.

Manager of the BHBR said that 16,000 tickets had been issued in that year between Belfast and Clandeboye (i.e. Helen's Bay). The line was first built as a single track but with the bridges wide enough for subsequent double-tracking which was carried out from 1897 to 1902. Thus what started as a branch line, ironically became the only part of the BCDR system that survived the cuts of the 1950s.

The eminent railway historian Dr DB McNeill gave the second talk to the newly formed Bayburn Historical Society attended by perhaps its largest audience ever – no less than 80 members. Quoting from Genesis, he recalled the BCDR was often likened to a 'creeping thing' though this was not really fair. On the occasion when the BCDR carried King Edward VII, the train arrived two minutes early to the consternation of the waiting dignitaries. It was true however that in 1848 both engines on the Belfast to Holywood line had broken down and employees of the company had had to push the carriages to their destination.

Up to the late 19th century, most large towns kept their own local time. Until the spread of railways this caused little inconvenience; for example, mail coaches took about 24 hours to travel between Belfast and Dublin. Up to 1862 the BCDR kept Belfast time, which was one minute and nineteen seconds in front of Dublin time. It is a little known fact that from then until 1916 when Greenwich time was adopted not just in Great Britain but right across the British Isles, its trains ran on Dublin time – 25 minutes behind Greenwich Mean Time. The change probably caused many to miss their trains, as previously they benefitted from the 79 second advantage conferred by Dublin time.

By 1910 the traffic was so extensive that no less than 160 trains ran into the Belfast terminus daily, the busiest station in Ireland.

The advent of the railway played a crucial part in the development of this part of the coast. In 1860 the population of Bangor was just 2,500 and the development of Helen's Bay had not begun in earnest. It was greatly helped by the long-standing offer from the Railway to all new residents of a free season ticket for two years. (McNeill commented wryly that many Ulster businessmen were more loyal to the half-crown than to the Crown.)

Helen's Bay was unique on the line as having an ostensibly private station. Arms associated with the First Marquess of Dufferin and Ava can

still be seen engraved on both sides of the stone bridge adjacent to the station, (though sadly the powers that be have allowed them to decay through previous neglect. They are described in Nicolson's book as 'dexter, a lion with a tressure flory counterflory or, sinister a heraldic tiger ermine'). His carriage would arrive in a wide sweep below the line and he could enter the station via a private staircase to a magnificent sitting room furnished with deep red upholstered armchairs with blue cushions embroidered with a coronet. Although the station was originally called Clandeboye, the late Margaret Garner, an eminent local historian, said that the then stationmaster Andy Moreland was reputed to have buried the Clandeboye sign with his bayonet and had it renamed Helen's Bay. (Nicolson tactfully gives Dufferin the credit for the name change. It had happened before 1886, as Bassett's *County Down Guide* refers to its being 'formerly called Clandeboye'.) In recent years access to the whole building including the waiting room has been denied to railway travellers, as it has played host initially to various restaurants, and to a spa.

There was in earlier times on the seaward side, a goods siding, a small hoist on the platform, with coal facilities and a hut. It was also where cattle could be loaded onto wagons for the market. The station and its employees have featured prominently in the life of the village over the years. Helen's Bay regularly won second prize as the best-kept station, behind the picturesque Marino. (It was rumoured that flowers were brought in to Marino from the Kennedy garden at Cultra just prior to the annual competition.) In 1964 the Helen's Bay track maintenance gang received the UTA award for the best kept section of permanent way in the district.

Top right: The railway bridge over Dufferin Drive. Bottom right: A view of Helen's Bay from Crawfordsburn, with Glenside Farm in the foreground. Opposite page: Station staff on parade at Helen's Bay Station.

The Station Square is effectively the centre of Helen's Bay and there have always been shops and services there. Mr Thompson was another stationmaster whose daughter ran Thompson's Hotel where the Post Office later stood before it in turn was replaced by town houses.

Margaret Garner had several tales from childhood of the railway. She recalled her mother used to take a short cut over the iron gates outside the station. To climb she had to gather up her petticoats and get on the first carriage. The driver always tooted in appreciation. Her uncle, Robert Workman, used to walk to church on Sundays along the railway track, there being no trains on Sundays in those days.

As noted above, the railway reached Crawfordsburn via a five-arched sandstone viaduct faced with Scrabo stone designed by Sir Charles Lanyon; it remains a fine sight. Tradition has it that, years later, a youngster fell off the viaduct but was saved from death by his clothes catching in trees on the way down. There is a fine account of the laying of the foundation stone in the local paper on 3 October 1863. As well as Lanyon and a Director of the line, Lord Dufferin, Major John Sharman Crawford and the chairman of the Company, Robert Ward of Bangor Castle attended. Those present were 'entertained to splendid dejeuner' at Crawfordsburn House. The foundation stone was removed in 1990, the centenary of Lanyon's death. A Victorian cache of Belfast newspapers and coins placed there in a hermetically sealed bottle 127 years before by Major Sharman Crawford was revealed. (The original sandstone parapets had to be replaced in steel, when the track was doubled between 1897 and 1902.) In 1903, King Edward VII travelled by train from Belfast to Bangor.

The station that served Crawfordsburn hospital and by extension the village over the years was initially downgraded to an unmanned halt in 1998, ironically just before the major redevelopment of the nearby Crawfordsburn House. This action was a far cry from the original requirement that another local station, Cultra, must be stopped at by at least one half of the trains or else the Company would be fined ten pounds a day.

The railway played a vital role in community life over the years. In the Second World War, one naval vessel coming into Belfast harbour accidentally depth-charged a shoal of cod. Some of the catch was put on the BCDR train and one local resident cycled to Helen's Bay station to collect it. Mr Rooney the stationmaster met him with a broad grin, saying 'I have a wee minnow here for you.' The 'minnow' was nearly four feet long and frozen solid; its new owner had to walk home pushing it on his bicycle.

John Crosthwait, the distinguished BCDR locomotive engineer, moved with his young family to the house they named Chillon at Grey Point in the early 1930s. His daughter remembers the telephone ringing at night – he had an extension in the bedroom, then a rarity – for example to report a derailment, which often seemed to happen at Ballynahinch Junction. She recalls having to reach the Presbyterian Church by 8.45 to be in time for the train taking her to Bangor Collegiate. The family enjoyed free train travel – in the case of his wife, for life. Mr Crosthwait was happy to see visitors thronging the beach as it meant more business for the railway, but his daughter Edythe has less fond memories of going out with sacks along with other local residents to pick up the vast quantities of litter left behind. She also recalled that in her father's day there used to be a carriage reserved for the Helen's Bay men, which the stationmaster would unlock to let them in. Despite the many changes over the years, and the demise of the BCDR as a separate entity, the railway has in practice turned Helen's Bay into a popular commuter location – just as the original architects of the branch line intended when they offered those free tickets to incoming residents.

Other Forms of Transport

In the late 19th century, the railway faced stern competition from ferries, associated now with the famous catchphrase 'Bangor and back for a bob', (although Morton asserts that this was actually coined by the BCDR as late as the 1930s). McNeill said that during the water shortage

Above left: BCDR sign on Helen's Bay crossing, warning trespassers will be prosecuted.

of 1933, Bangor wits retermed it 'Belfast and back for a bath'. Indeed the company itself acquired ships such as the Slieve Donard and from 1894 the Slieve Bearnagh (both built by Thomsons of Glasgow) which plied the route between Belfast and Bangor. By 1912 Erin's Isle had come as a replacement vessel, on which McNeill himself remembered travelling. It is interesting to note there was integrated travel over a hundred years ago – steamer return tickets were also valid for train travel, an increasingly attractive option after 1897 when the BCDR put a number of new coaches on the line. The first and second class were upholstered in luxurious fashion, with lighting by Pope's Patent Gas System in connection with Thompson's Patent Horizontal Flame Burners.

McNeill also stated, in his book on *Irish Sea Passenger Steamship Services*, that for the period between 1853 and 1862, the Bangor steamer (the 'Pilot' operated by Robert Henderson, a Belfast shipping agent) called at Grey Point. It seems possible that passengers may have disembarked in rowing boats, as there is no landing stage at Grey Point marked on the *Ordnance Survey maps* until the 20th century.

By the start of the 20th century the Belfast and County Down Railway had undertaken pioneering work on road services. Nevertheless early motor transport was an uncertain affair. In 1904 one of the first cars produced by the Belfast-based Chambers Motor company was taken for a run to Bangor. To reassure their family left behind in Belfast, a telegram

Above: View from Helen's Bay across the Lough, from Rev Archer's Illuminated Address.

was despatched from Bangor, announcing their safe arrival.

From 1922 many private omnibus companies were operating and they were quickly followed by freight and passenger services. Fares were lower than rail and the public accepted the novelty of a bus passing the road end.

There was an excellent network of roads throughout County Down and the County Council responded to public demand by improving road services. Road competition developed during the early 1920s, Matthew Morrow inroduced his Enterprise, solid-tyred buses from Belfast to Bangor in 1924, running four services daily, three via Clandeboye and one via Crawfordsburn. (Return fare 1s 6d (equivalent to today's 7 1/2p) compared to that by rail of 2s 4d (12p).) The Bangor Queen was another company who operated on that route.

In 1927, there were 27 rival bus services competing against the BCDR to the delight of the public, as their service was more flexible than the railway. The County Down railway was slow to react positively to road competition and it was not until May 1927 that railway-owned buses commenced rival operations. The inescapable fact that the distance between urban areas was shorter by road meant that the railway had lost its initial advantage. Today the A2 road remains a busy commuter route.

The Ulster Way, a circular 625mile (1000km) long distance walking route, was officially opened on 16 September 2009. Wilfred Capper who played a key role in the creation of the Ulster Way was himself a Crawfordsburn resident. Clandeboye Way, ie the former Dufferin or Carriage Drive (as it is often still known) features as an eight-mile woodland walk on a mix of old lanes and tracks starting at Helen's Bay Fort Road car park, across the A2 and then branching off to finish in Whitespots Country Park at Newtownards, having passed Helen's Tower en route. Another recent designation, again reflecting the beauty of the local environment, is Cycle Route 93 which also goes from Helen's Bay to Newtownards, though nearly all on public roads; in the other direction it follows the Coastal Path to Bangor, (a shift from not so former days when cycling on that Path was prohibited).

Chapter 3

Farming and Business Life in Former Times

Businesses in Helen's Bay and Crawfordsburn serve both communities due to the villages' proximity and have reflected the changing needs of each community throughout the centuries. While some businesses and landmarks remain the same, others have disappeared without trace. The two large landowners provided employment for local residents, and the progression from mail coaches and tracks to railways and roads created many new forms of employment to meet the needs of the expanding communities.

This chapter aims not so much to set out the current businesses, as to provide an account of those that flourished in previous years, drawn both from contemporary records and personal recollections. A very brief synopsis of the current operations, which vividly demonstrates the greater breadth of business now undertaken, from home as well as from business premises, is provided at the end of the chapter. (The *BayBurn Life* Newsletter, published biannually, is a further source of information on these.)

In times past, Quarry Port at the end of Helen's Bay beach was used to unload lime from luggers, which had sailed across Belfast Lough from quarries on the Antrim coastline. The lime was either taken from there to Smelt Mill Bay where it was burnt and prepared for building construction purposes, or spread on the fields. There may have been a bigger track running from Quarry Port along the coast to Smelt Mill Bay, at the bottom of Strickland's Glen, Bangor, (where during the second war a long-gone boatyard flourished).

While Crawfordsburn is the older settlement, the advent of the railway provided Helen's Bay with the greater incentive to set up a range of business activities, including two hotels. It was no surprise therefore that the area around the Station Square became a centre for local commercial activity.

The Rural Scene

It would be right to start with an account of the local agricultural scene, although only a partial record is here provided. (It is the intention of residents on Crawfordsburn's Cootehall Road to set down a more detailed history of that part of the community and the wider village, which will be very welcome.)

One written historical source is the account provided by Bassett in his *County Down Guide and Directory* dated 1886. Under the heading of Crawfordsburn, in Ballygrott there are six persons in the category of 'residents, farmers etc' – Hugh and James Patton, John and Patrick Moffatt, Robert McConnell and SC Magee. (The Pattons gave their name to Patton's corner, where Bridge Road joins Craigdarragh Road.) There is a Samuel Cargo at Ballymullan, along with Hugh Nelson and William Wallace in the same townland. Then under Craigavad, there are four at Ballyrobert – Samuel Crothers, John Duke (of Glencraig school one presumes), Samuel Gibson and E Taylor. However a separate heading of Clandeboye also covers Ballygrott and Ballygilbert, which records William Bradley at the former and his brother Robert in the latter.

As recorded elsewhere, and in line with the approach taken by a number of landlords, the Sharman Crawfords created a modern model farm around 1890, and built houses for the Estate workers both in the village and in The Square (buildings now demolished off Old Windmill Road). In his book on the *Buildings of North County Down*, Brett rather discounts the suggestion that the model farm was designed by Vincent Craig. It seems generally accepted that the slightly later gate lodge was designed by the architects Watt and Tulloch. In the 1920s the model farm, with its chiming clock after which it was sometimes better known, had an innovative railway system for moving materials such as animal feed around the site. Some residents can still recall its manager, Mr Robert Brown who lived with his large family in the farm's gate lodge, fondly known as Chass or 'Yaass' Brown for the pronunciation of his typically positive response to others' remarks.

In more recent times, there were still several farms in the Crawfordsburn area; these included the dairy run by John McEwen at Hillhead Farm, off the Cootehall Road. As his son Joe – with input from his brothers – has written an account of the farm, we are grateful for the opportunity to draw on that.

Joe's father John (Jack) came to the area from South Armagh in 1928; he bought 30 acres, 2 roods and 14 perches of land at Ballymullan from John Gilmer who had acquired it (for a larger sum) in 1912 from Thomas Montgomery who in turn had taken it over in 1884. (This may have been the same Captain Montgomery who moved to Bangor where he owned the lime kilns behind the gas works, according to William Seyers' account, as he records that Robert Gilmer held the farm later. The annual rent paid to Lord Dufferin in 1884 incidentally was some 80% higher than that nearly 30 years later. There is evidence how agricultural values moved up and down in those days.)

After some years, Mr McEwen bought over the local milk run (from the Moffatts), while still milking the cows by hand. Although the high voltage cables crossed their land, electricity did not come to the farm until the early 1950s. So in the 1930s John bought a coal-fired steam wagon which he used to clean the milk bottles. (Lighting the fire was a very early job every morning.) His boys helped with the milking, had a quick breakfast and then did the milk run in the van to Crawfordsburn, Helen's Bay (in harmonious competition with Sam Bradley) and Carnalea, all before going to school. John then acquired a further 50 acres from William James McKee, for which Bill McCormick (of Glenholme) rigged up a generator to light the cow-byre and dairy. In the later 1950s the milk delivery business was sold to Billy Johnston who lived in The Square, as it was no longer possible to sell milk direct from the farm unpasteurised. So the milk was sent to Bangor Dairies from which Billy purchased it. Hillhead Farm was converted to beef production and cereal growing. Over the years many local people worked on the farm and the milk round while others helped out at times, including southerners keen to find work in the north. The Conn family also moved from South Armagh to help on the farm and with the house. They bought a property in the Lowburn Cottages on the Ballyrobert Road. The photograph shows John McEwen with John Conn delivering milk in the Main Street in 1933.

As recorded elsewhere, Sam Bradley from Ballygilbert also delivered milk from Helen's Bay as far as Holywood. Milk was brought in from surrounding farms, pasteurised and bottled on the premises. His son Sam still has the own-label bottles. The photograph on page 39 shows Mr Bradley with his horse and cart, briefly offering a lift to Geoffroy and Estelle Shuttleworth at Grey Point in Helen's Bay. The round included buttermilk, and Grade 'A' milk from Hugh Moore's Jersey cattle which fetched a premium price. Sam's son remembers German prisoners of war digging up potatoes in the season, under their captors' watchful eyes. There would have been local youngsters still doing the same job until the mechanisation of 20 or so years ago. He also recalls the deep snows of the harsh winter of early 1947 when hedges and gates could be walked on top of, not opened. Terence McKeag, who had started out as a helper on the van, later bought up the milk run from Mr Bradley. He recalls that it meant a 4.30 am start each day, and no day off for seven years. Later still Mr Russell (of alliterative nickname) delivered milk – and sometimes newspapers.

In the late 19th century there was a smithy on the Crawfordsburn Main Street (where the craft and pottery shops are now), for which William Warnock is listed in the *Village Directory*. Later there was a blacksmith's forge at the Devil's Elbow, with another at Ballyrobert run by Davy John Taylor. His daughter said that he had found it particularly difficult to plate the mule that Colonel Sharman Crawford had brought back from the first war. Also in the row were the Ballyrobert Stores owned by Willie Taylor. Colonel Crawford latterly also had his own blacksmith, housed in courtyard buildings. He made metal supports for the heavy limbs of specimen trees on the Estate, recalls Gary Graham who, when he was working at the children's hospital, heard accounts of the Colonel's doings.

There was a wheelwright's workshop belonging to Jim McClements' father at Rosevale, off the Cootehall Road. Two of the stone-built cottages at Rosevale, now restored as self-catering accommodation from their former use as a pig unit, are potentially three to four hundred years old and likely to be among the oldest surviving

Bottom left: John McEwen delivering milk to Crawfordsburn assisted by John Conn, 1933.

Above: Sam Bradley (senior) delivering milk with his horse, Sally, with Geoffroy and Estelle Shuttleworth.

buildings in the two villages. An original building that butted on to the current Rosevale (which was built in the 1920s when Colonel Sharman Crawford sold 43 acres to Robert McClements) and which had to be demolished, had only cob walls. There were also a number of traditional linear white-washed cottages in Helen's Bay, demolished not so very long ago, including one that housed Alfie Neill, his wife and their three daughters on Fort Road nearly opposite Rushfield, close by a small quarry and a spring. He was the sexton for St John's for many years, his wife helped the Gilmers and Maureen was a most popular nurse at the Crawfordsburn hospital. There was the cottage too where 'Wee Mary', or later 'Old Mary', lived, with an earthen floor and a pig out the back, further along Fort Road at Bell's Hill. The cottage was roofed with corrugated iron which Thomas and Derek Lindsay would re-tar annually to stop it rusting. One neighbour recalls an imposing grandfather clock which was used to help prop the ceiling up. Mary was a real character who knew everyone in the village as a consequence of her babysitting and paper round. (On Sunday mornings she bought the *News of the World* on which she would then sit, in church.) Mary was the daughter of Langford McGarrell who had been born in Glenavy in 1853. At the age of eleven he had come to Crawfordsburn to herd cattle for the son of William Sharman Crawford, walking from Lisburn. (Margaret Garner had a story about Mr Aston who had lived in a similar Fort Road cottage, since demolished. One day Lord Dufferin and his agent had driven down to the Bay, to consider his plans for its development. As they were passing by the cottage, Aston had asked them to wait a moment as he would be just back. Mr Aston was – with a gun. Lord Dufferin and the agent moved on quickly. It is clear that concern about untrammelled development is not new. James Aston is recorded as a farmer in the 1892 *Ulster Directory*, with the definitive address of 'The Cottage, Ballygrot'.)

As noted above, William James McKee had a farm at the top end of the Meadow Way estate, and the Lane that runs from there up to the

A2 is still known locally as McKee's Lane. Perhaps as an early exercise in agricultural diversification, a small shooting range was created off the Lane. Known as the Clandeboye Miniature Rifle Club, its doings were recorded in the *Spectator* in December 1933. That year, the Clandeboye A Team held the record for the highest score in a match in the Ulster League. The Team also beat English teams across the water. Some of those recording high scores included J Mairs, J Donaghey, J Cammock, J Gribben, JP Robson and WJ McKee himself. Kerry Greeves remembers his father shooting there, before the war. Maurice Lindsay recalls seeing patrons, of both sexes, bringing their rifles in bags out to Crawfordsburn to which they travelled by bus.

Before the second war there had been fields along much of the upper side of Ballymullan Road, owned by the Mairs, between their house, Morningside, and the Main Street. John Lindsay rented a few fields behind their house (no. 20 Main Street) where he kept some cows and hens. Maurice recalls that the cattle would know by his voice which field to return to, after milking. Thomas Lindsay, Derek's father, similarly kept cattle in a field above his house at 3 Ballymullan Road. Derek recalls his father working out in the fields until midnight cutting the hay in June and July. Robin Lindsay rented some land at Lowburn. During the war, an aeroplane made a forced landing in his field above the cottages, and it is said the two occupants spent the night in the Old Inn, none the worse for their experience. Emma Graham's recollection is that it happened in a snow storm in the afternoon, and the aeroplane was later put under a police guard. However both Kerry Greeves and Derek Lindsay managed to acquire treasured items from the wreckage which they put away with other keepsakes, though they have them no more. Kerry recalls Robin Lindsay giving him and his brother bantams' eggs and letting them ride on the ruck-lifter. Robin also had a tar boiler which was towed behind his horse and cart when the road needed maintenance.

The Crawford family farmed at Sunnybrook; there were both wooden chalets (built as temporary accommodation for Belfast residents after the Blitz) and caravans there too. Once it rained so hard they got flooded out, and Derek's father gave the caravanners dry sanctuary in his barn. The only formal access to the farm was over the railway crossing just outside Helen's Bay station. People living there could however walk to Crawfordsburn across the fields. Returning to Sunnybrook late one Saturday evening after a session carousing in the Old Inn, a group was terrified by the jangling of chains beside them in the dark - the Geddis' pony had accidentally been left yoked to the cart.

For many years Jim Holden, with his sister Winnie, farmed at the end of Ballywooley Lane. His father had moved there in 1905, from Antrim. Their 36 acres provided for a variety of crops, including wheat, barley, potatoes, turnips and flax, as well as grazing for half a dozen cattle, with poultry in the yard. Jim recalls how lovely the blue flax flowers were. The farm did not have its own lint hole in which to ret the flax, but if the weather was right it could be 'dew retted'. After drying, it was formed into sheaves (or beets) which in turn formed a big round stack, before that was taken to a scutching mill in Newtownards. The farm was self-

Above left: The Neills Cottage, looking along Fort Road.
Opposite page: Crawfordsburn from the field up the Ballymullan Road.

Crawfordsburn Co. Down.

sufficient in many ways; it had both natural springs and a well from which water could be pumped. Jim still prefers the taste of well water to the modern mains variety.

The Holdens used horses for ploughing for many years, before they acquired their first Ferguson tractor. They would buy horses at Allam's sale yard in Oxford Street in Belfast; if a horse did not take to the traces when they got it home, it would have to be returned. (A good horse could be obtained for about £60.) Latterly they went to Herbie Smiley's smithy on Beatrice Road in Bangor, though they had also used Sammy Orr and Davy John Taylor. Jim recalls that until recently they still had a harrow made at Taylor's smithy, which proudly bore the maker's name.

The cattle were milked by hand. Jim recalls that even with long experience, it was not always possible to stop the cow kicking over the pail. The milk was then churned into butter in a large vat, which was churned by a paddle turned by a horse going round in a circle outside the barn. Their butter was sold with the imprint of a thistle as the farm's motif. Butter was sold from their cart, though people came in for the buttermilk; little was better tasting, Jim recalls, than newly-made buttermilk with wee bits of butter floating on the top. In the old byre, straw had been put under the roof for warmth. This spot was favoured by the farm cats for giving birth to their kittens. The cats coexisted with hens, ducks, geese, turkeys and even a pair of peafowl.

Feet were the main mode of transport. Jim walked to the Ballymullan School every day. John Lindsay was then the postman; for a long while until he got a bicycle, his round had been carried out on foot too, and Jim pays tribute to the distances he covered. Yet John still had energy to spare for other jobs at the end of his working day, such as gardening and hedge clipping. Jim would have walked into Bangor for groceries; toffee bars could be had as a treat, for tuppence.

Jim McClements recalls that neighbouring farmers would help each other out; several spending a couple of days in each location, bringing their horses and carts to ensure the harvest was safely gathered in, before moving on to repeat the procedure at the next farm. Vermin were a problem; one farmer with what would now be described as good hand-eye coordination could skewer two rats on the tines of a pitchfork, while both estates had their own, larger-scale means of keeping the rodent population down.

Top left: The McGookins' wedding day in 1920: first left Ethel Holden (James Holden's mother), James' Uncle and Aunt Jack and Cec McGookin, Adamson Holden. Above: Mr William Cheatley (born 1847) and his wife Jane, with David Cheatley, father of William (third from left in the back row); note the two sets of twins (the photograph was taken between 1900 and 1906).

The Cheatleys came to Brookmount farm from Donegal, via New Zealand. When the family left their farm at Kilmacrenan in Donegal around 1920, they emigrated to New Zealand. However some returned, including David Cheatley who had been born in 1878, and his son William born in 1915. The story is told that when sailing in to Belfast up the Lough, he asked his wife which side she wanted to live on. Thus they came to Crawfordsburn, living initially in a single storey cottage, with a byre at one end, before building a new house. All the farm buildings are located within a large and very clear rath or fort, the five foot ramparts of which still exist in places.

William (or Billy) Cheatley went to school on the Ballymullan Road, through Maggie's Glen, passing curious squirrels on his way. When he took over the farm, William bred horses, himself being a judge at Balmoral and Dublin. (His elder brother George was killed in the RAF in the second war.) The well in Well Field was the source of water for the house, guarded by a fairy hawthorn tree. Clay pipes and – intriguingly – old ink wells have been found in the fields. The two family photographs illustrate three generations of an Ulster farming dynasty, now all passed on except Mathena.

A little way further up their lane, in the valley below Coyle's Lane which runs parallel at this point, are the remains of several dwellings. While some were for summer use only, Mr and Mrs Martin lived in one house with their four sons, all year round. The boys went to work for Shorts. Mrs Anne Cheatley recalls her husband being asked one day by Mr Martin what he was sowing. Anticipating, rightly, that Mr Martin would be after some of the seed, he replied brussel sprouts. His neighbour was disappointed to discover some months later that he had been fooled into growing kale fit only for cattle rather than human consumption.

George Henderson's brother, Eric, has recorded aspects of farming at Millbrooke Farm in Ballysallagh. Their cattle were hand-milked until about 1940; it was only then too that a piped water system was installed to provide water to the byre when they were over-wintering. He recalled turning the cut hay for drying with hand forks or horse-drawn hay-tedding machinery which was prone to breakage. It was built in rucks for a month or two before it was brought into the stack-yard. In the war farmers were encouraged to 'make two blades of grass grow where one had grown before'. Kale and turnips were grown to supplement the hay; they had to be hand weeded and singled in drills, and then carted in winter to the yard. Their first silage was made in 1955, though before machinery was available, the green heavy grass had to be levelled by manual labour. Arable crops consisted mainly of flax and oats. The flax was pulled by hand and then weighted down with stones to ret in the lint hole, before being spread out to dry. Flax went out of favour, except for a period during the second war. Oats were rolled for cattle feed, having been cut by reaper and then tied by hand in sheaves. In 1948, a Ferguson tractor could be bought for under £500. After the late 1940s and the advent of combine harvesters, barley took over from oats. It was usually sold off to feed mills, where it was mixed with imported proteins and sold back to farmers for cattle feed.

In the Helen's Bay area, there were similarly a number of farms and farmsteads. Hugh Moore, who lived at Rockmount, had a herd of pedigree Jersey cattle, grazed in a field that is now Woodlands Avenue, which he was wont to show in competitions as far afield as Dublin. Individual cows and even bulls were regularly walked on halters up Kathleen Avenue and elsewhere, in readiness for such appearances, and

Above left: Mr David Cheatley (born 1878) and his family, William next to his father; Mathena is on her mother's lap, the others from left are: George, Molly and Jean (this photograph was taken around 1923).

his son Stuart would drive the cattle down Bridge Road. John Jess from Seaview in Crawfordsburn was his right hand man. He had previously owned land at Skelly Hill which he sold to Tommy Wardle who created a caravan park there. (Mr Moore owned a factory in Belfast making hessian bags. His son Stuart unfortunately lost a leg in an accident at the station.) Alan Cook thinks he was paid one shilling a week for helping out.

After the second war, horses were still used for ploughing the field between Mut's Lane (which runs from Craigdarragh Road to Coastguard Avenue), Coastguard Avenue and the railway bridge on the Craigdarragh Road.

Mr John Cumming leased the land for a market garden off Kathleen Avenue, and supplied fruit to the neighbourhood, up until 1965. 'Rene Shuttleworth said she enjoyed the social occasion of going on a Saturday morning with her friends to purchase their vegetables there. John, a Scot, had previously been the immaculately turned out head gardener on the Sharman Crawford Estate, and was responsible for the Colonel winning many trophies for 'his' horticultural prowess. There are two roses, (which are still commercially available) named respectively *Mrs RG Sharman Crawford* (pink) and *Molly Sharman Crawford* (white and fragrant), which were developed in conjunction with Alexander Dickson the younger of Newtownards. Mr Cumming and his family had lived in the Nash-designed gate lodge on Old Windmill Road, until the Colonel died and the house in effect changed hands. The Colonel's will left an extra one year's wages to many of his staff including 'the Head Gardener'. Mr Cumming, described by Frederick Harte as 'that solid, capable and agreeable Scot', wrote articles on horticulture for the *Belfast News Letter* under the soubriquet of 'Spademan'. (For the saga of the Crawfordsburn Fern, see page 147 below.) On Skelly Hill, George Downey, (who was a senior manager in a Belfast bank), had a poultry farm, with a poultry maid who lived in a small property nearby. (Records under the 1925 Land Act show Mr Downey as holding 15 acres on Skelly Hill, at an annual rental of £14, with the title being claimed as going back well into the 19th century.) There was also a pig unit at the top of Craigdarragh Road for some time.

There was continuity at the farmstead at Glenholme for several generations, culminating in the McCormicks. The farmstead included a duck pond and various outbuildings such as the bothy (see also George Best in Helen's Bay on page 136 below), and an orchard. Several commentators have paid tribute to Billy McCormick's skill with his hands; he was an early creator of go-karts, fitting them with independent suspension. He also helped Kerry Greeves build a car out of two old Fords. Glenholme was close to the railway line and one story was that a

spark from a steam engine had started a fire that destroyed the original farmhouse. Their land had included what are now Carolsteen and Chimera Wood, with its extensive caravans.

Blackwood Crescent was built on what had been the local Helen's Bay team's football pitch. Early residents, such as Betty McCartney, moved into the newly-constructed Crescent in 1954, benefitting from a Government subsidy then available for the purchase of such properties. (It is said that the Dufferin Estate offered it to the Golf Club at one time, but the swampy ground was not deemed suitable.) After the Gilmers, the Irelands had the farm called Glenside, reached off the road between the two villages. On the other side of the road was, from 1945, the farm of

Above: Glenholme farm house, Helen's Bay.

Ignatius Geddis' father Francis who kept some fine horses, and acquired the first Land Rover seen in Helen's Bay. (It had previously belonged to James McKee of whom it was reputed that when he had drink taken, his horse would find its own way home, bringing his master safely with him.) Ignatius recalls his family being asked (by the police) not to ride their own ponies on a Sunday, at the request of Helen's Bay residents. Their farm supplied the Old Inn with fresh eggs. He has commented that he was probably the fourth generation in his family to be in the haulage business, his great-grandfather having been involved in bringing building materials by horse and cart for the construction of Stormont Castle. He himself constructed the bases (out of black concrete) and the water supply for Mr Wardle's caravan park at Skelly Hill.

One of Mrs McCormick's first memories was being taken down to the beach as a young girl, to see the Titanic sailing by on Belfast Lough on its way out to sea. She also recalled as a young girl venturing on to her father's penny farthing bicycle which had careered down the hill and tipped her off into the burn. Her parents, in early agricultural diversification, made some of their land into one of the first caravan parks in Northern Ireland, having campers there as early as 1908. This was one of the reasons why the authorities facilitated their licence for many years. Derek Lindsay recalls helping his father, assisting the McCormicks to bring the caravans into their yard for the winter. This involved a hazardous journey across the railway line, keeping a wary ear out for approaching trains. A between-the-wars anecdote about business acumen concerned Sir Thomas Lipton and Mrs McCormick's father. Her father had asked Sir Thomas, in a relatively light-hearted manner, how he had been able to make money so quickly. Sir Thomas was very swift in his response – 'by minding my own business.'

Fishing was another source of food, as well as sport. Before the second war, lobsters could be caught not far off the bay. One resident recalls an outing with Harry Gilmer and his daughter in his lobster boat which ended in them all furiously hand-paddling for the beach after it sprang a leak. Tales are also told of salmon poaching and trout tickling in times gone by in the Crawford's burn.

In living memory women pulled flax in local fields and steeped it in smelly water. Many of the farms had their own lint hole for retting the flax. Some local residents also recount days of poteen-making and acquisitive raids on the property of better-off neighbours.

In Craigdarragh Road, before the arrival of mains water, the water supply was piped from Clandeboye. This often allowed small worms, frogs or even fish to arrive at unexpected destinations. Even prior to this arrangement, water had to be drawn by pump from a dam built on the eastern side of the road. During the summer, this supply was in serious danger of drying up. In Crawfordsburn village there was a different arrangement, with a pump being provided in front of the (later location of the) Country Club, providing good quality water.

Residents of Helen's Bay were not in favour of modernisation, when electricity arrived, for some, in the mid-1930s. A petition was got up opposing the introduction of street lighting, fearing it was the start of urbanisation.

Later after the second war, there were still several local milkmen including Billy Johnston; one was from Crawfordsburn, the other Ballygilbert, with a horse and cart sometimes still in use. However in the 1920s, residents in Crawfordsburn had a choice between two local suppliers, Bolton McKnight or the Moffatts, each of whom had a couple of cows which provided milk, carried in enamel jugs. (Emma Graham

Above: Church Road, still with no street lights.

recalls that the aged and grimy state of Johnny Moffatt's waistcoat pointed at least some customers in the direction of the competition.) The Ormo Bakery provided a regular bread delivery too. The fishman, with his pony and trap, was a familiar sight and sound, with his cry of 'Herrings alive'.

In the Two Villages

In Helen's Bay, Station Square has always been a focal point. Jean Blair's mother recalled that long ago there was an annual fair held in it.

The station itself was a key element of the community, with a staff of four. A fire was always lit in the ticket office, and there was a separate Ladies waiting-room. As recorded elsewhere, George Rooney, McFarland and Harry Parkhurst (who had initially been the ticket collector) were respected stationmasters, the last-named retiring in 1966. Although McFarland's was the other stationmaster's house, quite a fine brick building with timber gables, (subsequently replaced by a block of three houses), the Parkhursts lived in the cottage opposite the station (now the Beehive). This provided limited accommodation for Harry and Rita's nine children (two of whom died at an early age in tragic circumstances). Harry had also found time for greyhound breeding and training, gaining many trophies throughout Ireland during the 1940s and 1950s. Prior to a race, he often gave the dogs a run along the Golf Club fairways followed by a dip in the Bay. (He set snares to catch rabbits in the local fields.)

A local transport service was provided by Hutchinson's jaunting car – very useful for getting commuters home faster in the rain (though kindly stationmasters also loaned their umbrellas to residents caught out on wet afternoons). 'Fiddler' (Bill) Hutchinson, who had a limp, lived off Pigeon Lane, the lane that runs between Golf and Church Roads. It was also called Duck Lane by some, recording the birds which used to waddle along it. Before the two cottages there were demolished and replaced in recent years, Alex Minty later lived in one; he was a prolific amateur artist who painted many golfing scenes and the local beach. Hutchinson's horse could graze in what was then a small field where 1 Church Road stands today. When in Crawfordsburn, Emma

Graham recalls that Hutchinson 'parked' outside the Orange Hall, waiting for his next custom. With a stable and communal pump adjacent to his cottage, he lived next to Joe Nelson who bred 'Clandeboye' Pekinese and was a ferocious competitor in dog shows. His expertise was widely recognised; if neighbours had a sick dog Joe would often prescribe a remedy, his favourite being a strong dose of castor oil. Ignatius Geddis recalls as a child, with his mother, showing at Balmoral a Pekinese that he had been given, following an early success at a horse show. Joe kindly advised them on how best to brush the dog and prime it for the competition, so he was not best pleased when their entrant beat his.

Top left: Crawfordsburn Main Street, with a horse-drawn bread delivery van.
Above right: Painting of Helen's Bay Beach by Alex Minty.

In the corner of the Square was a long wooden hut used some days of the week by Jim Robinson, a cobbler. (He and his brother had a shoe shop in Abbey Street in Bangor.) This met one very important local need, and was also a hang-out for local boys returning on the train. Adjacent was Sunbeam Cottage, yellow-painted, owned by the Bucklers, let out to summer visitors; at one stage the cottage was home to a dress-maker who provided a valued local service. Then came the two shops owned by Mr and Mrs George Buckler, (where the off licence has been since 1971 and the hairdressers now are. A petition was got up against the advent of an off licence, although some believed they were signing up in its favour.) The smaller building nearer the station was a sweet shop cum newsagents, and the larger a grocery store. The business had been started by George's father on his return from service in India. Paddy Buckler understands that he had acquired the premises from Mr Randewich. (Mrs Randewich later lived in a wooden house on Bridge Road. During her time in Africa, she had acquired the knack of removing ticks from dogs, which she now put to good use to help neighbours out, as Joan Bushell recalls.) Sammy was the Bucklers' delivery boy, initially on a bicycle and then in a van. The Bucklers also had a hall with a fine sprung floor, behind the shop, facing towards Golf Road, which was used for dances and other entertainments between the wars. The premises also housed the telephone exchange, and for a time the post office, Mr Buckler then being the postmaster, the office being managed by Mrs Peck. (One of the sad duties in wartime involved delivering telegrams to local residents informing them of the deaths of their loved ones in battle overseas.)

Paddy Buckler recalls the approach of many residents who preferred to charge their shopping to their account, rather than pay at the time. (One went a stage further: he said openly that he put all the bills into a hat at the end of the month, and paid the first three he took out. But he cautioned against too much pressure to pay any particular bill, as that could lead to its mysteriously not even getting into the hat in the first place). The Square was accordingly often known as Buckler's Square.

George Simpson later ran the sweet shop element, and for a time it served coffee too.

Residents fondly recall the excellent ice cream which the Bucklers made in an outbuilding behind the shop; (if the odd bit of ash dropped into the mix it was regarded by at least one appreciative young customer as simply a bit of extra body in the batch). Some still rate it as the best they have ever tasted. The day when Mr Buckler made his first batch of pink ice cream and brought free samples to the schoolchildren across the road waiting for the bus has gone down in folklore. Clearly 8.45 am is not too early for ice cream.

Betty McCartney recalls that two girls who assisted in the shop lived in above it; on occasions they would lean out of upstairs windows exciting attention from young men passing below from the station.

On the other side of the Station Square, Dummigan's was a hall, used for dances and other activities such as Brownies, behind where the pharmacy now is. After the war, it seems that it was also used for a period manufacturing firelighters. For a period, there was another tearoom cum sweet shop run for a while by Andy Anderson and before him by Mr and Mrs Dobson, (where the dentist now is). The toffee made there is still

Above: Bucklers, Station Square, Helen's Bay.

remembered fondly by some with a sweet tooth. On the same side of the Square was the post office, before it moved along Bridge Road. Bobby Crawford ran another grocery for a period, but smaller than the Bucklers.

In the second war, a canteen was set up in the Square, under YMCA auspices, to provide refreshments for the passing soldiers. (This was located broadly where the dentist now is). One resident recalls being taken by her mother there, regularly, to help with the washing up. She was strictly advised to keep her eyes in front, not looking right or left.

Before leaving the Square, mention must be made of the chemists or pharmacy. The former proprietor, Gordon Smyth, produced his own distinctive cough medicine, having acquired the recipe from a pharmacist on the Woodstock Road in Belfast when he was a travelling representative, according to his daughter Val. It is widely considered to have near miraculous qualities. The present owners still produce a

potent linctus, which satisfies contemporary requirements while maintaining the historic tradition. This Helen's Bay nostrum has from its beginning, when Gordon started in the village in 1957, benefitted many overseas as well as local customers, as far afield as Australia and New Zealand. Gordon could be outspoken on occasions, and dispensed advice on patent remedies. Jeanette Neary recalls being told by him, when she was troubled by a stiff back, to knot a piece of string around her. She reflects that as she does not have one now, it must have been successful. Another traditional cure, for a sore ear, was to heat a sally rod and pour the sap into the afflicted organ.

Where there is now Helen's Way, there used to be several buildings. At times, the premises on the corner, Helenville, housed an antique shop and then a hairdresser's salon run by Jeanette Neary. Well sited in many respects, very close to the route to and from the station, Jeanette recalls being prudently counselled by Mrs Buckler, not to be seen out in her garden on a hot summer's day. (This was to avoid an endless succession of pleas from passers-by to use her loo etc, as she soon discovered.)

Bolton McKnight (at 10 Bridge Road) provided an important local service mending bicycles.

Opposite what is now the telephone exchange was Thompsons. Originally a hotel, this was later run as a tea room by the two Miss

Thompsons (Sarah, stationmaster James Thompson's daughter, and her niece Elizabeth) who kept hens in their orchard. (In the 1930s it was still providing bed and breakfast facilities, as James Douglas's father stayed there on the night before his wedding.) In the *Belfast and Province of Ulster Directory* of 1892, the stationmaster and postmaster was James Thompson born in 1847, (with Miss Waugh his counterpart at Crawfordsburn post office). William Seyers recorded in his 1930s *Reminiscences of Old Bangor* that Thompson moved from Bangor where he had previously been stationmaster when the BCDR took over the running of the railway from the original BHBR in 1884. He was 'most obliging and liked by everyone'; his son Samuel was the booking clerk. Helen's Bay was clearly fortunate in its succession of railway staff.

Above left: Helenville, Station Square, Helen's Bay in the 1980s. Above right: Station Square, showing Helenville as Helen's Bay Hotel next to Helen's Bay Stores, much earlier.

Alfie Mairs recalls a succession of daffodil teas organised at the Thompsons by the Presbyterian Church to raise funds for its new hall; just as the target would nearly be reached, the cost would increase again. The premises then became a successful grocery as well as post office, managed from the 1960s by Sandy Dalzell who retired by 1990. While the shop's popularity continued under the management of Judy Aiken, the premises sadly suffered from several break-ins and are no more. Thus while comparatively recently there had been post offices in both Crawfordsburn and in Helen's Bay, residents now have a couple of miles to travel for this facility.

Finally, beyond Thompsons was Gray's Builders Yard situated almost on the railway line to the left of the level crossing at Railway Cottages. (Bobby Gray had been a professional dancer before the second war.)

On the western side of the Carriage Drive was a Garage (and taxi service) run initially by Tommy Shiels, briefly by John Patterson and then from 1964 up to its closure by Marshall Pritchard. Although Tommy Shiels' initial response to a request for a taxi was regularly 'possible but not probable', it usually turned out to be possible. He drove his own car and wore a suit and hat as part of the service. Mary Strahan remembers she enjoyed, as a four or five year old sitting on his knee and pretending to drive the car. Kerry Greeves recalls that he could be both generous and humorous. One time Kerry took his Austin 7 in to Tommy, and helped him in the repair process; but when he asked the cost, Tommy said 'We'll see about that next time'. Tommy never did. On another occasion when Kerry was in the garage, someone came in asking 'Did you see Mr Mann here?' 'There was'na a man about the place', came the droll reply.

As Frederick Harte noted on coming to live in Helen's Bay in 1939, 'in some respects it is the most convenient place in which I ever lived. The railway, the post office, the grocery shop, the police station, the cobbler, the garage, the golf links, the sea are only a few minutes away.'

Gary Gillespie's father, Bob, set up a business in the 1960s doing property repairs and alterations, based in Granville Cottage down what might be termed 'Gillespie's Lane', between the Carriage Drive and Church Road. 30 years later there was hardly a house in the district which hadn't had some of his men in it or on it at some point. He had previously, during the war years, been involved in work at Grey Point Fort.

The Coastguard Station, down Coastguard Avenue was for many years a prominent feature of the local community. It merits a section in its own right – see pages 134-136.

Before the second war, in the fields below the Coastguard Cottages, an annual tented camp was held for unemployed men. They were paid a small sum by the Dufferin Estate to fell the trees down to the shore line.

After the advent of the railway to Helen's Bay, the older village of Crawfordsburn had comparatively fewer commercial establishments in the post-war era. Considerable local employment was of course provided

by the Old Inn and the Country Club. We know however that in 1892 both Adam Magowan and Robert Wallace were designated as grocers of Crawfordsburn, while Frederick Stevenson was a saddler.

Local transport was available with the Lindsays – Thomas had a taxi business before the second war, while Robin had a jaunting car, also used for runs to and from Helen's Bay station. According to one account, the diminutive but musical Alec Cleland had a small garage close to the

Above: Helen's Bay Coastguard Station.

Orange Hall. It is recorded that he mounted his motor bicycle using a wooden block. He used to take photographs on Helen's Bay beach, the old-fashioned way with a large black cloth over both his head and the camera. At the other end house in the Main Street, some residents recall the Misses Warnock briefly ran a small shoe shop, and also gave out balloons marked with the family name. There had been a stone cottage between the Club and the burn, which suffered from severe flooding many years ago and was subsequently demolished. The Cammicks lived there, with at least one daughter, Nellie, being a noted seamstress and dress-maker. It is believed the outbuildings behind the cottage housed a smithy.

The saw-mill closed a few years before the second war, while the huge wheel was taken away during the war. The mill had been owned, until around 1922, by Jim McClements' grandfather, who had sold it to Colonel Sharman Crawford. One theory, which seems plausible, is that the earlier windmill (Paddy Wightman's) had effectively been replaced by the water-driven corn mill in the village. In turn the corn mill had been converted into a saw-mill, which was then replaced by the more modern Ballyleidy one. The Crawford Estate had no longer such need.

It is recorded however that the pitch pine which was extensively used in the Colonel's model farm, was all processed at the Crawfordsburn saw-mill. One of the huge stones from the mill when it was used to grind corn still exists, as do the remains of two adjacent lime kilns, which were at least in part fired using offcut wood from the saw-mill. They may date from around the 1860s.

The thick-walled cottages adjacent to the saw-mill are around 250 years old. The Old Mill House, allowed to become derelict before it was converted, was originally a fine Georgian farm house. A road ran past it down to the saw-mill. It is believed that Glen House, which was extended in 1903, was built as a Dower house for Crawfordsburn House; it was the home of Colonel Lindsay for many years.

It was some years after the second war before there was a public telephone in Crawfordsburn village. The village post office has been in different locations. Mr Stanley Milling lived in the end cottage, No 1, now called Otira Cottage. Apart from being a cub-master and a great yodeller, he was involved in an escape from capture by the Germans in the second war. The post office was for a while run by his wife in their house. It was later taken on by Mr George Graham in the 1930s who had worked for Major Workman at Craigdarragh House. (A section of wall that he built still stands on the Craigdarragh Road.) The post office

was run in its final location, before it closed in March 1992, by Emma Graham and her sister. Initially they had only provided one 'national' English newspaper – the *Daily Express*; this could be partly explained by the fact that for many years the national papers came by ferry thus arriving in local newsagents only in late afternoon. (Sarah Reid then ran a coffee shop there.) In the early 1950s there was a hardware, china and stationery store run by Mr Cannaway.

Among residents of note was James Young, the well-known Ulster comedian, who lived along the Cootehall Road. Many residents speak of him and Jack Hudson with affection.

There have also been several developers who have built apartments, houses and other premises both in the two villages and further afield. Another book would be required to cover more recent developments.

In the more recent past, Helen's Bay station hosted a restaurant, for a time 'The Carriage' run by Domenico Traversari, but also 'Deanes in the Square', owned by Michael Deane from 1993 who moved to Belfast in 1997. (He was Northern Ireland's first Michelin star chef.)

Suffice it to say that Station Square in Helen's Bay continues to be an important little commercial centre, now with a pharmacy, an off-

Above left: Lime kiln and mill stone behind the Water Mill, Crawfordsburn.
Above right: Main Street, Crawfordsburn.

licence, hairdressers, and a dentist. There is also a beauty spa coming to the old station building, now renovated.

Crawfordsburn Main Street, now as ever a key part of the village's appeal, houses a pottery, a craft shop and an architect, as well as the Inn. Gertie Gribben recalls a former Secretary of State making a purchase in Cottage Crafts the cost of which she advised him amounted to £16.90, a figure he should note. The recently-appointed Roy Mason only looked blankly at her. Douglas Hurd's wife had more success learning to spin on her wheel.

Alas the street no longer has the resident tea leaf reader whose clientele at one time extended as far as fashion houses in Belfast and beyond.

The Crawfordsburn SPAR and independent garage run by John and Linda McCormick provide an important local service, open for long hours. It is the development of Jack McCormick's garage which opened on Christmas Eve 1955. The first tanker of petrol delivered then cost just £500 – less than a hundredth of today's price. At a time when one could buy four gallons for a pound, Linda recalls filling up a Daimler with no less than 28 gallons, (compared with the 3 gallon tank in the original Mini). One resident recalls wheeling the punctured tyre off her Mini, right through the village, to be mended by Jack McCormick.

Crawfordsburn Country Park has the Woodlands Café, set in an attractive location. Helen's Bay Organic Gardens, off Coastguard Avenue, supplies a wide range of organic vegetables and other produce, and provides a home for Helen's Bay Community Gardens. At the top of the Cootehall Road is Dicksons, the popular garden centre, occupying a field once farmed for his lifetime by Mr Rowley who worked for Clandeboye Estate.

There are also an increasing number of businesses now run from premises outside the traditional village centres, or indeed from individuals' own houses. While no list can be complete, they include bed-and-breakfast and self-catering accommodation, coach hire, a catering company, a coffee shop, computer repair, jewellery, horticultural expertise and gardening assistance, management consultancy, health practitioners, building and interior decorating services, information technology expertise and handymen.

In both villages there have been a number of writers, actors and artists, either resident or regular visitors. They include Harold Goldblatt, renowned as a leading member of Belfast's Group Theatre before and after the war, whose brother lived in Helen's Bay, and in Crawfordsburn the writer Meta Reid and the playwright Arnold Hill. (However one suggestion that Daphne du Maurier and her husband lived for a short while in Crawfordsburn during the war has not been substantiated.) The area still has a thriving creative arts community, including painters and those interested in the media and cinema, as well as individuals involved in running international charities.

Top right: Jack McCormick's Service Station at Crawfordsburn, shortly after opening.
Bottom right: Filling up at Crawfordsburn Service Station.

Chapter 4

Schools

Schools in the Two Villages

In the field of elementary education it would seem that our local townlands were progressively minded, encouraged by the interest shown and financial assistance given by local proprietors, notably Lord Dufferin, William Sharman Crawford and Mr Turnley of Rockport. By 1836 there were five schools in all, with just over 300 children on the rolls. These schools were generally built by public subscription and teachers' salaries were met by weekly or monthly payments by the children's parents, augmented by annual sums from the wealthy patrons.

Interestingly, Crawfordsburn village was the site of the two biggest schools. The longer established school, Ballymullan (East) or Crawfordsburn School, was a long, low, rectangular building 26' x 20', whitewashed and slated, though probably thatched in its early days. Sam Cargo was one of those given a grant of land in the 1780s on which to build the school. (The family gave their name to a road in Crawfordsburn, one notable descendant born in 1842 emigrated to New Zealand in 1861. After trying his hand at mining, this Samuel Cargo became a farm manager and finally in 1885 acquired 142 acres of his own at Seadown. One local historian suggested that he took out some Crawfordsburn sheep which became an antipodean breed but enquiries of the New Zealand Sheepbreeders' Association have drawn a blank.) The school stood at the Bangor end of the village below the small dam beside the river. It had been completed in 1792 and maintained by the people of the four adjoining townlands, Ballykillaire, Ballymullen, Ballygilbert and Ballygrot. In 1832 it was placed under the National Education Board, which paid the master £20 a year. In addition he received £18 from William Sharman Crawford and £5 from his pupils who numbered 84 in 1836 'including 4 Catholics', according to the contemporary *Ordnance Survey* memoir.

The first school at Ballysallagh (the *townland of the willows*) dating from the 1820s is now a dwelling house. It was said to be the successor of a hedge school where the pupils worked in the shelter of a hedge or in the shelter of a bank, often taught by hedge schoolmasters. Summer afternoon Sabbath schools met in Ballysallagh. Occasional evening prayer meetings and services were held there also till the school passed into the care of the National Board in 1851.

The newer and bigger school Ballymullan (West), built by Lord Dufferin in 1834 on an elevated site at the opposite end of the village, provided elementary education for 114 pupils in 1836, 'including 2 Catholics,' and from 1854 accommodated all the children of the neighbourhood. (It is interesting to note that here too we find something of the apparent competition between the two large land-owners.) Both Ballymullan schools in the mid-1830s had roughly a two to one ratio of boys to girls, perhaps comparatively emancipated for the time.

Emma Graham remembers attending this facility, at the top of 'School Hill', across the road from the Masonic Hall, though she left while only 13 to help her mother in the post office. A portion of the stone wall surrounding the school still remains. From 1928 James Donaghey was the Principal, initially prior to the arrival of electricity. (James Pyper had been Principal from 1897-1920, followed by Isaac McLoughlin up to 1928.) He was particularly keen to promote horticulture; three drills of potatoes, peas and beans were grown along with other things. The boys were taken each spring to Sunnybrook Farm to collect beech twigs to use as pea sticks, and were taught the skill of grafting fruit trees by Colonel Greeves's gardener (Mr Lindsay). In one photograph Mr Donaghey looks on; the Masonic Lodge can be seen in the background. Emma Graham recalls that when Mr Donaghey turned up at school wearing his plus fours, he was always

Above: Crawfordsburn Village viewed from the start of Ballymullan Road.

going on to play golf that afternoon. Mr Stevenson was the last Principal. Brian Kennedy, whose family had moved to the newly-built Altanagh at the Ballyrobert end of Ballymullan Road in 1926, remembers sitting the Eleven Plus exam, in the year it was introduced, at Ballymullan School. It had clearly prepared him well, as he won a scholarship to Sullivan. (He recalls reading a book about Wagner's operas, at the school.) Emma Graham remembers learning in depth about the counties of England, but no teaching was provided on Irish history, even if asked to do so.

Kerry Greeves, who did not attend, remembers there was an air raid shelter for the children behind the school, on the roof of which one could climb – out of school hours. His family was living down the road at Coolnashee which had been built by his father in 1925. The schoolmaster had a house provided by the Clandeboye Estate on the Ballyrobert Road, until the school closed.

Nicknames, often first awarded at school were much more common in previous times. They could last – not necessarily to the individual's pleasure – for a lifetime. Some local examples include Larky, Spud, Soda and even Plonker.

The present, replacement, Crawfordsburn School was completed in 1952, built for 120 pupils, at a cost of £30,000. It was described in glowing terms in the *County Down Spectator* as

*'without exception the finest country school in County Down…
Spacious lawns, an imposing entrance and a sweeping carriageway
add to the attractiveness of the building. Scholars attending this bright,
new and modern school situated in such an attractive spot
should be both happier and healthier',*

the article concluded. A bus was provided to convey children from the outlying districts of Helen's Bay and Ballyrobert. The first Principal was Mr Stevenson, succeeded by Mr Andy Francey, who had previously run the Clandeboye School.

The *Northern Herald* recorded the official opening in May 1953. As Rev Park put it, the children had entered the promised land, after many years of wandering and tribulations. Alderman Thomas Bailie MP and Mayor formally opened the school, under a cloudless blue sky, describing it as the best of its kind in the six counties. He noted that both Rev Park and Mr Donaghey had separately been told when they first

Above left: Ballymullan School, Crawfordsburn; note Mr Donaghey in plus fours (on a golfing day), also including Emma and Kathleen Graham, Viney Lindsay, Eileen and Maureen Neill.
Above right: Ballymullan School; including Jim and Winnie Holden (centre back row), Sadie Derby, Peter Irwin, Nan Graham, Elizabeth Thompson, Maureen Neill, Kathleen and Lilian Graham.

arrived that a new school would be built within two years. The old school had been 'lamentably unsuitable'. He then achieved popularity with the children by informing them that that day's holiday would not be deducted from the Coronation holidays, as the education authorities had proposed, at his request.

The school has subsequently been significantly extended, although not until after a period in the 1960s when the P5 children had to use the Terence Memorial Hall across the Cootehall Road.

While a Montessori pre-school is currently very much in business, at least two schools have come and gone in Helen's Bay. In the early part of the last century, the house at the bottom of Church Road in Helen's Bay (Seahaven) was Boyce's Academy for Girls. There are first-hand accounts of senior pupils having tethered the ponies on which they had come to school at a large ring at the back of the house, while they attended lessons. Indeed one girl rode over from the Ballymoney Road, accompanied by her groom who then took the pony away and brought it back for the end of classes.

A longer lasting private school for younger children, and one better regarded among its alumni, was run from the 1930s by Miss Jefferson at Seamount, 24 Church Road, with the help of Mrs Cook who owned the house. Carol McCartney was one who has happy memories of her time there, in particular Miss Jefferson's reading and acting in plays in the garden in the summer. Kerry Greeves recalls the pupils being taken onto the patio every morning to do their daily callisthenics. Mary Strahan recalls that naughty children were smacked with a ruler. One day, as the children were waiting outside for the school to be opened, the brakes on Miss Jefferson's bicycle failed, and to their great amusement she went flying past on down to the bottom of Church Road before she could regain control. Her brother James fondly recollects Judy Nelson, the junior teacher, instructing him in reading. The school kept going during the war; whenever the air raid siren sounded, the children were bundled into the cloakroom until the 'all clear'.

The school was latterly run by Mrs Winifred Bailie, a very keen Girl Guide leader, (whose father was Mayor of Bangor), assisted by Jean McArdle. Jean came to the school in 1951 which then catered for up to 20 four to seven year olds, and stayed with it in various premises (latterly on Bridge Road) up to its end in 1975. She remembers acquiring a second hand piano for the princely sum of £1.50 which Mrs Buckler, who was a great supporter, arranged to be delivered. It was as well it was so reasonable, because Jean recalls not all Helen's Bay parents were diligent in paying the school fees. The school provided a rounded education – on a fine summer's day, formal classes might end at 11 am and the school would decant to the beach. Not all the children were keen on initial attendance; one child made a point of crying till he made himself sick in the porch, until the day Jean presented him with a basin under his chin and graciously invited him to be sick into that. She also remembers a special invitation from Councillor Sawers' son to tea with his aunt, which was followed by a precarious climb up a ladder to inspect the pigeons he kept at his parents' home, Rust Hall. He also built a raft which was launched off the beach with due ceremony but from which he had to be rescued promptly when it started sinking. (Jean's association with the village includes a stint as organist at the Presbyterian Church and a remarkable record of teaching Scottish country dancing for over 50 years.)

Since 1999, in a single-storey building adjacent to St John's Church, Helen's Bay has had a Montessori pre-school for up to 16 children aged 2 to 4. In January 2008 the local children joined in the centenary celebrations by releasing 100 golden balloons into the sky and planting a rose tree. Montessori Helen's Bay is currently owned and run by Directress Joanne Mills.

(By way of background, Dr Maria Montessori, the founder of Montessori Education, was born in Italy in 1870 and was an influential pioneer in early childhood education of the last century. She was the first woman to graduate from the University of Rome Medical School and she became interested in education through her work as a doctor, using the classroom to observe children and developing the best ways of helping them achieve their full potential. The result was a method of education, the central idea being freedom of the child to work within a carefully planned and structured environment. Maria advocated that all children are intrinsically motivated to learn and that they absorb knowledge without effort when provided with the right kind of activities at the right time in their development.)

Nearby Schools

Although they are a little outside the geographical scope of this book, it would be right to mention three other nearby schools attended by local children.

Glencraig School:

There has been a school at Glencraig since around 1820, initially at the corner of Seahill Road and the A2. It was a church school overseen in the latter part of the 19th century by the redoubtable Canon John Hare Duke (who had changed his name by deed poll from Ducke), Vicar of Glencraig who was born in the year of Waterloo. Coming to Glencraig in 1869, he served until his death aged 90. When 61 he married for the second time, and then had no less than seven children.
(It is recorded in the family that one of his brothers, a missionary in Brazil, was eaten by cannibals.)

Canon Duke wrote of Glencraig School
'that the farmers and labourers of this parish, can, for one penny a week, secure for their children a thoroughly good secular education, fitting them for an efficient discharge of the duties of their position in life, ought to be a sufficient inducement to their largely availing themselves of so great an advantage'.

The Canon himself selected the schoolmaster, who received £40 per year with a 'free house and coals'. The children were to be reminded that when they meet 'the Vicar or Mrs Duke outside to show courtesy, the boys to make a bow – the girls a curtsey'. (Some might think that an admirable precept for today.) Duke was clearly hard to please; in selecting the Master in 1895, he wrote in his diary about the successful one of four applicants – 'nothing better'. This was the unfortunate Mr Sloan, who is recorded as being called a pig by one of his young charges who then threw stones at the school door when asked to step outside, and was three years later given notice to leave on Boxing Day. So perhaps Duke's judgement was not faulty. The faithful infant teacher, Miss Clokey, stepped into the breach. George Woodhouse was the Canon's last appointment in 1903, and a sound one too, as he continued as Master for 39 years. In 1926, the running of the school was transferred to the Ministry of Education. The present building within the old walled garden of Rockport was opened in January 1966, and then extended 11 years later.

Tom Cave attended the former Glencraig School, although he was initially sent back home when it was discovered that he was too young to attend. He recalls being regularly caned for poor spelling by the then Principal, (Ed Caves), but bore no malice as Caves also frequently rewarded him with a penny tip for getting paraffin from Craigavad Stores for his use at home. Tom and his brothers used to wear clogs; his brother was soundly told off by the formidable lady teacher for walking too loudly in the classroom. When they got outside, the disused section of the old Belfast Road, which had shortly before been straightened out at the Devil's Elbow, was the pupils' playground.

Clandeboye or Ballysallagh School:

Clandeboye or Ballysallagh School moved to the site of the modern day Clandeboye Lodge Hotel in 1859 and remained there until its closure, when Mr WJ Henry was Principal, in 1969. The school was built entirely using locally produced materials, apart from the roof tiles.

Isaac McLoughlin was appointed Headmaster of Clandeboye School in the 1890s. He took lodgings at the house of a widow with a small farm on the Ballysallagh road, (where the Ulster Way now crosses it). He married one of her daughters. Shortly thereafter he was elected Secretary of the Irish Protestant National Teachers Union, in which capacity he served up to Partition. He was presented with a splendid illuminated address in 1920, though he became the first President of the Ulster Teachers Union (in its place). At about this time he transferred from Clandeboye to the Ballymullan School in Crawfordsburn. This had

Bottom left: Canon John Hare Duke, Rector of Glencraig, 1869-1905.

the advantage of enabling his daughters to travel to Belfast by train from Helen's Bay for their work, although he himself continued to travel considerable distances by bicycle. As a Clandeboye employee, he and his family had the right to walk up the Drive to Ballygilbert Church on Sundays.

George Henderson has these memories of the School. (George adds that it should not be taken as a reflection on the school that these memories are less about education and more about survival skills.)

'My mother Kathleen McCracken lived on the Ballybarnes Road and attended Clandeboye School from 1908. She walked over the fields to the Ulster Way sign at Cochrane's Hill on the Ballysallagh Road opposite the old Ballysallagh School and then walked down the road to school. A photograph records the pupils attending in 1910.

In the next generation, we lived on the Millbrooke Road at Hillview Farm. Our family consisted of eight boys and two girls and we all attended the school between 1930 and 1952. Some walked to school while others got the bus, but we all walked home. While waiting for the bus opposite the end of Ballybarnes Road (if we hadn't missed it) we sat on a wall outside the gate of the house at the road side. The wall consisted of flat horizontal stones with upright stones at intervals making perfect seats. This arrangement was not appreciated by the owner as he tarred the wall so we were unable to sit on it anymore. The older ones looked after the younger ones – no adults were deemed necessary. My own

Above left: The illuminated address presented to Isaac McLoughlin in 1920.
Top right: The former Clandeboye (or Ballysallagh) School, 1910. Bottom right: The former Clandeboye (or Ballysallagh) School, 1949; (note the Henderson boys all turned out in ties and waistcoats).

memories of school from 1942 to 1948 are of soldiers and prisoners of war marching past the school frequently; they were stationed at Helen's Tower (camp gate) and Fairview (Finlay's Farm.) The American soldiers walked across the Dufferin Drive and two fields to Hillview looking for eggs and they gave us children chewing gum. Pupils used to collect used bullets and when someone found a blank it was put in the pot-bellied stove and after a few hours there would be a loud bang, this did not go down well with Mr Francey. We enjoyed the daily 1/3 pint bottle of milk; lots of pupils did not like theirs so my brothers and I sometimes drank two or three bottles each. In the winter the milk would often be frozen solid. Between the school and the Clandeboye Estate there was a grass area which was changed into a vegetable plot, where we grew potatoes, carrots, parsnips, peas and beans. Mr Francey got us to dig a deep trench and pick up all the stones. I have never seen longer parsnips since; I think Mr Francey exhibited the produce in local shows, this was just after the war.

In the woods beside the school there were lots of red squirrels and we picked hazelnuts and enjoyed them as much as the squirrels.

When walking home from school we passed Brown's Orchard at Ballysallagh House which was handy for apples to eat on the way home. Occasionally we would hear a shout and have to run for it and climb the fence which got higher each year. They also had a field of turnips and we would nip in for one to eat on our way home. Barney Hughes Bread Van would pass us regularly and we would chant:

'Barney Hugh's Bread sticks to your stomach like lead
No bit a wonder you fart like thunder
When you eat Barney Hugh's Bread.'

The driver would make the van backfire when passing, much to our delight. School-boy humour.

My first teacher was Mrs Williamson and then I progressed to the other side of the curtain which separated the room into two classrooms to Mr Francey's class before I moved to Bangor when I was 11 years old. Mr Francey moved to Crawfordsburn School in 1952 as Principal and afterwards two other teachers at Clandeboye were Mrs Marie Fulton and Mr Henry. My elder brothers Edward and Zander were taught by Mrs Longmore (the mother of Robin, the golfer) and Mr Grant. My brother Eric and sisters Ellie and Jean were also taught by Mrs Longmore and then Mr Robey. Mrs Longmore's name was described by a child 'as something to do with cutting grass.'

Mr Francey came after Mr Robey. When we boys were kept off school by my father eg for threshing or other harvest necessities, his note never varied – 'Name of child' was 'unavoidably detained'. Mrs McKee was the Education Welfare Officer, she cycled around the countryside to check on school attendance and was known as 'Ma McKee'. (The *Spectator* paid tribute on her retirement in 1959, noting that she had in over 20 years in the post cycled many thousands of miles round North Down, having only taken on the job when her husband became too ill to do it himself. Joe McEwen records her frustration when boys would turn up for school late, having helped out on the milk round beforehand.)

Mabel Jess was brought up on a farm in Ballysallagh. She recalls walking to and from school, from the age of five, being trailed along by her elder siblings. Jim McClements attended the school for one year. His grandfather Mr Rowley was the Clandeboye chauffeur (for some 60 years); it was tremendous to be collected from the school in a Rolls Royce.

Rockport:

Rockport School was opened in September 1906. It has always been housed in the property originally built by John Turnley in 1817. The school was started by Geoffrey Bing (of Keble College, Oxford) with a matron, an assistant master and just four boys. (At least one of the original boys was killed in the first war.) The local connections were however strengthened when Bing married Canon Duke's daughter, Irene, the following year. By 1909 cricket matches were being played against Campbell College and Holywood Ladies. In 1913, there were 35 boys at the school. During the war, Bing bought 27 adjacent acres on which to raise cattle and grow produce for the school. Although he was succeeded in 1945 by Eric Tucker, who in turn was Head for just on 30 years, for a long while the Rockport pupils were known in the neighbourhood as 'the Bing boys', (see photograph on page 60).

Kerry Greeves went to Rockport during some of the second war years. When the air raid warnings sounded during the Blitz, the staff and pupils stayed in a basement. On one occasion, he insisted he needed to go to the toilet upstairs. He managed to take a look out of the window and vividly recalls seeing, against a clear evening sky, massive waves of planes droning along the Lough on their way to attack Belfast. One of the Rockport cows was killed in a blast. Kerry and a friend found on one of their rambles two large cylinders on the shore. Intrigued by the military markings on them, they struggled with them back to school where they hid their booty under a building, raised on stilts. Mr Bing lost no time in sending for the Army to take the objects away and blow them up, safely. Mr Bing, he recalls, had a limp and could be very cross. You could tell by the way his eyebrows knitted up, when he was going to beat someone. Pre-war, there had been a jetty on the beach below the school, and a large boulder in the sea. Swimming trials, with 'colours' awarded for successful completion, were held for pupils to swim various distances. It was not only boys; Caroline Blackwood was one of several girls in the late 1930s. Indeed she beat all the boys to win the Under 14 athletics prize.

Continuity has played an important part in the Rockport story – Chris McFerran was a governor for over 30 years. On the other hand things have changed over the times. Mrs Sinclair, who was Mr Tucker's secretary, recalls taking her sons into her office in their pram from when they were only a month old, so she could return to carry on her work.

Sunday Schools and Other Children's Organisations

Sabbath, or Sunday, Schools have played a significant part in the history of youth organisations in Helen's Bay. The first Sabbath School in Helen's Bay was held in the Presbyterian Church around the time of the erection of the

Congregation on 6 August 1895, and that of St John's Church somewhat later, in the early 20th century. In Crawfordsburn, a Sunday School was run in the 1940s in the Terence Memorial hall by Mr Wallace, who was the clerk of Session at Ballygilbert Church. It appears from a photograph taken outside the hall, clearly shortly after its completion, that this followed an earlier precedent. The Hall also housed an evening service taken by Dr Park, on alternate Sundays.

On the occasion of the Silver Jubilee of H.M King George V and Queen Mary all the children in the Sunday Schools were presented with splendid *New Testaments*. These bore the inscription: 'The English Bible, the first of National Treasures and the most valuable thing that this world affords, His Majesty King George V.'

A Girl Guide Company and also a Brownie Pack were started in Helen's Bay in the early 1920s by Mrs Trelford. Meetings were held in the loft above the garage of her home, Ballygrot House, her three daughters comprising the nucleus of the Guide Company. It is generally considered that it was after her daughter, Kathleen who later married Major Robert Stephens, that Kathleen Avenue – previously called 'The Middle Road' – was named. However another school of thought attributes it to Kathleen Brown of Tordeevra. Others involved in the Guides were two kindergarten teachers from Glenlola. Helen's Bay (B) Company Girl Guides, whose standard is kept in the Presbyterian Church, was formed in the early 1930s. Their uniform in the early days was a heavy cotton drill material worn with a felt hat. This was superseded by a lighter weight, more modern, uniform.

Some 16-20 girls attended, the numbers made up by a small contingent from Crawfordsburn and one girl from Craigavad, who,

Bottom left: St John's Sunday school, 1944. Top right: Sunday School outside the Terence Memorial Hall; including (it is understood) Samuel Graham, James Reid and Mr Black, John Comac, Samuel McClements, Jane Holden, Jack McClements.

Above: Aerial view of the lower end of Kathleen Avenue.

incidentally, arrived and departed in a chauffeur-driven limousine. One of the Patrol leaders was the daughter of the stationmaster, Mr Rooney. The first meeting was held in the drawing-room of the old Presbyterian Manse, Fort Road, but subsequent meetings were in Buckler's Hall.

An early youth organisation was the 'Leprechauns' – or good Irish fairies. These were started by the Thompson family who lived in the Old Manse on Fort Road. Although a well-to-do family, (Sammy Thompson was a senior Government official who had come from Dublin to help set up the Stormont Civil Service and his wife was Daisy), they had a great awareness of poverty, for Mrs Thompson's brother, Canon CHP Lyndon was the Rector of St Paul's, York Street – a parish in what was then a very needy part of Belfast. (Canon Lyndon had won the MC in the first war, and sadly lost an arm during the second when taking a 'horse-drawn' funeral; a US Army jeep passed at speed and the horses bolted.) The Thompsons brought handicapped Brownies and Guides for a day out in their lovely Manse Garden, carrying the youngsters to tables groaning with food for them to enjoy. Shortly before Christmas, the Leprechauns would gather provisions and funds through 'pound days' held at the Thompsons' house, local residents donating tea, sugar, butter etc topped up with purchases from Smyth and McClure in Bangor. On Christmas morning, they would deliver boxes of goodies to the poorer folk of Newtownards who were startled to receive this generosity from the Leprechauns.

By contrast, Scout troops have never flourished for long in Helen's Bay – perhaps partly because in previous years many local boys went to school in England or belonged to troops allied to their school. The first troop established in 1933 did though last for a while. Their meetings were held in a small hall (now demolished) at the back of the present chemist's shop in Station Square. Cubs have had more success and there has been a Pack on and off from the 1930s to the present day.

Above: Rockport School, summer term, 1910. Mr and Mrs Bing are in the centre seated. The boys include members of the Workman, Robson, Ross, Hardy, Herdman families, and also WW McBride and JM Inglis who were killed in the first war.

Chapter 5

Growing up in Crawfordsburn and Helen's Bay

A Range of Reminiscences: 'Things were so different then'

Although any account can at best be only partial, it is worth recreating some elements of the childhood that those who grew up in Crawfordsburn and Helen's Bay enjoyed between the 1930s and the 1950s. It is clear that many look back on those days with affection, even though times were hard, school teachers caned regularly and there was not much money around. On the other hand, it was an attractive environment in which to grow up, with freedom to enjoy the fields, the shore and the sea, with a population small enough to ensure that everyone was known. As many have commented – things were so different then.

One perspective comes from Tom Cave whose father was a farrier, who lived in a wooden bungalow for the first 11 years of his life from 1940, then with seven siblings, beside the labourers' cottages at the top end of the Craigdarragh Road. He remembers his father paring the feet of the donkey owned by Charles (later Sir Charles, though still known to many as Charlie) Brett who lived across the road. Davy Cave was good at making wrought iron, a skill he had acquired with the Services in Germany. In all that time, they had neither electricity nor running water, even though these had been installed in the posher houses on the Craigdarragh Road in the 1930s. (Separately a tale is told of one lady who came to consider buying a large property on Craigdarragh Road but recoiled in horror when she discovered the house had only one staircase, which she would have to share with the domestic staff.)

A pump serviced the cottages about 100 yards distant, and Tom still remembers the pain of the pails' metal handles cutting into his hands. Nevertheless his father was punctilious about his children providing a mug and fresh water for those traipsing thirstily along the Craigdarragh Road on a dry summer day.

The original labourers' cottages each had some surrounding land on which they kept hens, ducks, and a calf or a goat too. Jimmy Girvan kept pigs. Jimmy often went to Bangor market on the bus; with drink taken after a successful visit, he would imitate the cries of the itinerant fish salesman – 'fresh herring O'. Tom recalls that Jimmy enjoyed chewing tobacco. When it was finished, he didn't spit it out (as they do in Westerns), rather he carefully dried it out on the range, and then smoked it in his pipe. An early instance of recycling.

Alec Lowry had a vegetable plot. He and his sons used to rise early to purchase additional material from the Oxford Street market. One morning when one son was reluctant to spring out of bed at 4 am, Alec was heard to exclaim in exasperation 'are you going to lie there all day, boy?' He also provided a local delivery service to the villages.

Goods travelled in the other direction too; one regular visitor was the bread server from Inglis's bakery in East Belfast who brought his goods with a horse and cart. The man who did his round selling paraffin was sometimes mystified to find that the tank behind his pony was lighter at his next destination if miscreants had turned on the tap behind him.

From an early age (amazing to think nowadays) as young as eight or nine, local boys were encouraged, if not required, to earn their keep. There were many opportunities then; when the potatoes were due to be harvested the schools would be visited. Tom Cave would hope that he would have the chance to work for Major Workman at Craigdarragh House. Not only did Mr Workman pay the handsome sum of 10 shillings a day, he also ensured that his workers were given a decent lunch at the house. The going rate for a day's work, for example for helping with the hay-making, was two and six pence. One favoured job was using the ruck-shifter to help stack the hay rucks. The sandy bay below Craigdarragh House, which could be reached discreetly through the glen, was a favourite haunt for a swim.

Milk was supplied by Sam Bradley who bottled it on his farm across the main road at Ballyrobert. Tom spent some time as Sam's mate, helping with the deliveries from the top of the Craigdarragh Road down to Grey Point Fort. Tom recalls that Sam was occasionally slow to adjust his driving technique from horse to motorised horsepower; he would tug on the steering wheel shouting 'whoa', before he remembered to use the brake. Sometimes when the van reached their final destination, Sam would go in for a little liquid refreshment at the NAAFI, while Tom would lurk outside hoping that he might be lucky and receive a small pudding or occasionally a wafer biscuit. Another job was picking up shoes from residents in the big houses and delivering them to be mended to the cobbler in the Station Square.

Caddying was another role often favoured by boys. Tom went to the Craigavad course and soon discovered that small stature and waiting politely in line to be asked did not offer much financial reward. A generous tip was a bob, but the more usual rate was a tanner (sixpence). Irwin Parkhurst, the stationmaster's son, also caddied on the Helen's Bay course.

Alfie Beaney's maternal grandfather had a blacksmith's shop at the end of their long thatched cottage at the Devil's Elbow. He recalls on one occasion a bullock broke loose when it was about to be butchered at Ballyrobert, charged along the road and careered into the forge where it did considerable damage. Alas it did not find sanctuary there. Seahill was then a haven for larks and Irish hares. As a youngster Alfie would help Dickie McBride ride horses liveried at Gibsons over to meets of the North Down Harriers at Comber and elsewhere. It is curious to think that they waited, and then rode the horses back again, after a full half day being ridden hard by their owners at the hunt. Horses going further afield would be put on the train at Helen's Bay station. His grandmother (who conveniently did not have to change her surname of McConnell on marriage) was given a traditional cure for whooping cough by an old lady near Ballynahinch where she had previously lived. Alfie confides that this

Top: Sam Bradley's milk bottles, Ballygilbert Dairy Farm.
Bottom: Two contemporary golfers in front of the former club house

consisted of a crust of bread, dipped in tea and then dipped in sugar, with a suitable incantation. He remembers a range of children coming to the house for the cure. Canon Capsey was also a regular visitor to the house, benefitting from Alfie's mother's baking of soda bread; he would ask her in her turn to visit sick children, assuring her of glory in heaven.

Life was not without its physical dangers too. One day when some boys were playing with discarded ammunition, (a hand-grenade which had presumably not come from the local factory), there was a partial explosion and Tom's friend lost his finger while his brother got shrapnel in his legs. Ashley Davis recalls that the shoreline of Belfast Lough was littered with burned out incendiary bombs – cylindrical in shape up to one foot long. His father used to give him the small parachutes, originally attached to the bombs, as playthings. Gary Gillespie found Grey Point Fort an excellent place for a young boy to play in, after the Army moved out. Not only were lots of plywood shooting targets left behind, but there was also a surprising amount of live ammunition scattered around the camp. In earlier, pre-war days, one exciting discovery was made in the thatch of the cottage at the foot of Ballymullan Lane, of a 19th century or even older pistol.

Proximity to the Fort could certainly provide interest. Carol McCartney remembers being invited to play 'housey-housey' in the camp – there was usually something good to eat. In the field next door, soldiers were trained to stab bayonets noisily into straw-filled dummies. Ironically the building of their house, Harbour Grace, had been completed the very day that war broke out. Her father had always wanted large plate glass windows in their new house, and joiners had to be sent for urgently to create solid wooden shutters. Her mother, a Canadian enjoyed camping out, so they would sometimes slip over the garden fence and pitch tents to experience the big outdoors. Her mother was, like many residents frustrated by the heavy clay soil. She would always go out for walks with a bag and it would be a bad day when she didn't manage to bring back some better soil to work into it. In later years her mother opened their garden which included fine alpines, to the public.

In 1939 Sheridan Drive consisted of only two houses - Kabakona where the founders of Glenlola School, the Misses Harte, lived and the thatched house that is now number 21 where first GC Lynn and then

Isaac Stewart resided. Mary Strahan says that the erection of Kabakona was funded by an uncle who made his money building railroads in America. Her aunts accordingly named it by the Indian word for *place of quiet waters*. The aunts never married as their father was a Methodist Minister who frightened off any potential suitor. Their nephew, James Douglas, describes how the energetic Crawfordsburn gardener Billy Keating used to sweep through the garden at Kabakona, putting all to rights, just as 'the Assyrian came down like the wolf on the fold'.

The garden at number 21, Hadley Edge, includes both an imposing air raid shelter, constructed of massive stones and thick concrete, and a croquet lawn. Carol McCartney recalls that when the coal boats that Stewart owned passed in the Lough below, the ships' masters were instructed to toot in respect. (Curiously the three steamers he bought in the 1950s were named simply 'First', 'Second', and 'Third'.) This house remained thatched until 1972, then in the hands of Mr Rutledge Hadley White who owned the Culloden Hotel. It takes its present name from his.

Terence McKeag lived with his family up Coyle's Lane; his father had been a professional jockey. Terence learned very early how to drive a tractor – about 10 years under the age for a driving test. He also had skill with horses which led indirectly to his first job after leaving school, as a trainee manager in the Belfast Faulat factories. The job came to include chauffeuring James A Faulkner and others some evenings. He owed his first pay rise to the future Prime Minister of Northern Ireland.

Branagh's shop was at Gibson's corner, initially in a wooden building, (where the Darragh architectural practice now is). The location was named after Sandy Gibson who then owned Enfield House. Gibson made one of the cottages beside the house available to Mrs Cluney in 1941 after she had lost her home near the Mater hospital in the Blitz. Tom Cave remembers when Coca-Cola first arrived at Branagh's, kept in an ice-filled cabinet; sadly he could not afford it. For many years the shop

Above: Hadley Edge, 21 Sheridan Drive as first built in 1938.

supplied a vital need, putting out buckets, spades and flags for visiting children to acquire on their way through to Helen's Bay beach.

Ashley Davis, as did Mary Shaw, testifies to the number of visitors to the beaches at summer weekends. He recalls hundreds of cyclists passing along Craigdarragh Road on the busiest weekend in the height of the season, as well as trippers queueing four deep up Church Road as they waited patiently for the extra trains put on by the BCDR to get them

back to Belfast. Mary was obliged by her parents to take daily sea bathes to improve her health, from Horse Rock, where in winter she left her clothes and a hot water bottle. In her teens she shared a pony, called Diana, which liked nothing better than lying down in the sea. (Mary was born in 1923. She told the tale that there was then a curfew, even in Helen's Bay. Her father had gone to the post office to summon the doctor but as no-one could be roused at the post office, he had had to get special permission from the police station to drive his own car to get the doctor.)

Pam Gilmer also used to swim in the sea all year round; the aim was to swim from Horse Rock to the boat-house at the far end of the

Top: Helen's Bay beach.
Bottom: Mary Shaw on a haystack on the golf course, outside Seahaven, Church Road.

beach and back. Pam took up golf at the age of eight and competed in juvenile competitions across the road. Her father had both a yacht at the RNIYC and a rowing boat which he kept in the boat-house at the far end of the beach. Pam recalls that many nights they put out a net, and the following morning would collect mackerel and the odd herring. Surplus fish would be given away to friends and neighbours. On one occasion a vast barrel of beer came ashore, off a travelling ship. Her father salvaged it with the help of some friends (the 'Brethren of the sea') and consumed the contents at the boat-house. He dutifully reported the discovery to the local authorities, but they found it empty.

Pam's grandfather had built in 1911 one of the first bungalows with a verandah in Northern Ireland, officially called Vancouver. Her father was reared on Glenside farm below Crawfordsburn, though he later became a manager in the Ulster Bank. In his retirement, he served as an ARP warden. Educated at the Ballymullan Road School and Inst, he achieved local celebrity for producing humorous and generally much-appreciated personal verses about friends and neighbours, under the nom de plume of 'Old Seaweed'. While several of these have rightly been recorded for posterity, we have chosen not to include any, to avoid any risk of offence. Many more serious though still whimsical poems of his were published in the Belfast Telegraph in the 1930s, again under various nom de plumes. While the majority concerned soccer, three verses from one by 'Phelim' on a different topic are included here. (It is self-deprecatory as he was an industrious gardener himself.)

> 'On Friday last, the die was cast,
> My fate was signed and sealed;
> You may assume that troubles loom
> Unless a poet's repealed.
> My little jaunts to soccer haunts
> Are up the pole I fear,
> My simple joys with all the boys
> Are dead as yester-year.
>
> A family tiff and in a jiff,
> If you can understand,
> It was decreed that I, indeed,
> Must henceforth till the land.
> A dreadful biz! My trouble is
> I own a garden plot,
> Which grows in size before my eyes,
> Believe me now or not.
> .....
> And all the while, you'll know that I'll
> Be toiling like a Turk,
> I'm telling you the worms are due
> To see some dirty work.
> I'll spoil their hash, the while I bash
> The beetles and the bugs,
> I'll trim the nails of tribes of snails
> And slice the slimy slugs.'

Harry Gilmer, for it must have been he, fulminated in vain in December 1937 at the impact of the house built by Tom Cull on Horse Rock. Writing in the *County Down Spectator* under 'Consternation in Helen's Bay', he grieved that this 'beloved bathing place of bygone generations' was being sliced up, first by the War Department and now by

Above: The Bungalow, Helen's Bay.

the builder who had erected a six foot fence to prevent access. A poem followed, entitled *The Longshoreman's Lament – My Right of Way (All rights – including rights of way – reserved!)*.

The poem included this verse:

> 'And never more shall I repair
> To catch my cockles on the strand,
> The wily winkle in his lair
> Is safe for ever at my hand.'

Joan Bushell pays tribute to Mr and Mrs Gilmer for never turning anyone away, during crowded summers, if there was a request to use the toilet, to boil the baby's bottle or to bandage cut feet. Gill Johnston recalls getting her feet cut all too often on broken bottles left by trippers on the beach. She had an Australian nanny who was a good swimmer herself, and taught her charges to swim well too. She has many memories of the freedom for children in the area, and always being outdoors. The golf course, accessible through a gate out of her garden, was a huge attraction. She had golf lessons from Tom McKinstry, while Pam Gilmer's sister, Nancy, taught her to dance.

Ashley Davis went to school in West Bangor. At the age of six he would cycle – or rather tricycle – round from his house to Helen's Bay station. He would leave the tricycle in the waiting room and repeat the journey on his return. But Ashley's favourite mode of transport was Hugh Moore's last Shire horse, Bruno. Another resident recalls riding his horse, Sugar, round Rushfield, long before the houses were built. Rabbits abounded in the neighbourhood; Ashley was fond of chasing them – unsuccessfully – in the same field. Mushrooms could be picked in good quantity before Sheridan Drive was completed. Michael Murray recalls shooting snipe, on Saturday mornings, in Rushfield – they liked the boggy ground. Other outdoor occupations for different generations include searching for clay pipes discarded by farm workers on Irish Hill and placing pennies on the railway line to be flattened by the oncoming train.

For successive generations of children in Helen's Bay, the beach has been a key focal point. A group of friends would make a fire and cook sausages; the Drive too was another haunt for many, including for impromptu barbecues. Going to the cinema in Bangor was for some, a

Top left: Grey Point, Helen's Bay.
Bottom left: Helen's Bay beach, showing Tom Cull's house at the end.

monthly treat. Sea fishing was also popular (with the occasional foray to snaffle salmon up the burn). Less popular was the charge levied by the Dufferin Estate for several years in the 1950s. Access to the beach then was through the turnstile at the bottom of Fort Road and then past the hut where Tommy lurked to take your money or check your annual ticket. Then at the far end of the beach, the archway into the Crawfordsburn side could be closed off, at least in theory, if not in practice for those able to scale the wall.

There were those who sought to sustain certain standards. One newly-resident mother enjoyed patronising the weekly library van. The redoubtable wife of a local colonel was wont to scrutinise her book selection for the week and comment loudly 'I wouldn't have that in my house with a young girl in it'. One of the first televisions to arrive in Helen's Bay was at Rathwyre in Kathleen Avenue, the home of the Grants. Mr Grant owned the Grand Central Hotel in Belfast. Derek Lindsay remembers Mr Grant with affection; he would drive up to the Old Inn, park in the street and – if he was in the right place at the right time – give Derek half-a-crown to 'go and buy sweets with'.

Before the Grants, Rathwyre had been owned by Captain Thomas Dawson Morrison MC who had joined the RIC in July 1920, after serving in the Royal Munster Fusiliers. He was adjutant of the Gormanston Training Camp until disbandment of the RIC two years later. He rose to become Deputy Inspector General of the Royal Ulster Constabulary in 1952. He is also credited as the founder of the RUC Athletic Association at New Forge, and the Morrison Cup is competed for annually still. In the Second World War, Morrison was in charge of the Special Constabulary and the Ulster Home Guard. His house was therefore kept under the watchful eye of two soldiers.

In the very early days there was no relay station in Northern Ireland, so local television reception was very patchy. Several more households purchased televisions in the immediate run-up to the Queen's Coronation in 1953, including the Grants. The photograph shows Mr and Mrs Field hosting a group of friends and neighbours at Carrig Gorm on the great day, including the McCartneys, Crosthwaits, and the McKeowns among others.

Again, few households could afford fancy cars – the first Jaguar was spotted in Kathleen Avenue. However many boys built themselves buggies, using old pram wheels etc. Ashley recalls not only many exciting races down Church Road, but also being given a lift back up the road by

Top left: Helen's Bay Beach on a busy day, showing the groynes and sand dunes. Bottom Left: Painting of the boat-house and Estate wall by Morrison.
Top right: Captain TD Morrison OBE, BL, MC. Bottom right: Mr and Mrs Field and a group of friends outside Carrig Gorm on Coronation Day 1953.

soldiers in jeeps, to start their next journey down again. Soldiers from the Fort also took a personal interest in the maids who were live-in servants in the big houses on Kathleen Avenue and elsewhere. For their part, maids enjoyed attending social functions such as whist drives at the Fort, (according to 'Rene Shuttleworth).

One man at the Coastguard Cottages was particularly skilled in salvaging large planks of wood that drifted down the Lough from the shipyards, and fetched up on the shoreline towards Grey Point. Many a barn or garage was roofed with such doughty timber. (While there is less material, beachcombing is a local practice that continues to this day.)

One resident recalls her feeling of frustration because her father was good with his hands and made her a wooden pram which he decorated. In vain did she try to persuade her friends to exchange their shop-purchased metal prams. Gary Gillespie's father took on the role of Santa Claus, trudging round the village on Christmas morning, delivering small gifts to any of his regular customers who had little children.

Entertainment was sometimes available for free. Jean Blair remembers the time when Mr Ewing's pet parrot escaped from its cage at Carrig Gorm. It flew from tree to tree; the unfortunate gardener was urged to climb each tree in turn until finally the bird was recaptured.

Music and dance were an important part of life, when the work was done. At Glenholme, an informal jazz club was located – the entrance fee was a princely three pence. One local dance band included Thomas Lindsay (melodeon), Bill McCormick (banjo) and Frankie Norton on the drums. They played in local venues, including Crawfordsburn and Ballyrobert Orange Halls. Mrs Shillington, at Windover Lodge on the Ballymullan Road, was reputedly a world ballroom dancing champion, partnered with Victor Sylvester. In Helen's Bay, a group of players met regularly at Sheridan Lodge, the Shillingfords' home. They included Tony Greeves, Clare Johnson and June Shuttleworth on violins, Anthony's father or
Mrs Marjorie Livingstone playing the piano, his mother on the cello, and then Anthony on the clarinet. Palm Court music such as *Lilac Time* was a favourite.

As in other parts of Ulster, motor sport was a feature in former years. Jim McClements recalls that his father, with a group of friends, would set off at 6 am, with their lunch, to walk to Bradshaw's Brae to see the Ards TT, returning only after the race was all finished. Jim himself went on to much success in motor sport competitions, both in Northern Ireland and further afield. His cousin, Sam, who achieved great renown as a biker, was brought up in Rosevale.

In June 1935 and again the following year, (the year of the fatal accident in the Ards race), there was a Bangor TT. This was a new circuit for the County Down Trophy. The *Spectator* provided good coverage. There were 20 entries, including an American who brought his car over on the liner Aquitania. The 5.9 mile circuit started at Bangor station and came out as far as the Cootehall Road, before turning back to Bangor, passing through Bryansburn, and down Gray's Hill and along Queen's Parade. It was a handicap race, with the less powerful cars being required to complete some five or so fewer laps. In 1935 the winner was an MG Midget which benefitted from six credit laps. The driver found the bumps at Bangor West 'disconcerting'. The fastest car was driven by the Brazilian Luis Fontes whose quickest lap took a little more than four minutes, at over 82 mph, 'truly a terrific performance'. Fontes said that the circuit was more difficult than the Isle of Man. That year, the marshals on Gray's Hill were troubled by dogs – one met an untimely death under the wheels

Bottom left: Carrig Gorm.

of a car, while in 1936 a dog caused another driver to retire when it bent his steering system. That race had been started by Northern Ireland's Prime Minister, and the cars were still 'head to tail at Crawfordsburn Corner'. The prizes were awarded at Caproni's Palais de Dance, where Princess Nina Mdivani and her party had several tables, the paper noted.

Additionally, a motor cycle rally route consisted of a different circuit, passing right through Crawfordsburn, along the Ballyrobert Road, out toward Bangor, and then roaring down the Cootehall Road.

Politics could also intrude, though with a sense of excitement for youngsters. Margaret Garner recalled seeing members of the Ulster Volunteer Force drilling on the lawn of Craigdarragh House in 1912. Thomas Workman was clearly a man of strong views. She said that Thomas forbade anyone to speak of Lloyd George in his house and when a Roman Catholic nun friend visited an aunt who lived at the big house, she was obliged to stay at the gate lodge, rather than Craigdarragh House, and the then residents in the lodge were cleared out for her. The approach to Home Rule was not unique however; another resident has recalled how their relative, while working for the Crawford Estate, was required to join the UVF and similarly take part in drills at Crawfordsburn House.

Margaret recollected another incident when she fell seriously ill on a family holiday in Cushendun; the doctor from Helen's Bay was summoned to attend in his pony and trap. (She did not recall how long it had taken the unfortunate man to get there and back.)

Bob Jess recalled one tragedy in Crawfordsburn, in the first part of the last century. He and his sister had been playing in the village, when they heard a man whose clothes had caught fire shouting to them. As young children would, they ran home up Jess' Lane (beside the Orange Hall) to Seaview, on the hill, to fetch their father. By the time he returned, the man could not be saved.

Emma Graham was one to recall the era before running water, mains drains and indoor bathrooms (the last of which arrived in her house in 1951). Traditionally water came from the pump across the road. Her father was the first, in the row of cottages on their side of the Main Street, to make arrangements to have water piped into the house. He had to pay the council the princely sum of five pounds, and do the work himself (starting at 5 am to reduce disruption to the street), though this was later reimbursed after inspection. The Grahams continued to pay the Dufferin Estate for their water supply for some years, until the Council engineer advised them that their water was now coming from the Silent Valley. Her family also had no electricity when they first moved into the post office; there was a precious Tilley lamp which she, as a young child, was not allowed to light.

The Lindsays in Main Street had their own well from which to draw water, but again no electricity for many years. Baths were taken in an iron bath before the fire, in water boiled over the range.

Times were sometimes hard. Emma Graham recalls that some people in Crawfordsburn could not afford to buy coal for their fires, so folk joined in collecting branches and other firewood to burn at home. One building that could always afford a fire in her day was the Ballymullan Road School; there was an oven on top of the fire, to which the children would take bacon and eggs and other local produce for what would now be called 'domestic economy'.

For sport, Emma learned to play badminton, along with the Shuttleworths' son at St John's Church Hall. This of course was in the original Church Hall over which the roof leaked badly, so on a rainy day the players had to contend with buckets on the badminton court too. Brian Kennedy helped his father, Gilbert, remake a tennis court on the lawn at Altanagh on the Ballymullan Road; space restrictions meant the doubles tramlines were narrower than regulation. The house had a clear view over the fields towards Helen's Bay and the Lough, in those days.

Nigel Kelso was 15 years of age when his mother and he arrived in Crawfordsburn in 1952. His mother 'Paddy' Kelso had secured an appointment as Manageress of the

Above: Nigel Kelso dressed to wait at the Crawfordsburn Country Club.

Crawfordsburn Country Club. His most vivid memories were of sunny summer days spent exploring the fields behind the Country Club and watching the magnificent white swans on the dam, which fed the stream that flowed under the road and behind the Old Inn. In the winter they would swoop in over the road to land on the dam but on one occasion the dam was frozen over and the swans skidded with a flurry of feathers and flapping of wings and ended up in the rushes at the far end.

Nigel used to ride his bicycle into Bangor to go to the pictures. There was a tobacconist shop in the upper half of the Main Street (run by Mrs Murphy), which had a large room at the rear where one could leave a cycle for a few hours for about 6d. (This 'accommodation' would not have been much use in the early days of the Tonic Cinema when to get to the film-show 'Toot' Finlay drove his blue Fordson tractor into Bangor.) Nigel would also ride down to Helen's Bay, buy an ice cream and eat it whilst watching the trains go by, before the long climb back up the hill.

Their accommodation comprised of two rooms, one round the back near the kitchen and the other upstairs above the front entrance, access to which was up an internal flight of stairs from a room which was then used by the members for some serious card games. Nigel recalls watching out through the keyhole, at the players seated around a large round card table covered in green baize and with hollowed out polished receptacles for their chips. The room would be filled with a haze of blue smoke and the drinks were liberally replenished from the wine cellar immediately below that room.

There was only one shop that he remembered – opposite the bus stop and as he waited for the bus to take him into Bangor, he would muse over the wording displayed over the shop window and door. On the left in small sloping print were the words 'Fancy Goods, Stationery' then in the middle in large letters 'S.CANNAWAY' and on the right 'Hardware, China'. The reason he remembered it was because he would translate all this to read 'Fancy! Good stationary, 's kind a'way hard we're China'.

Maurice Lindsay lived almost next door to the Club. He also worked some evenings there for a spell in the 1950s. He remembers being lulled to sleep by the 1930s tunes played by the fine bands that came to the Club. On a quiet evening, if the band was playing softly, it was possible too to hear the swish of the ladies' dresses as they glided around the dance floor.

Alan Cook was born in 1931 and lived with his Mother in a detached house half way down Church Road in between the two semi-detached houses. Opposite, there was a wicket gate to the Golf Course.

His father decided that he should have 10 successive golf lessons with Tommy McKinstry. It stood him in good stead as he played off a 12 handicap and as a 17 year old he was able to drive the first hole (319 yards) provided he got the right bounce. During the war he recalls Northern Ireland went through a major change – societal and religious. Peaceful, undisturbed Helen's Bay found itself suddenly involved – troops and WRNS in the Fort, an anti-aircraft battery on the 6th fairway with a searchlight battery on the 4th. Sheep grazed on the golf course in lieu of the mower (no diesel) so that when playing an approach shot muck and ball flew together to the green.

Tommy McKinstry went away to join the Services but Dick Ross remained. He played off 3 and Alan was lucky enough to play with him on quite a few occasions during the early 1940s. Dick was clad in a trilby, a sports jacket and he smoked a pipe. Thus attired, he set about the course in relaxed and winning mode. Alan's mother was twice Ladies Captain (1930 and 1958).

Subscriptions in those days were very reasonable. Aged 19 and up to the age of 26, they were: Helen's Bay Golf Club – £4, Royal Belfast – £3, Royal North of Ireland Yacht Club – £3, and the Country Club in Crawfordsburn was £4.

Sport was essentially amateur then and it was almost considered unacceptable to be outstanding in any one. In Alan's case rugby, tennis, golf, sailing and athletics were what he enjoyed most although he slightly

Above: The ARP bell rung to sound the 'all clear'.

bucked the trend by running for Ireland (400 m) when he was 18. When at home on holiday from school in Dublin he used to train at Cherryvale with the Queen's undergraduates under Franz Stampfl. He did starting practice with, inter alia, Jack Kyle. Jack would be 5 yards up on him for the first 10 yards and Alan would be 5 yards up on him in the second. Training was a bit different in those days and even somewhat original. During the school holidays Alan worked out his own training schedule. If he was taking the train to Belfast Mr Rooney, the stationmaster, would arrange for the upcoming engine driver to whistle as he came over the Crawfordsburn bridge. At this point Alan would leave the house, sprint up the road, down the underpass, catch the second or third carriage and jump on board just like the guard. This always got a cheer of approval from Rooney, Parkhurst the porter, the engine driver and whoever else. Needless to add, such considerations as insurance had no part to play.

In addition Alan pegged out a rough measured circle on the golf course which didn't bother the committee provided that he trained before 10 am.

In the War, his house was the local ARP station and his mother would receive the phoned green, yellow and red warnings. The wardens would be summoned, congregate in the house and be prepared to mount their bikes to patrol their routes if the signal went to red. The warning required the warden to blow his whistle every two minutes. However, by the time the raids started in earnest a siren had been installed on the roof of the police station. The 'all clear' was a personal delight as it required Alan to stand on the running board of the red Lanchester of Miss Praxeda Oswald (at Breathtulla) as she toured Helen's Bay's main roads ringing a large bell akin to those used by the fire brigades - clearly very important war work for a boy of 11. The house wasn't just the ARP station as they had Squadron Leader Taylor, his wife and daughter billeted with them and Seamount School took up the sitting room. Subsequently two ATS girls arrived. Alan didn't care for the officer as she said that he ate like a pig – a lesson well absorbed. The private was a driver – Sheelah Blakiston-Houston – complete with gauntlets and the mirror image of Sam in 'Foyle's War', he recalls.

Alan had bought a Canadian redwood canoe from the grandson of Mrs Brown who lived in what subsequently became Bennet House and whose husband had brought it back from Canada in 1890 on his yacht. It held four people and he had rigged up a lugsail with jib and lee-board which could run fast at 16 – 18 knots. It was duly registered (A 39) and Alan kept it originally at the Gilmers and subsequently at the Fort jetty where it was used, with his special permission, to bring two of the WRNS out to the Motor Torpedo Boats which couldn't make the jetty except at full tide; morale-boosting war work in a way which he didn't realise at the time. Alan had two lobster pots and he could make a few pennies selling their contents.

Chapter 6

The Churches

The Beginnings – the Presbyterian Church at Ballygilbert

In the early 1800s there were no real villages except Crawfordsburn in this part of Down and there were a number of Church of Ireland and Presbyterian people among the rural population who were almost entirely spiritually uncared for locally.

Where spiritual provision was concerned, the nearest places of worship for any of the denominations were in the towns of Bangor, Holywood and Newtownards. Regular church attendance was obviously difficult for many and church connections were often nominal. To meet the problem of reaching well over 2000 Presbyterians in the area, the Home Mission Society, founded by the General Synod of Ulster in the 1820s, working in association with Bangor Presbytery, commenced outreach work in Ballysallagh, a townland on the west of Clandeboye Park.

Many of the population at this time were not well off. It appears from the 1841 census that about 20% of all families lived in thatched clay cabins with just one room, although a further 45% lived in so-called class 3 houses, superior clay cottages with as many as four rooms and glazed windows. The next 30% lived in stone and lime-built farmhouses, thatched or slated, with one or even two stories. (It is recorded that in 1835 Holywood had only three two-storied buildings.) While these standards seem low, in fact the County of Down was ahead of the rest of Ireland in housing terms, at that time. In addition to a significant increase in the population in the 1830s, other societal changes were apparent, with the introduction of the national school system, new tithe arrangements and the imminent construction of the Newtownards workhouse. In 1840 the union of the two major Presbyterian branches to form the Presbyterian Church in Ireland took place.

A contemporary narrative, probably written by the Ballymullan schoolmaster towards the end of 1843, records:
'The Reverend Abraham Liggat came in March 1841 having been introduced to the people by the Revd W Graham of Dundonald, now missionary in Palestine. Mr Liggat commenced his work by preaching in the Schoolhouse of the district two sermons each Sabbath, one at 12 o'clock and the other at 6.'

Having found that the district of Ballysallagh was too small to form a congregation and having been shown that the village of Crawfordsburn and the surrounding districts were destitute of the Word, Rev Liggat commenced to preach in May in the Ballymullan Schoolhouse. He continued to preach on the mornings of the Sabbath in Ballysallagh and preached in the evenings in Ballymullan. Rev W Graham assisted him in forming a Sabbath School in the latter place which soon increased from 50 to 120 children and from 10 to 20 male and female teachers.

(Rev Graham was later murdered in the Damascus massacre of 1860. Coincidentally Lord Dufferin first achieved some of his reputation as an international diplomat through his pronouncements on the Syrian and Lebanese issues of the time.)

Such was the beginning of a ministry that culminated in the founding of the congregation at Ballygilbert. Only 14 months elapsed between the calling of the young licentiate and the opening of the new church on a site obtained from the Dufferin Estate in Ballygilbert townland after involved and difficult negotiations. (The former Lord Dufferin died in 1842, and although William Sharman Crawford's ready offer of land in Ballymullan had first been accepted, the Rev Blackwood, acting as guardian for his young Lordship, did consent at the second time of asking.) Rev Liggat travelled to Glasgow, Edinburgh, other towns in Scotland and Liverpool to raise funds for the building. James Sharman Crawford laid the foundation stone on 25 April 1842. Both Sharman Crawford and Francis Gordon who later built Craigdarragh House are recorded as donating £1 in the collection at the first service on 13 September 1842. The church, accommodating 310 people, and roofed with Bangor blue slates, was built at a cost of £300. It served no less than 13 adjacent townlands and a total population of over 2600 in the catchment area.

Rev Liggat, a protégé of the formidable Rev Dr Henry Cooke, was the Minister of Ballygilbert Presbyterian Church until his early death at the age of 34 in 1851. It is recorded that Rev Liggat lodged at one time, early in his stay in the locality with the Hanna family, grocers in Crawfordsburn. In a ceremony conducted by Dr Cooke in 1844, he married Sarah Wardlaw, niece of John McDowell who was then living at Sarahfield (or Sarahville as it is shown alternatively on the *Ordnance Survey* map). They lived first in a damp, rented house in Ballydavey, before coming to live at Sarahfield. It appears the house served as the Manse from about 1846 to 1858. The house is a charming Georgian farmhouse or 'gentleman's cottage orné' as Charlie Brett suggests in his book on the *Buildings of North County Down*. (The house was renamed Gulladuff by a subsequent resident.)

More information, including insights into the social history of the congregation at this time, is provided in the official history of Ballygilbert Presbyterian Church 1841-1991, *A Light for the Road*. The present Minister is the Rev Roy Patton.

The church is continuing to expand, though not in one regard. Sam Bradley can recall the shed behind the church where members of the congregation could stable their ponies and traps for the duration of the service. Considerable quantities of hay were consumed during lengthier sermons.

Rev Liggat did record personal notes about the families in his congregation, though he only got as far in the alphabet as the letter H before he died. His records show that many farmers also had other occupations or crafts, for example weaving, shoe-making or even watch-making. One was a coastguard; there were three shopkeepers, two grocers and one owner of a spirit shop. There are eight entries of people going to America, including two families.

It is not recorded how far this congregation was affected by the famine, although the number of Ballygilbert families had increased from 115 in 1844 to some 160 seven years later. It is known that in May 1848, 460 inmates of Newtownards workhouse were Presbyterian. (It is also recorded that at the worst in March 1847 the Newtownards workhouse built for a maximum of 600 housed no less than 832 'paupers'. The Newtownards Poor Law Union was however able to keep going on its own resources, unlike many others which had to have recourse to the Treasury.) It is clear that the population in this particular locality in Northern Ireland were not so dependent upon the potato, with more scope for mixed farming or supplemental income, which therefore reduced the full extent of the famine.

Helen's Bay Presbyterian Church

As long ago as 1882 there had been talk of building a church in Helen's Bay. Ballygilbert Church was then the nearest available and it was a long walk for many. As Lord Dufferin, on being asked to lease a piece of ground for a mission hall, declined for the time being to do so, a tent was acquired in 1883, in which services were held during the summer months. Mr Thomas Workman also carried on a Sunday school at his home, Craigdarragh House, featuring lantern talks. He showed slides to illustrate Bible stories.

In the spring of 1892 the Presbytery of Ards was asked to make provision for services to be conducted in the Temperance Hall, at the Station Hotel, Helen's Bay, which request was readily agreed to. The Temperance Hall was built and owned by Mr and Mrs Williams, the former being a retired coastguard, although in the *Ulster Directory* of 1892 the hotel is shown against Mrs Williams only. (It is ironic that an off licence is now adjacent to where the hall functioned.) There is no record of those ministers and others who preached in the tent or in the hall. The only reference to be found is in a letter from Thomas Workman to his daughter Jane, in which he describes an evening service when he led the service and preached the sermon. It is known that Mr Mollan also conducted many services. He and his family lived in Thornleigh, Kathleen Avenue, where he held a Sunday school in his own home. These services must have been very popular, as it was felt in 1894 imperative to build a church.

It was at this point an important event took place. The Rev John Quartz of Ballygilbert (who had succeeded to the ministry in 1852 after preaching three trial sermons in three different churches) and Mr Thomas Workman of Craigdarragh had a disagreement. Rev Quartz wanted to spend a sum of money on stabling and Mr Workman wanted an organ. Mr Quartz's opinion prevailed and Mr Workman removed himself and his family from Ballygilbert where he had worshipped since 1881. Thomas Workman had been a leader in the founding of a society called The Presbyterian Association for the Defence of Scriptural Liberty in the Service of Praise. As honorary secretary, he was keen to promote the movement. He decided to do everything in his power to hasten the building of a church in Helen's Bay. This was no idle dream as the Workman family had played a large part in the building of several churches: May Street, Alfred Street, Elmwood, Fitzroy and Belmont, and his cousin Robert was the Minister at Newtownbreda, having begun his preaching during the Revival of 1859.

The Ards Presbytery report for 5 June 1895 records a *'memorial, signed by seventy six persons, representing about thirty families resident in Helen's Bay, praying to be organised into a congregation'*.

Among the inhabitants of Helen's Bay were other prominent industrialists, merchants and professional men who were also prepared to give time, effort and money to establish the congregation. They included WS Mollan, linen merchant, a clerk of session of Fisherwick Presbyterian Church and honorary secretary of the YMCA for 50 years; G Herbert Brown, of Tordeevra, High Sheriff of County Down and a keen yachtsman; George McIldowie, a Belfast solicitor; James Mackie DL head of the famous firm of J Mackie and Sons (initially of Alton and later of Fairholme both in Helen's Bay); Hugh Ross, a linen merchant and a director of the Midland Railway Company who lived for some time in Rust Hall, and John Smith who built Dalry on the Craigdarragh Road.

In 1895 Lord Dufferin presented, free of rent, a most suitable site for the church. This was felt to be a propitious moment to issue an appeal for funds. The appeal referred to Helen's Bay as 'this favourite and rising watering-place'. In accordance with the direction of the Assembly a congregation was erected by the Presbytery of Ards, at Helen's Bay on 6 August 1895. At this time the Rev Thomas Johnston took charge of the congregation. Although he retired in 1890, he was living in Helen's Bay and was soon at work helping the infant congregation.

The building of the church began in 1895 and was very quickly finished. The estimated cost was £1200, (though the final sum was £400 more). Mr Kerr was the builder and according to contemporary accounts gave much satisfaction. (Gary Gillespie's maternal great grandfather, Andrew Auld, was however called in to advise at a later stage of the construction of the church. He was involved in trying to find a solution when, for some unaccountable reason, the two sides of the church roof refused to meet and form a perfect peak.)

A small but interesting fact is contributed by Captain Young, grandson of the Right Hon Robert Young, the architect and founder of the firm of Young and Mackenzie. The agreement for the building was written on a half sheet of notepaper. Robert Young was a friend of Thomas Workman, which was probably one of the reasons for the choice of architect. Many important buildings were designed by the firm including the Presbyterian Church House, Belfast.

On Saturday 24 October 1896, came the great event, the laying of the memorial stones. The description of this momentous occasion is well reported in the *Belfast News Letter*:

> *'The ceremony was fixed for half past one and a numerous company were conveyed by special train from Belfast. The church and its locality were gaily decorated in honour of the occasion and when the Marquess and Marchioness of Dufferin, accompanied by Lady Hermione Blackwood arrived they were met with a cordial greeting. They were received, on behalf of the congregation, by Mr Workman, who introduced to them quite a number of visitors. After refreshment, provided by the ladies of the congregation, had been partaken of in the hall of the Helen's Bay Hotel, the company then adjourned to the church for the interesting ceremony.'*

Several other stones were laid by distinguished ladies, but Mrs Sharman Crawford was unable to attend though her husband presented a cheque for a handsome sum, the Moderator informed the Assembly.

On 9 May 1897 the Moderator of the General Assembly, Rev Dr Williamson, opened the new church for public worship. The *News Letter* stated: 'The new church is a very handsome structure, built of Silurian stone from Ballygowan quarries and faced with white granite from Scrabo.'

The Marquess of Dufferin and Ava was asked to collect at this service and graciously agreed to do so. As a prominent benefactor, there was a 'Dufferin Pew' set aside for many years, marked out with a red tasselled silk cord, at its entrance.

Faced with dressed basalt with sandstone dressings, the building consists of a five-bay nave defined by buttresses with off-sets. The style is a rudimentary First Pointed Gothic, with two lancets piercing each bay on the liturgical North and South elevations. The West elevation consists of a large gable wall pierced by three small lancets with foils above which is a Second Pointed window with bar-tracery subdividing it into five tall lights over which is a sexfoil flanked by two quatrefoils. The truncated tower (which was originally to have consisted of three stages capped by a broach-spire) has clasping buttresses and is pierced by small lancets and an elaborate First Pointed entrance with vigorous dog tooth mouldings and a hood-moulding terminating in carved heads as label-stops.

Particular features of note are the stained-glass windows, including in the second bay from the liturgical west, a pair featuring The Sower and The Reaper by the London firm of Clayton and Bell, erected in memory of Thomas Workman (1843-1900). In the fourth bay from the west is another pair on the themes of Hope and Faith, erected in memory of Rev Williamson and his wife, based on designs by Sir Edward Burne-Jones and made by the firm set up by William Morris. Three lights in the west wall (commissioned by James and Mona Taylor in 1900, in memory of their infant son, Waldo) also feature typical Morris treatment of the background foliage. The presence of the two Clayton and Bell windows and five by William Morris's firm led to the listing of the church as a historic building 96 years after it was built.

Rev WJ (John) Archer served as the first Minister in Helen's Bay from April 1898 until 1909. He married Rowena Brown, younger daughter of John Shaw Brown. Some time at the beginning of Rev Archer's ministry the Manse was built and a long struggle to pay off the debt was begun, though an 'At Home' in the Manse held in 1898 raised £650 which paid off half of it. Mrs Finlay recalled her family attending evening services at Helen's Bay Church in order to enjoy the hymns accompanied by the harmonium. She was a member of Ballygilbert Church where an organ was not installed for many years, and where only psalms were sung. In 1903 an organ was presented to Helen's Bay, given in memory of Margaret and Thomas Workman by their children. In those

days metal communion tokens were in use and the Helen's Bay tokens, incorporating shamrocks, were unique.

In 1909 Rev John Edmund Hamilton was called, succeeding Rev Archer. The magnificent illuminated address presented to Rev Archer, containing coloured scenes of Helen's Bay and Crawfordsburn, was later given to the Congregation by his daughter Mrs Weston. (Three illustrations in all by JW Carey from the address are included in this book, by kind permission of Helen's Bay Presbyterian Church.)

At a reception in Mr Williams' Hall the ladies of the Congregation presented Mr Hamilton with robes. Mrs Crozier remembered vividly that Mrs Taylor and Miss E Workman, being of low stature, were obliged to stand on chairs in order to robe him, Mr Hamilton being very tall.

In 1912 the Solemn League and Covenant was made available for signature on the communion table in Helen's Bay Church. This showed clearly the feelings of the majority of the Congregation in opposition to the Home Rule Bill and determined to remain under the British Crown.

The *County Down Spectator* reported a funeral at the church in 1913, for Dr TH Gibson, at which George McCorry played the organ.

Above: The Manse on Fort Road, from Rev Archer's Illuminated Address.

The visiting minister said of Gibson that 'he was almost as well versed in Plato as in Justinian… (yet) he was as remote as the poles from pedantry.' Crawford McCullagh was noted to have accompanied the coffin from his house.

1914 – 1918 First World War Years:

On 21 August 1915, Mr Hamilton left to be a Chaplain. He served in France with the 2nd Battalion Lincolnshire Regiment. In 1918 he was attached to the 2nd Battalion Royal Berkshire Regiment, both part of the 8th Division. In March 1918 he was transferred to the 15th Division and attached to the London Scottish. He was awarded the Military Cross and his Brigade Commander Major General Clifford Coffin VC, DSO said of him:

> 'He was always ready to share the dangers and difficulties of the men and earned the esteem and affection of all ranks.'

The war years were difficult for the congregation despite the efforts of Rev RA Hill and the Rev H Cupples. A large number of men went to war from Helen's Bay. Many were in the Ulster Volunteers and as soon as war was declared they went into camp at Clandeboye. A Roll Of Honour was compiled at the close of war to commemorate those who had served.

On his return from service Rev Hamilton accepted a call to ministry in the Church of Scotland. He lived to become 'The Father' of the General Assembly of the Church of Scotland, and died at the age of 101. Two Helen's Bay elders visited him in Edinburgh. Still alert, he was interested in what had happened in Helen's Bay, in the 62 years following his ministry there.

Rev Francis McCaughey was ordained on 16 March 1920. He was a churchman of high principles and was meticulous and accurate in everything he did. On the material side, the church owed a debt of gratitude to Rev McCaughey, for it was he who introduced the envelope scheme of Free Will offering. The church was able to show a balance of income over expenditure for the first time for many years.

On 1 June 1926 the Session held an important meeting. It was suggested that Helen's Bay should link up with a neighbouring congregation. It was placed under the care of Rev William John Currie of First Bangor for three years. The Rev JC Boggs acted as Minister in Helen's Bay until he was called to a congregation of his own in 1928.

In 1930 electricity was installed. The son of the sexton, Alfie Jess, recalls that his father would wake his family at 5 am on a Sunday morning to get the original coke-fired boiler going and so heat the church for the benefit of the first congregation. The arrival of electric heating meant his family could get another two hours sleep, as well as him avoiding the asphyxiating fumes of the boiler-house.

The following year, Mr Leslie Martin (whose wife was the sister of Lord McDermott) was called to the congregation and his ordination ended the association with First Bangor, (although notes of the Helen's Bay Church's activities were included in the First Bangor magazine until after the second war).

Above: Helen's Bay Presbyterian Church, by Carey, from the Illuminated Address presented to Rev Archer in 1909.

1939 – 1945 Second World War Years:

Some extracts from minutes reflect the life of the Congregation during the War years:

26 Oct 1939 the subject of 'Blackout' was first mentioned.

24 Nov 1940 buckets to be purchased to hold sand, also shovels.

24 Feb 1941 an additional shovel, another bucket for water purchased and two sandbags had been filled. 'Thus the defences of the church were completed.'

27 April 1941 an appeal marked 'urgent' was launched to aid people in Belfast who had suffered the horrors of enemy action on the night of 15 and morning of 16 April.

4 May 1941 police had been informed that church premises would be available for the reception of evacuees should the necessity arise. Fortunately this was not found necessary.

At a point early in the War, the stained-glass windows were removed and stored for safety in a large coal cellar at Craigdarragh House.

Around December 1942, the use of the church for services was granted to German prisoners from the Craigdarragh Prisoner of War Camp. Their own chaplain, Pastor Schmidt, conducted these.

On Wednesday 13 June 1944 a service of prayer and dedication was held at the time of the opening of the second front in Normandy, in accordance with a request by the King that all churches should hold such services. The Session decided that the Church would be open for private prayer between 8am and 9am on each succeeding Wednesday during the remainder of the conflict.

During the war the National Anthem was sung at the end of the morning service as it had also been sung during the 1914-1918 war.

24 August 1945 in a minute of the Committee 'Reports were received that the stained-glass windows had been replaced.' This year also saw the setting up of a branch of the Presbyterian Women's Association.

4 June 1946 'Thanksgiving of Peace' collection to be taken on Victory Sundays.

A Roll of Honour was compiled.

The Post-War Years:

A Jubilee service was held on the first Sunday in 1947. In April 1951 the Manse on Fort Road was sold and the proceeds used for the purchase of a new Manse in due course.

The question of a church hall had been discussed for many years. The Dufferin Estate Company agreed to grant a conveyance of additional ground at the rear of the church at the rent of £1 per annum. Mr Edgar Robertson laid the foundation stone of the new Church Hall. The hall was built by Mr F Boyd & Sons of Ballymiscaw and cost over £3000. Tom Boyd, remembered building it with his father Fred and brother Reuben. In memory of his wife, Mr Robertson gave £1,000 towards the building of the hall. This made it possible to open the hall free of debt. The inaugural service was held on 26 February 1955 when the hall was officially opened by Lord McDermott who was Mrs Martin's brother. Among those present were Mr JL Yeames and Miss McGonigal, both of whom saw the laying of the memorial stones in 1896 and were present at the opening of the Church in 1897.

In 1963 Rev Martin, who had done much good work with local scouts and guides, retired. In the following year Rev Robert Gilmore was installed as Minister. (He passed away in July 2011). The congregation agreed to purchase a new Manse at 13 Church Road.

In 1969 the Church was extended, with a new Minister's Room, Choir Room, toilets and foyer added to the rear of the building. The organ was removed and rebuilt. New lighting was installed and the interior was completely redecorated. The Moderator conducted the re-opening service on 15 May 1970. A number of donations were made, including a new communion table and cross, and a lectern.

In 1985 when Rev Gilmore retired, a more modern Manse was purchased - 2 Rockmount Gardens. The following year Rev Colin Megaw was appointed Minister; the Moderator, Rev JT Williamson, conducted the ordination service. Rev Megaw, who initiated a summer scheme for young people, celebrated his 25th anniversary in 2011.

Church activities continued to thrive and expand far beyond Helen's Bay. In 1987 support was given to Miss Kerry Bullick to join the

African Inland Mission in Kenya, and four years later the Congregation agreed to assist Mr Mark Henderson who was going to Brazil to help with voluntary work on mission projects there, and Miss Helen Murray to Cognac in France.

In 1996 the Scheme known as 'Project 100' was launched. The Committee felt it necessary to take immediate practical steps towards keeping faith with the vision of the founders of the Congregation by undertaking necessary repairs and renewals to counteract the ravages of climate and time over 100 years to the exterior of the building and to update and improve the facilities and decoration of the church building and halls. It was planned to complete the work before the centenary of the first service.

In 2002 Odesola Funso came to Helen's Bay from Lagos, Nigeria. He studied at Belfast Bible College. On returning home to Nigeria he was posted by his denomination as coordinator in Southern Africa, including Zambia and other land-locked countries. The link between Helen's Bay and the Redeemed Christian Church of God has grown out of Odesola's involvement in Helen's Bay Presbyterian and his invitation to Rev Colin Megaw and computer skills tutors Colin and Debra Anderson to carry out Pastors' Seminars in 'Doing Ministry' and 'Computer Studies' in July 2003. The team also visited highly populated compounds and a Church Farm Project at Kasupe. As a result Helen's Bay agreed to raise the necessary money to provide irrigation on the Farm which involved sinking a borehole, providing a pump, tank and pipes. Thus began a long-term, on-going project which resulted in Bible clubs, computer facilities/ internet café, building an orphanage, school, church and skills training centre.

In 2008, a link spanning the church hall and church was built (contractor, J & K Campbell). This provides a comfortable area for meetings and discussion.

Two years later the church clock on the east gable facing Church Road

was restored and relit, at the initiative of John Orr, Trevor Edwards and colleagues. It is Helen's Bay's only public clock, having been installed in the late 1940s, a donation by the Ross family of Golf Road in memory of their mother Jeannie Ross who lived at the former house called Dunrobin on Golf Road. It was accepted after discussion with local residents and the Church Session, on the strict understanding that it would not chime.

The Church of Ireland – Church of St John Baptist, Helen's Bay

There was in ancient times a church at Craigavad. In the *Taxation of Pope Nicholas* in 1188 the 'Ecclesia de Craigevada' was valued at 8 marks, along with its rectory. In 1622 it was reported by the Protestant bishop that the church was a ruin.

The present parish of Glencraig was carved out of the parishes of Newtownards and Holywood. It came into being in 1850. Helen's Bay was part of this parish. The Church of The Holy Trinity at Glencraig, Craigavad was constructed in the Gothic style in 1858. It cost £1,164 and seated 132 people. Miss Symes of Glencraig House made a gift of the site. An extension to the nave was added in 1868 with provision for a further 92 people; the cost of the vicarage built the same year was more than that of the church. Sam Clokey served as sexton for almost half a century to his retirement in 1907 with a pension from the vestry of £10 a year; his daughter was the infant teacher.

The parishioners of Holy Trinity who lived in Helen's Bay had a long journey to Glencraig. A few wealthy families had transport but the majority had to walk. An early member of the congregation recalled that on wet Sundays the family would therefore attend the Presbyterian Church and hear Mr Archer preach. The Episcopalians did as the Presbyterians had done and started to rent a room near the station. This was a hall behind the former Post Office and belonged to Mr Dummigan.

The first service was held in Dummigan's on Whit Sunday, 1906. Services continued there until enough money was raised to begin the construction of a proper church building in 1909. Ford, Whitcombe and

Bottom left: Restoring the clock on the east gable, Helen's Bay Presbyterian Church 2010.

Above: The first church of St John Baptist, Helen's Bay.

Cogswell, architects of London, designed it. It comprised what is now the chancel. The design of the windows was 'Early English Lancet'. The foundation stone was laid by the Marchioness. There was in addition, a temporary structure attached, made of corrugated iron, which housed the entrance porch and was known locally as 'the Tin Tabernacle.' The cost was a substantial £800, most raised locally. The first service in The Church of St John Baptist, Helen's Bay was held on 7 November 1909. The average congregation in those days was 90. This little building played an important part in the life of Helen's Bay.

1914 – 1918 First World War Years:

The officers and men at Grey Point Fort paraded to the church every Sunday and some played a full part in the life of the parish. The Credence Table in the North Wall of the Chancel bears witness to this:

> *'This credence table was erected by Major FJ Hill OC RGA September 1914 to July 1919. To the glory of God and in memory of the Officers who served under him at Grey Point Battery and gave their lives for King and Country in the Great War.'*

Two flags hanging in the church are associated with the original Ulster Volunteer Force, set up to defend Ulster at the time of the Home Rule crisis in 1912. Many inhabitants of Helen's Bay would have been members. The UVF formed the nucleus of the men who went on to be part of the 36th (Ulster) Division, which famously fought in the Battle of the Somme in 1916.

Lady Dunleath presented the Union Flag, on the south wall, to 2nd Battalion North Down Regiment, of the Ulster Volunteer Force, Newtownards, on 2 January 1914. The other flag is the regimental colour of the Regiment presented by the Marchioness of Londonderry. Once green, but now faded, this banner has the Red Hand of Ulster and UVF embroidered in red silk. A brass plate on the sill of the west window has the dedication:

'To the Glory of God and in grateful commemoration of the devotion and courage of the men and women of the Parish of Glencraig who volunteered and served in the two Great Wars 1914 – 1918 and 1939 – 1945.'

It is understood that Mr JP Ewing, of Carrig Gorm, who presented the bell in 1925, then presented the flags to St John's, where they were initially hung at an angle in the sanctuary, before being framed for better preservation in their present location in the nave.

One of the finest brass memorials is in the chancel. It is inlaid in coloured enamels and surmounted by the Arms of Sharman Crawford. Lieutenant Terence Sharman Crawford of the 15th Hussars was killed at Aldershot in a motor bicycle accident at the age of 21 in July 1913. Colonel Sharman Crawford was a great supporter of St John's. He paid out of his own pocket for a curate to come from Bangor parish to lead a Sunday morning service in St John's (as the vicar of Glencraig could not take services in both churches from 1918 on). Another memorial lists all those who gave their lives in the First War; perhaps the most poignant is that to RAF Lieutenant John Mercer Grimshaw Bell MC who is recorded to have died on active service on 11 November 1918.

The East window commemorates Captain Harold Hardy, 13th Battalion Royal Irish Rifles, killed in action at Kemmel Hill on 15 April 1918. He was a member of a prominent Helen's Bay family and was one of four brothers who served.

The lectern is dedicated;
'To the glory of God and in loving memory of Sub-Lieutenant Patrick Hugo Irving Vance, RN of HMS Shark. Killed in Action in the Battle of Jutland 31st May 1916 aged 19. 'Fear God and honour the King'.'

The Battle of Jutland was the most famous naval battle of World War 1. Patrick was an only son, killed manning the forecastle gun. (The lectern is a replica of that in the church that served the Royal Naval College at Osborne.)

The Vicar of Glencraig remained responsible for the whole Parish and the services held in both churches. There was one Select Vestry for the whole Parish covering the two churches.

There are a number of stained-glass windows; one in the chancel is in memory of Robert Trelford who lived for many years at Ballygrot on the hill above the church. As the inscription says, he was: 'a founder of this Church.' Another window, unusual in colour and composition, is in memory of Mary Gardiner, MA, who died in 1942, having been a headmistress.

Subsequent Development:

In 1924 the first part of what is now the Nave was built. This included steps down from the Chancel to the central space with its fine wooden roof. The style did not entirely harmonise with the existing church as the walls were built with stone dressings and rough dash, as opposed to the crisp

ashlar and graded slate rooves of the original. The architect was a local man, Percy Jury. The windows were designed on Tudor lines – described as severely stripped, minimalist Perpendicular or Third Pointed. It cost £3,393. The Nave and organ chamber were erected by public

Above: After the extension of St John Baptist in 1924.

subscription. In aid of this fund a huge bazaar was held at Crawfordsburn House. Members of the Congregation gave most of the furnishings at the east end of the church as memorials.

The children and grandchildren of Thomas Lee and Elizabeth Hardy gave the pulpit. Trelford, Hardy, Matthewson and Ewing are names that recur in the memorials of St John's. A Reading Desk was gifted in memory of Arthur Greeves.

In 1925/26 a Committee of Management was formed. Colonel Crawford informed them that due to the worldwide depression, his income was considerably reduced and his subscription would now be £75 towards the stipend of the curate in Bangor Parish. (It had previously been £150. In his will he required whoever took over Crawfordsburn House to continue to provide support for St John's Church as he had done and to augment the stipend of the curate.) In 1929 a committee was appointed to decide with the contractor on the best means of lighting the church with electricity. Three years later the vicar outlined the proposal for building a Parochial Hall.

In the mid-1930s a wooden church hall was built. Emma Graham's father, George, was centrally involved in its construction. He used some of the 'unemployed' men who came down from Belfast in the summer to camp below the Coastguard Cottages. This hall stood for some 50 years and served a variety of useful purposes.

In 1942 to safeguard the stained-glass East window, it was removed in sections and stored for the War's duration in the stoke hole. The next year, it was decided to advertise the Parochial Hall for sale, the cost of repairing it after use by the Military being more than the committee wished to pay. There were many enquiries but no offers the Committee were prepared to accept, £500 being the sum they had in mind.

In 1944 it was noted that there were not enough parishioners going to both services. In the Canon's opinion, 'occasional attenders at church were those who made a compact with the Devil.'

In 1953 a font was placed in St John's in memory of Canon Capsey. Two years later, Mr H Page, organist for 37 years tendered his resignation. Colonel Ronald Greeves who died in 1988 was the choirmaster for over 50 years. Mrs Greeves was said to have 'a hot line to the Almighty' – she was a spiritual and caring Australian, who had been at school with the

Above: Colonel Ronnie Greeves, aged 3 and a half years, with his sister.

wife of the Australian Prime Minister. (When Dame Patty Menzies came to launch the Canberra she stayed with the Greeves.) Christmas parties at her house were much looked forward to by local youngsters.

In 1961 the Select Vestry of the Parish decided to adopt the Stewardship Scheme of fund raising. This received the enthusiastic support of St John's Church Committee and proved to be very successful. At the suggestion of Archdeacon G A Quin, Helen's Bay at last became an independent parish and St John's became a separate entity in July

1962. St John's now appointed its own Select Vestry. 3 Church Road was bought as a Rectory. Rev ECL Dunne MA was appointed as Bishop's Curate and was inducted by Bishop Mitchell in September 1962.

The Congregation had grown and an extension to the building became essential. This was completed in the early autumn of 1964 and comprised the completion of the nave, porch and extension of the vestry.

The walls were built of stone dressings with rough dash. The ceiling was barrelled in timber, with the windows once again conforming to English lancet shape. The cost was £22,500. This part was consecrated on 31 October 1964. The architect was Arthur E Jury, son of Percy, and the builders were Messrs David and Rainey, of Belfast. Like the 1924 extension, the third phase was rendered with grey roughcast with sandstone dressings.

The *County Down Spectator* recorded the formal opening of the extension.

> 'The clergy processed round outside the church, singing Come, Holy Ghost, our Sounds Inspire. Then the Bishop of Down and Dromore, Rt Rev Dr EJ Mitchell, knocked three times on the church door. Two other bishops were in the party, including Dr Elliott who had attended the opening of the previous 1924 extension.'

The tablet in the south wall of the sanctuary commemorates the first full Rector, the Rev Ted Dunne. He was instituted in November 1964, but sadly he died suddenly in May 1965. Rev Canon Alec Stewart was then appointed Rector. In 1969, Mr Stanley James retired as sexton after 25 years of faithful service to the church. The three subsequent rectors were Canon Dr Michael Dewar, Rev Alan Abernethy and Rev Ronnie Nesbitt.

In 1986 the earlier church hall was replaced. It was a much appreciated improvement. As Doreen Ricketts put it of the former hall 'if you met someone carrying an oil stove and a rug, you knew where they were going.' The current hall now hosts, as does its Presbyterian counterpart, a number of community activities, especially during the winter months.

For many years Mrs Kay Coulthard has maintained a close link between St John's and the international charity Love Russia. The church is also involved in work in Africa, with ties to Ethiopia through the current Rector.

The church has been floodlit at night for a number of years, in part following an initiative by members of the Congregation to undertake an annual Christmas swim in Helen's Bay's chilly waters for charity. (It is curious to think that this action which lasts in terms of immersion all of one minute, is considered worthy enough to raise funds, given that not so long ago, a number of local residents thought nothing of swimming all year round.)

In 2004 the then Archbishop of Armagh, the Most Rev Robin Eames attended the festival service, taken by the Rev John Medhurst, to mark the 40th anniversary of the consecration of St John's as a parish in its own right. The current incumbent, Rev Canon Tim Kinahan, was instituted by Bishop Harold Miller in 2006. For some years the church has held very successful May Fairs, including a local art exhibition and sale.

St John's has recently been presented with a Book of Remembrance for those whose ashes are interred in the garden at the church. A display case containing the book is situated at the rear of the nave. The earliest recorded date of birth is 1889 and access to read the entries may be obtained by contacting the Rector.

Above left: The Clergy processing at the opening of St John's extension, 1964.
Above right: St John Baptist's original church hall, with its replacement under construction.

Chapter 7

In the Wars

Grey Point Fort

The two World Wars had a big impact on the area. Many local men went to fight, some sadly not to return. Especially in the second war, significant elements of the Services were either stationed or billeted here. Moreover because of the Belfast Blitz in 1941 there was a large influx of civilians, living in temporary accommodation or caravans to avoid the danger of further air attacks. Everyone was affected by rationing while donating surplus metal was another contribution to the war effort. One

resident regrets the passing of the iron gates that used to grace the entrance to many driveways, as did her father who disliked having to paint the wooden replacements much more often. The photograph shows local residents gathering a collection of old pots and pans, in their cart.

However Grey Point Fort has been a constant feature in Helen's Bay for over a century now.

Apart from historic Carrickfergus Castle and others of its ilk, the oldest examples of coastal defences around our shoreline are Martello towers which date from the Napoleonic wars. It became obvious by the end of the 19th century that something more modern was required to provide protection for the thriving port of Belfast against external naval attack. Accordingly, the decision was made to establish two batteries, one at Kilroot on the north side of Belfast Lough (subsequently demolished to make way for the power station), with the other at Grey Point. Between them the batteries covered the full width of the Lough.

Grey Point was built as a pentagonal fort between 1904 and 1907 on land bought from the Marquess of Dufferin and Ava for £8,400. The construction work was undertaken, for a similar sum, by Messrs WJ Campbell & Son of Ravenhill Road, Belfast who had recently completed the Lough Swilly forts. It was surrounded by an 'unclimbable' wall and palisade. Two six-inch Mark VII breech-loading guns, built by Vickers Sons and Maxim Ltd., were mounted and tested during May 1907. The barrel of each gun was 23 foot long, and weighed 7 tons. The guns were capable of firing shells weighing about 100 pounds a distance of up to 6 miles. A 10 person crew was required for each gun. In addition three Maxim machine guns were mounted on infantry carriages. (It is quite likely that the visit of Earl Roberts included an inspection of the new Fort, as he was the Master Gunner of St James Park from 1904 up to his death in France in 1914.)

The photograph of the Fort and the surrounding area dates from 1960, but it shows the scale of the whole site. It was garrisoned during both world wars although it did not in practice ever fire a shot in anger at

Above left: Helen's Bay salvage collection, autumn 1941 (left to right) Mabel Shillingford, Judy Nelson, Kitty Stephens, lower row – Mrs Tate, Miss Livingston, Mrs Simpson, Mrs Mussell.
Above right: The jetty created below Grey Point Fort, around 1950; the gentleman by the wheelbarrow is Harry Gilmer.

an enemy vessel. The Fort itself was abandoned in 1956 when the guns were disposed of, although the adjacent hutted encampment survived into the 1960s; after restoration the Fort was opened to the public in 1987, in a ceremony that included some of those who had served at it during the war. The two current 6 inch guns were acquired from the Irish Republic, one from Spike Island in Cork. As well as being the only monument of its kind preserved in Northern Ireland, (although there is a similar site at Fort Dunree in Donegal), the Fort has played a significant part in the development of Helen's Bay, so it is right to treat it fully. A visit is strongly recommended; it also now hosts a most interesting radio, uniform and photographic exhibition built up by volunteers.

The Fort was manned by the Antrim Royal Garrison Artillery, (Special Reserve), during the First World War. In 1915 a hutted camp was constructed to accommodate six officers and 172 other ranks. In addition thousands of troops trained at Grey Point before despatch to the front. The Fort's practical defensive use was limited by the absence of searchlights. Ironically the 1905 Committee on Armaments of Home Ports concluded the threat at Belfast was lesser than in Lough Swilly and that no searchlights were required at the former.

Above: Aerial photograph of Grey Point Fort and surrounding area, 1960.

Charles Milligan, writing *My Bangor from the 1890s*, recalled a serious incident in 1914. This was the story leading up to the execution of Carl Hans Lodz as a spy in the Tower of London on 11 November 1914. Posing as Charles Inglis, an American from Chicago, he arrived in Belfast from Scotland. He paid some boatmen to convey him down the Lough where he took a close interest in the boatyards. Becoming suspicious the boatmen took him to the examination vessel at the entrance to the Lough and were instructed to take Inglis ashore at Grey Point Fort. Milligan's brother, as a Reserve Captain, had been posted there. As luck would have it Milligan had lived for ten years in Chicago. During cross-examination, Inglis's lack of knowledge of the city beyond what might be acquired from a guide book was revealed. Milligan contacted the Police. Inglis was subsequently arrested in Killarney. At his trial it came out that he had reported on Zeppelin defences and naval intelligence.

A First World War anecdote concerned the dashing Captain Leslie Porter of Ballywooley House who had joined the Royal Flying Corps. He was very famous in the area for having landed his plane in Ballywooley field, taking it home 'on leave'. He had played a part in establishing a motor business in Belfast. Sadly he was killed on active service in October 1916. A memorial in the grounds could be seen for many years, until builders removed it.

In 1926 the Grey Point huts were sold and removed. Periodic annual camps were held by the Lancashire and Cheshire Heavy Regiment. Harry Garner, later Colonel Garner, had joined the Territorial Army in Liverpool in 1921. His unit camped at Grey Point for a fortnight in the summers of 1932 and 1933, to practise gunnery. An invitation to tea at the Yeames' in Old Mill House (off the Craigdarragh Road) led to his acquaintance and ultimately a long and happy marriage with Margaret, both living in that house.

It is recorded that the master gunner at Grey Point from 1924 to 1934 was Basil Lloyd, who lived in the house at the entrance to the Fort now occupied by the Country Park warden.

In 1936, two of the searchlight emplacements were built (with the central, final one being added in 1940) and several other modifications carried out within the Fort, including the arrival of electricity. The three feet thick concrete roofs that now protect the guns against air attack were

added by summer 1940. Bob Gillespie, who visited the Fort in 1987 after it was reopened, recalled working on the construction projects, and that he and his colleagues had been soaked by the autumn gales when building the searchlight emplacement. He also told a story about Captain Marsham who had accidentally ordered an excessive quantity of camouflage paint from the stores in Holywood Palace Barracks. The Captain had discreetly buried the entire consignment in a large hole, near where the car park now is.

In June 1938 the first camp of the new Territorial Army unit, 188 (Antrim) Heavy Battery Royal Artillery, was held at Grey Point. The tents were successfully erected in spite of gale force winds. The RUC Band played at the sports meeting during the camp. The keenness displayed by all ranks was 'most refreshing' according to the official account. An open day for families was also held that year, as Mrs Patton recalled visiting the Fort where her husband was posted.

The unit was mobilised for a fortnight during the Munich Crisis from 26 September 1938. On that first night most of the men were billeted in St John's Church Hall, with the permission of Canon Capsey. Although they set up tents the next day, within a week many had blown down.

Following a further camp in June 1939, they were again mobilised on 24 August 1939, two weeks before war was declared. The establishment of the unit which at this time also covered the Kilroot Fort was set at 6 officers and 179 other ranks.

In the second war, the Fort also housed both the headquarters of Northern Ireland Coastal Command and an ATS detachment. Grey Point was remarkable in the extent of the operational role played by the women, which included deploying the searchlights and range-finding. There were also WRNS signallers posted there; one recalls:

'We were either on top of the Royal Hotel, Bangor or at Grey Point Fort. The fort was a cold, grim sort of place but at that age you made the most of it. Lots of laughs and companionship. At that age, 18 or 19, you don't take in the seriousness of it all'.

There were other ladies present. The redoubtable Kitty Stephens was called up to Grey Point in August 1939; as she recalled 'Two stripes and you're in charge of the cook-house!' She was in the process of cooking scrambled eggs when the first shot was fired. (Could those eggs have come from 'Battery hens' one wonders?) Kitty's cooking prowess later stood in her in good stead, when she served lunch for the Queen at Hillsborough Castle. At the other end of Kathleen Avenue in Helen's Bay, lived Nan McCammon who also joined the 43 County Down ATS, served at Grey Point and later gained a commission. She married Colonel Claude Kirby-Smith. Her cousin, Belinda Hill, remembers cycling with Nan to visit aunts in Belfast. The photograph shows Nan and Kitty with other members of the Company at Grey Point in September 1939.

As well as the main guns, the Fort also contained two howitzers for defence against shore-based attack and anti-aircraft material. In the second war, it was also protected by metal barriers across the road where the Grey Point road crests the hill, through which it was just possible to squeeze with a bicycle. The Commander asked the owner of 11 Grey Point to cut his hedge lower so that the soldiers when coming from the Fort had a clear view of the beach, in case of invasion. The large house at Horse Rock was initially intended to be built close to the sea below Coastguard Cottages, and the foundations remain to this day, but ironically the Army objected to that location. So it was that Tom Cull built the three-storey house (rather than the bungalow which had been anticipated), and it then had to be camouflaged during the War.

During the second war, as in the first, the role of Grey Point Fort was to protect Belfast Lough from naval attack. When a ship entered the

Above left: Contemporary aerial photograph of the similar area. Above right: 43rd County Down ATS Company at Grey Point, with Nan McCammon and Kitty Stephens second and third from right respectively.

Lough it would have been contacted by the coastal defence and asked to make itself known. If there was no answer the ship would be signalled to 'Heave to or be sunk.' If the ship still maintained its course or again failed to reply, a plugged round would have been fired across the ship's bows. If there was still no response the next round to be fired would have been a high explosive shell. During the war the gunners carried out regular target practice. A tug from the Clyde towed a barge a mile behind with a chequered target. Twice a week the gunners fired at the target. Ahead of this, local residents had to be warned to open their windows and doors to prevent damage due to the blast. The gun crew were warned to keep their mouths open, when the shot was fired, to prevent internal damage from blast waves. Reports from those stationed at the Fort would suggest that the target was usually missed.

Two days after the outbreak of the Second World War, a merchant ship, the 'E Hayward,' entered Belfast Lough apparently unaware of the change in conditions. When it failed to respond to a recognition signal, a plugged round was fired across her bows. Interestingly the local newspaper of the day reported that two shells were fired over the bows, one of which passed over houses in Carrickfergus before landing in a field near to the residence of Mr Henley of Woodburn.

According to the official Grey Point booklet, this was the first and only shell shot fired in anger from the Fort – though see the account below. It was reputed that on another occasion the plug of the gun was accidentally discharged. This ricocheted off the water and landed somewhere above Carrickfergus. It is said that a cow was killed and a cowshed demolished by the impact.

Over the years, the Fort had some distinguished visitors. Anthony Eden, then Secretary of State for War visited the Fort on 24 July 1940, accompanied by the Chief Controller of the ATS. This was immediately after the completion of

the anti-aircraft shields for the main guns. Just four days earlier the 'SS Troutpool', with a cargo of grain all the way from Argentina, hit a mine off Strickland's Glen and sank. Eleven people were killed. For some time her superstructure was still visible, as the photograph shows. (A Dutch coaster, the 'Santa Lucia', had also struck a mine in Belfast Lough and sank in November 1940.)

A boom to deter U-boats from entering was slung across the Lough, recalls Carol McCartney, from a point below the Fort that is still marked with a War Department post.

According to Bill Clements' book on the *Fortifications of Ulster*, the Grey Point battery was placed on a care and maintenance basis as early as December 1943, once the German threat had diminished and as the new battery at Orlock Point had taken over its role in protecting that side of the entrance to Belfast Lough.

In spring 1944, in preparation for the D-Day landings, many naval ships of different nationalities, including three American battleships, the 'Arkansas', 'Nevada' and 'Texas', were moored in Belfast Lough. It is estimated that the total number of officers and sailors on board was around 30,000. One young crew member recalled: 'I had never seen so vast an armada of ships'. The Belfast Lough ships were a major part of the bombardment fleet in support of the landings and left on 3 June. General Eisenhower had earlier visited the fleet while it was off Bangor. Alan Cook recalls that he identified no less than 80 warships, using his 1943 edition of *Jane's Fighting Ships*, from his observation post at the turret window in Mrs Brown's house. Joan Bushell remembers plentiful fruit being washed ashore at that time, in quantities not seen for several years, discarded from the well-provisioned US ships.

The remnants of groynes (both in wood and steel) that can occasionally be seen at low tide on both the Crawfordsburn and Helen's Bay beaches actually pre-date the second war.

Bottom left: 'SS Troutpool' after hitting a mine, off Strickland's Glen.
Top right: Naval ships in Belfast Lough, shortly prior to D-Day, late May 1944.

A 'whiskey galore' incident occurred when rationing as a result of the Second World War was at its height, when one of the Sunderland flying boats made by Shorts, that were moored off Cultra, broke loose in a heavy wind and went aground at Grey Point. Attempts that afternoon by two tugs to pull it off the rocks failed. Naturally the next thing to be done was to rescue the petrol, to lighten the flying boat. Two large tanks were floated down from Harland and Wolff for that purpose, and were then moored off Helen's Bay beach overnight. One eye witness account, then a teenager, has recently recorded seeing two vans parked by the sand dunes at the top of the beach later that evening. It is further suggested that some of the petrol was offloaded by local residents, initially into jerry cans, and then into empty 5-gallon drums brought in the vans. The witness then persuaded two of his friends to don official uniforms and promenade in the moonlight along the beach. This brought proceedings to a premature halt. The police were subsequently called in to find out who had taken this valuable 100 octane fuel. Many years later one of the policemen involved in the follow-up observed that it appeared several local residents had secreted petrol in various containers in their gardens or around their houses. It may however still be prudent not to name the names of those suspected of involvement.

Barrage balloons were flown over the Lough to deter enemy planes. One resident recalls one early morning, during a summer storm, seeing one large barrage balloon hit by lightning and bursting into flames. Kerry Greeves recalls another breaking loose and being washed up on the shore at Rockport.

Above: The Sunderland Flying Boat ashore on the rocks at Grey Point.
Bottom right: Barrage balloons over Belfast Lough.

From 1946 the Battery was maintained by the newly-formed Independent Maintenance Battery R.A. Formal entry was still past the sentry at the gates. The guns were sold to Eastwoods for scrap in 1956, but the camp was then used until 1 April 1960 by the Headquarters of 39 Brigade. Queen's University OTC also used the site at weekends.

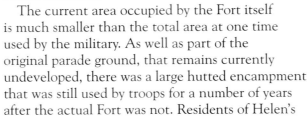

The current area occupied by the Fort itself is much smaller than the total area at one time used by the military. As well as part of the original parade ground, that remains currently undeveloped, there was a large hutted encampment that was still used by troops for a number of years after the actual Fort was not. Residents of Helen's Bay still remember with great affection the horse shows that were an annual feature of local life before and after the second war; competitors came from as far afield as Ballymena, such was the quality. There was also an annual cricket match held on the parade ground between Fort personnel and local residents. The troops also played a full part in the life of St John's Church, and the Helen's Bay Players were created by a captain stationed at the Fort.

The last word might go to the *Irish Builder* which wrote percipiently as long ago as November 1904: *'The fortification of Belfast Lough, so often projected and so often postponed, has at last taken shape. Over 50 years the project dates back, and one cannot wonder if the fortification of today will be so obsolete half a century later as that of 50 years ago is today.'* Its assessment was spot on.

Recollections of Colonel Bertram Cotton

In 2011, Lieutenant-Colonel Bertram Cotton kindly gave an extensive interview, (an audio copy of which is available elsewhere). Colonel Cotton had served at the Fort as a subaltern from 1939 to 1940 in 188 Antrim Coast Battery Royal Artillery TA. He later commanded the subsequent Regiment – 429 Antrim Coast Royal Artillery, also a TA Regiment.

Colonel Cotton explained that the Territorial Army in Great Britain was established following the Territorial Force (commonly known as the Haldane) Act of 1904, although the militia continued through the first war in Ireland up to 1922. In 1937 the first TA regiment was formed – 188 Antrim Coast Battery – as a successor to the Antrim Artillery Militia. (In 1899 this Militia had contained no less than 821 all ranks, the strongest Militia Artillery Regiment in Ireland.) On the first recruiting night for the new Regiment between three and four hundred men assembled inside, and outside, the drill hall.

Top left: On guard at the entrance to Grey Point Fort. Top right: Pre-war camp at Grey Point, with in lower row from second left: Ronnie Greeves, Oscar Graham, Major General Pollock, Maynard Sinclair, Sam Toppin; back row includes: Harold Glendinning, Patrick Cooke, Arnold Breene, Donald Shearer, Michael Marsham. Bottom right: Manning the guns at Grey Point Fort.

Commissioned in 1938, Colonel Cotton attended his first camp at Grey Point the following year. Attendees at the camp included, in addition to the then GOC Major General Pollock, Major (later Colonel) Rollo Carew – the Adjutant and ex-Royal Artillery full-time training officer, Donald Shearer (an Irish soccer international and later the first CO of 429 Regiment), Ronald Greeves and Maynard Sinclair amongst others. The camp was in tents in a field at the back of the subsequent hutted encampment. Both the guns and the searchlights were tested at that time. In addition to the gun crew, there was a magazine crew of 12. Once the shells were hoisted, numbers 7 and 8 of the gun crew moved them from the lift, whilst they were loaded by numbers 3 and 4. Close coordination was needed between the gun crew, those in the Observation Post, and the soldier manning each searchlight. The gun layer would set the direction and the range-finder the range. Allowance had to be made for the tide. Depending on the supply of shells, up to four or five rounds could be fired each minute.

Before the war, Colonel Cotton recalled that the Regiment trained two nights per week in a drill hall in Great Victoria Street in Belfast. Two of their officers – Donald Shearer and Patrick Cooke – both lived in Londonderry. To spare them the longer travel, both went regularly in uniform to Fort Dunree in Donegal where they trained alongside the Irish Army.

In the war, an Examination Vessel, manned by the Royal Navy, was moored in the Lough, roughly between Whitehead and Bangor. A separate code was created each day by the Royal Navy headquarters in Belfast Castle and passed to the examination battery at Grey Point, (though in 1941 the Orlock battery took over this role). Every vessel entering or leaving the Lough had to be given the pass, which was flown in flags by day and lights by night. Entrance up to the harbour was only permitted when the right signal was hoisted. Colonel Cotton said that he and his colleagues claim to have started the war. The 'E Hayward' had been a coal boat returning from Wales on 5 September 1939. He himself

Above: Church parade at Grey Point Fort.

had been on duty all night, and observed that the boat did not close with the examination vessel. It was comparatively close to the Grey Point battery. Contact was initially attempted through the Aldis lamp, before Colonel Cotton went off duty, handing over to a colleague. He described how he had not had time to start his breakfast (being cooked by Kitty Stephens) before the alarm was sounded and as he raced back to the Fort, the gun was fired. He recalled that the shell had ricocheted several times on the Lough before landing behind Castle Dobbs at Carrickfergus. The explanation was that the coal-boat had been very lightly manned and the skipper had not been on the bridge at the time.

After Dunkirk (May 1940), he said that up to 180 vessels had been moored in Belfast Lough. The Fort was given the coordinates of each ship and none could move without notification being passed from Naval Headquarters. Colonel Cotton recalled that he had been on duty at 3am one morning when it was a noticed that a county class cruiser, HMS Somerset, was getting underway and was starting to move out, without notification. Efforts to make contact first through the Aldis lamp and then the searchlight were to no avail. Colonel Cotton therefore authorised the firing of a round, laid off alongside the vessel. As he described it 'all hell broke loose'. He himself was asked for a full explanation, and subsequently his Commanding Officer was called to see the Royal Navy Flag Officer. However, the Navy recognised it was their mistake and an apology was duly made.

A number of improvements were made to the guns and the associated arrangements, in the early war years. This included a mechanised system which improved the range-finding, and automatic electric switches for the searchlights. It was about this time that the additional 4 inch naval gun was placed halfway along the shore hole of the golf course. Although this was used as part of the anti-aircraft defence battery during the Belfast Blitz, it was in practice of limited value. The hutted encampment had been completed by Christmas 1939 – not Nissen huts, but double-lined, using good timber. A 30 yard rifle range was in the trees on the Bangor side of the guns.

There had been between a dozen and 20 ATS girls at the Fort, under the command of a very efficient sergeant major, Nan Campbell. Initially they had done clerical and administrative work, though they were later used also to man the searchlights and range-finder in the Observation Post. A weekly church service was held in the camp; they had no resident chaplain, so Colonel Cotton was deputed to pick up the Rev Eric Barber, a curate in Dundela, to take the service. On one occasion Barber had lost his voice, so Colonel Cotton stood in. The service was in effect a full parade, requiring the attendance of all the 140 or so officers and men stationed at Grey Point. Medical services were provided by the Helen's Bay doctor who lived in Church Road.

In October 1939, a central order required all officers below the rank of captain to learn to ride a motor bicycle. Colonel Cotton's learning was supervised by a retired sergeant major who stood in the centre of the field while he rode round him. Every Friday he would collect the pay from the bank; each section in turn was paraded, paid and signed for. A NAAFI was provided, which also laid on bingo and other entertainment for the troops. (He recalled that they were well fed – the two sergeant cooks had both been butchers by trade. However even their culinary prowess was defeated when another officer asked them to cook a cormorant he had shot off the Point.)

After the Second World War, the Fort was again put on the care and maintenance regime. However when 188 Regiment was reformed as 429 Antrim Coast Regiment in 1948, Grey Point was the Regimental Headquarters; the Regiment also manned Kilroot and a mobile battery consisting of anti-aircraft guns and a six pounder. The Regiment had a fine pipe band led for several years in the 1950s by a pipe major who lived on the Falls Road. The headquarters was built in the middle of the Fort, but subsequently demolished. In the mid-1950s a splendid new headquarters was built at Firmount on the Antrim Road. However the Regiment was disbanded in 1957, when Colonel Cotton was in command. (The unit converted to the Engineers in an appropriate ceremony at Ripon.)

He recalled that some 30 or so of the gunners attended the 1987 re-opening ceremony at the Fort.

Wartime Recollections

by Jim Page (resident in Helen's Bay during the Second World War)

During the Great War (1914-1918), Grey Point Battery regularly garrisoned 300 troops, who trained on the 6-inch guns. Open trenches, dug during 1915, ran the entire length of the Back Shore, from Grey Point to the Coastguard Station, the cottages in the row of which had a rental of £12 per annum.

Between 1930 and 1939, the Lancashire and Cheshire Heavy Brigade, 550 strong, consisting of RA and RE units came each summer by boat and train, marching down Church Road to the strains of *'The Stein Song'* to train on the guns and searchlights, with nightly shoots on towed targets in mid-Lough, against the Kilroot Battery. The order of the day was,

> *'Open your windows tonight, please. There will be gunfire from the Fort tonight,'*

Between the wars Grey Point was for many years the setting of the popular Horse Show, when dozens of magnificent mounts were on view in jumping, trotting, and style and general appearance events. However by 1938 war clouds were again looming over Europe and many of the local young men and women enlisted in the reserve units. Air raid precautions (ARP) lectures filled Buckler's and Thompson's all to learn from Mr Carlisle of Newtownards. War, declared on Germany on Sunday morning 3 September 1939, brought vast changes to this small and peaceful community. An immediate influx of hundreds of soldiers and ATS to Grey Point, Crawfordsburn, Seahill, and even Nissen huts and searchlights on the third and fourth fairways of the golf links must have doubled the population. The black-uniformed Local Defence Volunteers (LDV) which soon became the khaki-clad Home Guard, was enrolled and armed against expected invasion in 1940, and was on continuous stand-by till 1945.

A large RAMC unit, the 16th Casualty Clearing Station, 180 strong, was billeted locally from 1940 – 43, when the first droves of American GIs arrived with tanks, lorries and jeeps to Seahill Camp, Crawfordsburn and the woods of Clandeboye. (The officers were put up in 7 Bridge Road, the Sergeants' mess was at Dr Blair's, and the nurses stayed at Mrs White's house on Craigdarragh Road. The nurses carried out their duties at Campbell College daily.) For months prior to D-Day, Seahill billeted paratroopers of the famous American 82nd and 101st Airborne Divisions, who would spearhead the Allied air landings in Normandy, as Belfast Lough filled with literally hundreds of US, British, Canadian and Dutch warships and transports. A few days after D-Day, the mighty American battle-waggons, 'Nevada' 'Arkansas' and 'Idaho' dropped anchor in the mid-Lough, their turrets black from firing hundreds of rounds during the Normandy landings.

What a contrast to the grim nights of 1941, when hundreds of German Heinkel Bombers had droned unopposed up Belfast Lough, directly over Helen's Bay en route, to blast and burn Belfast and kill a thousand of its citizens.

As the invasion rolled on to its inevitable victory, hundreds of defeated Wehrmacht prisoners were incarcerated at Seahill, and only two years after Germany's surrender, were they permitted to walk in twos around our roads.

The Home Front, including Helen's Bay Home Guard and Volunteers in Crawfordsburn

There is sadly little on record of the Helen's Bay detachment of the Home Guard, but the *County Down Chronicle* of 11 April 1944 reports on the use it made of that Easter weekend.

> *'Most Home Guard units were given a holiday over Easter, but one or two made full use of the weekend for extensive training. Helen's Bay Platoon are accorded full marks in this respect as they turned*

Above right: Mr EV Page talking to Officers from the 16th Casualty Clearing Station next door at 7 Bridge Road, Helen's Bay.

out 99% on Saturday afternoon, went into camp with the Military
and carried out a full programme of work including PT, bayonet
fighting, firing practice with rifle and Lewis Gun, field training, and
an exercise at dawn and various lectures.
A Senior Staff Officer inspected the men on Monday. He was
keenly interested and chatted with each man. The men dispersed
to their homes late on Monday evening after 48 hours experience
of training under military conditions, and although each was
thoroughly tired, it was the unanimous opinion that much had
been gained by the training. Congratulations are due to
Mr Jackson for his enterprise and co-operation with
local military, who, it is learned, left nothing undone to make the
Home Guards comfortable and the work interesting.'

A further article in the Chronicle of 25 March 1944 reports on shooting competitions at Comber and recorded that,

'.. special and deserved mention must be made of Portaferry,
Helen's Bay and Ballyhalbert-Portavogie Platoons who turned out
two teams each, and had to call on every man in the platoon to
do so.'

Frederick Harte who retired to Helen's Bay six months prior to the war, noted in his book

'It was prepared for all eventualities. We had a platoon of the Home
Guard well drilled and equipped, commanded by Mr Maurice Jackson.
My son Noel became Corporal and finally Sergeant. He made a record
for attendance, since during the whole four years of the Platoon's
existence he never missed a single muster for duty'.

Harte also paid tribute to the work of,

'.. ladies, among whom Mrs Stephens was an untiring worker,
assisted by young people, (who) collected large quantities of waste
paper, bones and other discarded commodities. Most of the
gentlemen of the village, under the leadership of Mr Hunter Tate,
were banded together to help any home which might fall a victim
to 'the terror that flieth by night'.'

He also gives credit to the housewives who, under the greatest difficulties and privations, kept the home fires burning. In coping with rationing,

'..the whole cry was about quantities, coupons and points. The art
of making a little go a long way had to be carefully studied by the
lady who held the keys of the pantry.'

It is very fortunate that this photograph of the Helen's Bay Home Guard survives. It includes Jim Davis, whose wife Kathleen's testimony follows in this chapter. It is sadly not now practical to identify every member in the photograph, but the names of all those who have been so far are recorded.

The Craigavad Home Guard was headed by Major Anderson (of Anderson McAuley) after the ex-Regular Army Major Hughes. Alfie Beaney had joined the Craigavad Home Guard, when he was 22, along with several of his friends. He recalls that initially they spent much time patrolling the roads. They met in Glencraig School, but went every couple of months to Kinnegar for formal training such as shooting practice on the range.

Top right: Helen's Bay Home Guard, including the Air Raid Warden Hunter Tate, and where identification has been made or suggested (broadly from left): back row – Messrs Gawley, Bannister, Mairs, Victor Galloway; middle row – Higgins (father and son), Jack Gray, Lieutenant or Captain Maurice Jackson, Sergeant Noel Harte, and Messrs Terence Hardy, Houston; front row – Messrs Jess, Hugh McCorry, Jim Davis, Crossey, Jack McClements, Charlie Meneely and Winston Brownrigg. Bottom right: Craigavad Home Guard 1944; back row (from left to right) – Alec Rainey, Matt Bustard,

It was a very mixed group, he relates, a community of workmen, middle and upper class – that was 'the wonderful thing about it; all the local people joined'. There were anti-aircraft batteries at Clandeboye and Islet Hill, Groomsport, which overnight once a month Craigavad Home Guard would man, alongside the regular soldiers. He had great praise for the courage of the pilot of the plane which towed the kite that provided their anti-aircraft target practice. As this was after the Blitz, Alfie never fired the guns in anger.

Harry Beaney, Alfie Beaney, Dickie McBride, Ernie Fisher, Robert Savage; middle row – Jack Wallace, unknown, Leathem Harris, William Coey, Thompson Gray, Douglas Gibson, Billy Hume, David Clarke, Harry McMillan, Norman Hume; front row – Unknown, Topsy Grant, Major Anderson, Major Hughes, George Hume, Sam Coey, Jimmy Bradley. (The three missing from the original photograph may include Eric Brown and Douglas Gibson's brother). Above: Glencraig Civil Defence Post L 1115, outside Sullivan School, February 1945.

A different facet of wartime life was recorded by *The County Down Spectator* in July 1940. A public meeting was held in the Terence Memorial Hall at which 'every household in Crawfordsburn was represented', to consider the inauguration of a Crawfordsburn Voluntary National Emergency Organisation. The leading light was Professor Montrose, though Mr Donaghy, the ARP Group Warden, took the chair. The purpose was to 'show the spirit of the people of Crawfordsburn'.

The programme would include basing a first aid depot in the village, a fire-fighting squad, a damaged buildings squad, air raid shelter provision, feeding and billeting of soldiers, and 'the administration of the village if it was cut off as a result of air raids or invasion'. Mr Montrose said that it was a peaceful village of individuals who looked after their own homes and gardens, but the residents had bonds which united them more firmly than the 'dragooned subservience to the commands of some Gauleiter'. They were all in the front line now, and must be ready for anything – bombs, parachutists, gas etc.

A pamphlet on first aid was handed out to all who attended, and residents were encouraged to train themselves to give first aid – they could not count on getting help from Helen's Bay, Mr Montrose said. (Emma Graham remembers attending a first aid course in the Memorial Hall.) He proposed a flowery motion in which the residents of Crawfordsburn pledged to aid and comfort each other in all trials and to make the fullest contribution to the national war effort. Seconded by WJ Stewart MP, it was unanimously passed. A committee was formed with Donaghy as chair and Montrose as secretary; other members were 'Mesdames' Greeves, Lindsay and Kennedy, with Messrs Stewart, Wallace and Falloon and Dr Park. (As another professor later wrote about the complex Montrose, whom he uncharitably described as a getter-up of backs, 'for Jimmy, the moment between conception and execution was now.')

Another element of the local war effort was the Civil Defence service. The photograph shows members of the local community in their Unit posing outside Sullivan School in Holywood. The personalities include Margaret Garner's father Mr Yeames, and Nikko Duffin's cousin, as well as the Glencraig Principal Ed Caves. Betty Lowry, a long-standing Seahill Road resident whose father Edward Beale was in the unit, has pointed out that it included residents from Ballyrobert and Helen's Bay right through to Marino, and people of very different backgrounds. The ladies' uniforms are those of the St John's Ambulance.

A propos of air raid shelters, Gill Johnston recalls that her family had a large dug-out in their garden, containing furniture, a table, bunks and even a cot. Once the siren sounded during family lunch when she was being pressed to finish off her rice pudding. Ah she thought, I will escape that in the dug-out, but no the nanny duly brought the remains down to the shelter to be completed. Two Polish pilots, who must have been stationed not far away, came to stay for a short break, and one played the piano beautifully. Sadly she learned later that he had been killed just before he got leave to spend time with the baby son he had not yet seen.

Mabel Jess was then living at Ballysallagh. She remembers one bad night in the Blitz when a bomb exploded in a nearby field and all the doors in their house blew in. The woods close by were all lit up with incendiaries and the water in the reservoir turned orange.

Irene Calvert, who lived with her family at The Chase on Craigdarragh Road, was appointed Northern Ireland's Chief Welfare Officer in 1941. This required her, among other things, to organise facilities for the several thousand Gibraltarians who had been evacuated from their homes on the Rock for the duration of the war. (Although there has been such a suggestion, it does not appear that any Gibraltarians were billeted locally.) Irene was in many ways a remarkable figure, being an independent Northern Ireland MP for Queen's University from 1945 to 1953. She was a strong voice for social reform and a pioneer for equal opportunities for women.

There were two or arguably three ammunition factories in the locality. Two were at Ballyrobert, and one at Glencraig, all were owned by Charles Hurst. The two at Ballyrobert were close to each other, one being in a converted byre, up what is now called Coyle's Lane. Lawrence McKeag and Alfie Beaney have confirmed the locations. It is likely that derelict outbuildings (adjacent to Ballyrobert House) are the last remnant of this factory. The other was on the site of the Vauxhall garage showroom. It does seem that there were no explosives used or manufactured at any of these premises, but we have been able to ascertain they made bullet sleeves in the two locations at Ballyrobert, and Bofors gun recoil gears and aircraft components at Glencraig.

It is recorded that over 200 (mostly girls) worked round the clock at Ballyrobert, in some cases perched on high stools to reach the machines erected on top of the cow stalls, with a further 45 (mainly men) at Glencraig. (It is fortunate that references to the factories were contained in the booklet commemorating the 75th anniversary of the founding of Charles Hurst which was produced in 1986.) The workers included Jack Argue, (previously employed as a farm labourer at Anderson's), Betty Lowry's cousin (who stayed in Seahill during the week to be close to her work) and Winifred McKee (Helen McCormick's aunt). Winifred said that she earned a better rate of pay there than she could elsewhere. Emma Graham remembers in the Crawfordsburn post office serving the factory girls early in the morning, as they walked back to their wooden bungalows in Carnalea, after working the night shift at Ballyrobert. They smelled strongly of oil, she commented.

Alfie Beaney recalls that the factory up the lane (which he states was then called Firth's Lane after a previous farmer who lived there and killed his cattle locally before taking the meat to his butcher's shop in Bangor) was on the poultry farm of the Thompsons. His brother Harry worked in the lower Ballyrobert factory. When it closed after the war, the head foreman, Murray who lived in Holywood, noting that it was next to the original garage on the corner of the main road and the Ballyrobert Road, suggested to Harry that he should think of buying the site. However the price was too high. The premises had extended by 1951 when Mr Lyle took over the petrol station and other buildings to start the current garage.

Alfie Beaney has clarified the story that there was a wartime BBC broadcast from the factory. He recalls that this was actually made from the Ballygilbert Church Hall, as one of the *Workers' Playtime* series. Those working in the factories would have all attended.

The third factory was in Glencraig. This was also in a cow byre, belonging to Mr Murphy, where the Scout Hall now stands. However the suggestion that Sir Winston Churchill visited the factories may have arisen from the name Churchill then associated with one of the local houses and a byre.

My Wartime Memories
by Kathleen Davis

Most of my wartime memories are of Helen's Bay, as I came as a bride to live here a month after war was declared. We soon got to know people through joining organisations set up to help the war effort.

The YMCA started a canteen in the Station Square to provide a meeting place and some extra food for the soldiers in Grey Point Camp. A group of ladies arranged a rota system to run the canteen. At first the food was fairly plentiful, the favourite meal being toast with sausages, beans, bacon and one, two or three eggs on top until quite suddenly our supply of eggs was withdrawn. Then other foods became scarce, but we did manage to keep open if only to serve tea, coffee and whatever scones or biscuits we could produce ourselves. Then came general food rationing, affecting everyone. This gave us fun devising recipes for eggless and fat free bread, cake and puddings. At that time some powdered dried eggs were to be had and I discovered they made quite good pastry. Some weeks the allowance of fresh food was only two ounces of butter or margarine, an egg or two and perhaps a little bacon. Ration books were issued and coupons had to be exchanged for various items of food. My husband kept bees and I was able to extract the honey, put it into jars and sell it in aid of the Red Cross. There was no sugar for jam-making so any available fruit was bottled in water or very light syrup for winter use.

Top left: Bullet sleeve production at Ballyrobert, supervised by Miss Edgar.
Bottom left: Ballyrobert Service Station around 1960.

The Home Guard was formed in 1941 to provide security and to watch for enemy planes, or German invaders by parachute. Jim was posted one night a week to Helen's Tower in the Clandeboye Estate on watch duty, leaving me trembling at home with a loaded gun under the bed as word had come through that Germans were on their way. Thankfully I did not have to use it.

During this time ships were mostly travelling in convoy and it was quite fascinating to see 20 to 30 lying in shelter in Belfast Lough, though I saw and heard two of these being blown up by mines and disappearing in a matter of minutes. As there was no television and very little radio it was difficult to know what was going on.

The next blow to our morale was the rationing of petrol. Coupons were issued to those who were allocated a little for essential purposes. We were able to use our car about twice a week for work only, so our bicycles were made good use of. Our yearly first class train tickets cost us £6 for the two, allowing us to travel as often as we wanted between Bangor and Belfast.

A sewing group was organised by Mrs Mitchell, at Rathmoyle, on Craigdarragh Road. One morning a week a dozen or so ladies met to make bandages, including Mrs Lindsay from Glen House in Crawfordsburn and 'Rene Shuttleworth. (Mrs Lindsay had been the Irish skiing champion in her day.) These were triangular pieces of cloth which had to be hemmed all round with a herringbone stitch. Our sewing had to be very neat and after careful examination masses of bandages were ready to be dispatched.

We heard the drone of heavy enemy bomber planes as they followed a route over Belfast Lough. This was very frightening as the sky was reddened with the reflection of the fires from the city shops, the City Hall and the Water Works on the Antrim Road. It was a very worrying time as most people had relatives in the city. Incendiary bombs were dropped on the farm buildings and houses in this area, so Jim and I felt it would be better to sleep out in the open. Laden with blankets we were about to open the front door when a land mine exploded in Cultra, demolishing two or three houses. The blast from this blew our door in and sent us flying down the hall. Our grandfather clock suffered the same fate, and as the song says 'never to go again'. We decided then not to go to the fields and for many weeks slept on a mattress on the floor of a small room at the back of the house as far from windows as possible.

The blackout gave a lot of trouble too. Curtains were made out of blackout material to make sure there wasn't a chink of light showing from the houses. The city and towns had only the dimmest lighting, no road lights here at all, and if a torch was used the beam had to be partly covered. Air Raid Wardens were always on the look-out for any slip up on these rules.

Ration books were introduced for clothing, even shoes. Jim and I spent a holiday on a lovely estate in Loughgall. From there we cycled over the border to Monaghan and while there we bought some non-rationed clothing, butter, sugar, etc, which we stuffed into our saddlebags. The rain never ceased for our 28 mile journey back to Loughgall. We arrived back drenched to the skin and lost all the goods as the black dye from the saddle bags had run through and ruined everything. We felt suitably punished for smuggling. Our hostess took one look at us, took our wet clothes to be dried and sent us off to have a hot bath, reminding us not to take more than the 5 inch hot water ration allowed to each guest. At that time beautiful dress material could be bought in Dublin, taffetas, satins at about 1/- per yard and pure silk for as little as 2/11 per yard.

Although there were many hardships, much suffering and loss of life, our family and friends came through this without being too badly affected.

The POW Camp at Rockport

The first part of this account is based on a conversation, on his return to Helen's Bay in October 1997, had by Robin Masefield with Rudi Brulz who had been a German Prisoner of War (POW) in Northern Ireland.

Rudi had initially served in Russia, but before the worst of the retreat, (from which none of the rest of his unit returned), they had asked for volunteers to serve as parachutists, so he had transferred as a paratrooper to the western front. After his capture on the Belgium-France border, he was first placed as a POW in camps in Londonderry and Dungannon. However in summer 1945 Rudi had been sent to the camp adjacent to Holywood Palace Barracks, from where he was transferred in 1946 to Rockport. He recalled that on Christmas Day 1946, the POWs had been allowed out within a nine-mile radius. He found his way to St John's Church in Helen's Bay where the sermon was on the text 'I was a stranger and you took me in'. A worshipper invited him home for tea. This was Mrs Greeves.

He did not leave Rockport until spring 1947 when the last POW camps were closed in Northern Ireland. For the first three months of that year the Government allowed POWs a few miles out of the camps. He thus got to know Colonel and Mrs Greeves and their friend Mrs Aickin, along with her son RAF navigator Cyril Aickin and his wife Evelyn, a wartime nurse at Holywood Palace Barracks. Mrs Aickin continued to send him food parcels in the Scottish work camp to which he had been moved, fearing that the Scots would not feed the prisoners. At Christmas 1947 the guards were most envious of the cake etc that he received. He was only returned to Germany three years after the War in 1948.

Rudi said that the prisoners sent to Northern Ireland camps were those considered to be the more dangerous, eg parachutists, submariners, SS etc. In Rockport, he made toys and cigarette cases – he still had one at home. He employed four POW colleagues in the end and they each made enough from their sales to British soldiers to buy a watch. However local manufacturers got the camp authorities to take away their tools, as the competition was proving too strong. It was not a large camp, with several hundred to a thousand at most he believed. An Army captain was in charge.

Rudi worked out of the camp for some sergeants, initially as a cleaner, but then as interpreter. On one occasion the local authorities feared the group was trying to escape and sent a police boat to investigate, but Rudi maintained they were only seeking to sunbathe. He recalled the POW teachers making notes on lavatory paper, e.g. on subjects as obstruse as the different properties of convex and concave mirrors. He also used to write choir music in the camp on wrappers from tins of food. They made violins from the bottom of tea chests. As a customer of the POWs, Trevor Boyd recalled purchasing iron crosses for sixpence each off the Seahill prisoners. History does not now record if these were the genuine article but one suspects that, if so, they would

have been sold for a higher sum. Others recall seeing less exotic items such as cap badges or epaulettes.

There had been, he said, escape attempts from Dungannon – one tunnel, and others tried going over the fence, where one prisoner was shot. Evelyn Aickin told of an escape attempt in Rockport, when the local policeman had been out on his bicycle looking for the prisoner; Mary Strahan herself observed a policeman with his hand on the shoulder

Above: Karl Schouau, POW number 20317, Rockport camp 22 April 1947.

of a POW bringing him in to the former Helen's Bay police station. Alfie Beaney and Betty Lowry remember local houses being searched, following an escape. Jim McClements remembers the high fences and barbed wire surrounding the camp. Nikko Duffin also recalls passing the camp one day, back from a swim below Craigdarragh, when he and his companions' eyes were stung, which came from tear gas which must have been used at the camp, perhaps to restrain the prisoners. Lionel Carew, whose family was then living at Fairholme (with a flock of chickens which he recalls had a particular propensity to roam across the Craigdarragh Road), remembers parties of prisoners on their way to work on local farms singing *Deutschland uber Alles*.

Margot McClements has evidence of the friendship between her uncle and another German prisoner – Karl Schouau, POW No. 20317. The photograph of Karl in his uniform is dated 27 April 1947, at Rockport camp though was no doubt taken a good deal earlier, as may be seen from the accompanying photograph of Karl in his POW dress with Anne McBride. It was given 'in thankfulness for received hospitality'.

It is understood that he had been allowed out to help those working with the horses at Enfield House at the top of Craigdarragh Road, and this was where he met Dickie McBride, with whom he then kept in touch for many years after his return to Germany. Their friendship is the more remarkable given that Dickie had been a staunch member of the Home Guard. Margot's father worked for the Demolition and Rescue teams in Belfast, drawing on his construction experience; he worked hugely long hours clearing up after the Blitz attacks.

It is understood, from a reference by Charlie Brett in the *Buildings of North County Down*, that the site at Seahill was initially built to house American troops prior to D-Day, and turned over to the prisoners of war when the Americans left. It is also recorded that a large contingent of American troops were stationed in the grounds of Crawfordsburn House.

Although there is no formal right of way nearby, the last remains of a part of the Rockport camp can still be seen, in the shape of several tiers of concrete foundations for the Nissen huts in a field and adjacent woodland just inland and east of the Seahill sewage works. It was here that Rudi Brulz did find the steps to the hut where he had slept, half a century before, as a homesick young prisoner.

Grey Point Fort Addendum

Prior to joining the RAF, Alfie Martin DFC spent nearly two years from August 1939 as a Sapper in the Royal Engineers manning the searchlights at Grey Point and its sister forts. As a Territorial, he too had been at the June 1939 camp at Grey Point. The Fort was a very pleasant place he recalls, but on duty at night you tried to catch some sleep on a blanket on the floor of the searchlight emplacement, hoping not too many alarms would go off. His usual position was the easterly one overlooking Helen's Bay beach. The searchlights could not be elevated above the Lough, so were of no use in the Blitz. He watched the first great raid from the Parade Ground, seeing flames over the docks and North Belfast, frustrated that they couldn't do anything to prevent it. As one of the few soldiers at the Fort to have a car, he was in demand to drive the officers, for example to bring Captain Greeves from Crawfordsburn for the Church Parade. Maynard Sinclair was his CO; he recalls however a degree of distance between the members of the Artillery and Engineer Regiments at the Fort. Life wasn't all work – Alfie still remembers fondly the dances at Ballyrobert Orange Hall. In 1943 he was shot down over the Franco-Belgian border, but after several months escaped to Spain with the help of the French Resistance. His remarkable tale is told in his book *Bale Out*.

Above left: Prisoner of war Karl Schouau, in his Rockport POW camp clothes, together with Anne McBride.
Above right: Barbed wire and the concrete bases for the huts that comprised Rockport Prisoner of War Camp.

Chapter 8

The Social Fabric

This chapter entitled 'The Social Fabric' aims to describe some of the many past and present organisations that have played an important part in the development and social cohesion of the two villages. The contents are set out in alphabetical order, in part to avoid giving any impression of precedence of one body over another. Nor is it a comprehensive list; for example it excludes the local branches of political parties; as might be expected, there was a local Unionist branch with which for example Dr Park, the Ballygilbert Minister and sometime Presbyterian Moderator was closely associated. One highlight was the annual ball at Clandeboye House. The two villages are fortunate in the wealth and diversity of interests and opportunities available to residents and visitors. Long may such commitment flourish; our community is the richer for it.

The Bayburn Historical Society

The Bayburn Historical society was founded in 1989, with Robin Masefield as its inaugural chairman. The society took as its purpose: 'to encourage the study of and where feasible to record and publish local history.' The Marchioness of Dufferin and Ava was asked to be the Society's patron and the first talk was appropriately on the First Marquess. The Society took Helen's Tower as its evocative motif.

The subsequent talks in the first season were a foretaste of things to come, covering the advent of the Belfast and County Down Railway, wind and water mills of North Down, Grey Point Fort, and the origins and natural history of Crawfordsburn. Eager audiences would pack into the Presbyterian Church Hall or the Country Park Centre for well-informed entertainment.

A photographic record was taken of aspects of the village, and residents were tapped for their reminiscences. The Society benefited in the 1990s hugely from the expertise and enthusiasm of Stuart White and Grenfell Morton as chairmen and Adrian Mencarelli as secretary.

Their contribution, and that of many others, was immensely appreciated. Stuart set out seven roles for the Society: research, collection of old material, collection of current material, maintenance of the record base, publicity and public relations, editorial and social. These guidelines have stood the Society in good stead ever since.

In the spring of 1990 the Society organised a first for Northern Ireland, 'an historical jog' around places of interest in the two villages. It was this research that formed the basis for the Society's four mile Bayburn Trail, which was published as a millennium project. Society members – Stuart and Basil White working with Adrian Mencarelli's map – attractively illustrated the Trail, which came out in November 1999.

Two large-scale displays of the Bayburn Trail, thanks to support from North Down Borough Council, can now be seen at locations beside Crawfordsburn Inn and at the entrance to the Fort Road car park in Helen's Bay.

The Society has also arranged an outing each year to add directly to members' knowledge of local history in other parts of the country. The subjects of its meetings have ranged widely over the years, including talks on local mills and mines, the Royal Irish Constabulary, Irish Lights, voyagers on the Titanic, Castles and Houses in North Down, the 1798 United Irishmen uprising, the Heritage of the Somme and aerial photography of Ireland. Throughout this period a regular feature has been the reminiscences of the Society's own members which have helped to bring alive the past for the modern generation.

Fifty Years of Brownies in the Bay

In 2004 the Brownies in Helen's Bay celebrated their remarkable 50th anniversary, together with Rainbow Guides, family and friends with a Thanksgiving Service.

This was conducted by the Rev Dr John Medhurst in St John's Church on 7 November. Rev Colin Megaw told the congregation that Miss Winifred Bailie started the Brownies in November 1954 and they met in the Old School House in Bridge Road near Station Square. Since then they have met weekly in the Presbyterian Church Hall and more

recently in St John's Church Hall.

The youngest Brownie, Emily Rohan, lit a candle to celebrate 90 years of Brownies worldwide, followed by five Leaders (Joan Bushell, Jean McArdle, Eunice McKerrow, Joan McShane and Etta McGucken) lighting candles to celebrate 50 years of Brownies in Helen's Bay. All Brownies renewed their Promise, followed by the Brownies saying prayers and singing *Give me Oil in my Lamp*. A former Brownie, Claire Hunter, read from *John 1 v 1-14*. Sophie Pollock carried the Brownie flag.

Following the service everyone enjoyed meeting in the Church Hall to see photographs from the earlier days and many pack holidays spent in Portstewart. Mrs Doreen Gilmore and Mrs Heather Knipe cut the anniversary cake.

Ten years previously there had been a lesser celebration, but again featuring a ceremonial cake.

Crawfordsburn Country Club

Set back a little off the road in Crawfordsburn is a picturesque cottage which, until recently, was the frontage of the Crawfordsburn Country Club. It is very old and reputed to be the haunt of smugglers in the 16th century and the hiding place of political fugitives such as Henry Joy McCracken in the 18th century. Previously owned by Mrs Reid, it is known to have been remodelled in Tudor style by Sir Emerson Herdman of Sion Mills, in the late 19th century when he used it as a summer cottage.

In 1910, local businessman Mr William Johnston, who also ran a small bus company called 'The Garden of Eden Bus Company' plying between Crawfordsburn and Belfast, took over the lease of the cottage, the Crawfordsburn Inn and surrounding land. He may well have acquired the land behind the cottage from Jim McClements' grandfather, with whom he was great friends.

Mr Johnston has left behind a short biographical account which is worth drawing on. His father having died in 1871 when he was five years old, William earned money singing at the Alhambra Music Hall at the age of just six. He then learned seafaring on the Gibraltar training ship for orphans. Abandoning a start in a linen office, he went off to sea, including rounding Cape Horn in a windjammer, and fishing for cod out of Halifax, Nova Scotia. After many adventures over several years, he returned to Belfast where, in his own words, he 'specialised in feeding humanity on the cheap' – serving chip potatoes, fish and polonies. This was at the Burlington on Ann Street which served the workers of Belfast for 14 years, until the premises' rent became exorbitant and he moved to York Street. But William was also looking to Bangor, among 'so-called God-fearing people'. He bought premises at Quay Street on the front in 1906, adding a 'palace ballroom' and survived a legal dispute with Bangor authorities that had to be settled in Dublin. (Both his sons David and Billy served in the Navy for a period during the war.)

The Old Inn at Crawfordsburn followed, as his next venture. Subsequently he built a ballroom behind the cottage across the road from the Inn and opened it to the public for dancing. Called the Cingalee, after a musical play he admired, the facilities which included tea gardens, flourished.

Johnston has recorded that his favourite client was the Nationalist Member of Parliament Joe Devlin, who on one occasion hosted a garden party for 850 people which he paid for out of his own pocket. 'He just loved this little heaven on earth, and no other place was good enough'. Devlin was well-known for bringing children from inner-city Belfast down to Crawfordsburn. Johnston noted too that wonderful crowds visited the old place, touring parties from England, Scotland and Wales in their thousands. 'In fact it was the pleasure and delight of my whole life and the devotion of my beloved wife who was one with me… the happiest days of our lives'.

Top left: Brown Owl, Etta McGucken, with (from left) Katie Megaw, Jenny Lawson and Saskia, celebrating 40 years of Brownies in Helen's Bay.
Top right: Billy Johnston in his Naval uniform. Opposite page: Cingalee Tea Gardens, main entrance.

His daughter Peggy has shed some light on the incident that led to the end of his connection with the Inn. It was deemed a place of ill repute, even though William was out of the country at the time and a lady of the night admitted his establishment had been 'set up'. He was taken to court and even spent a short period in prison rather than pay the fine. (A well-intentioned friend paid the fine off, for his release, reportedly to Johnston's chagrin.) The consequence was that he lost the licence for the Inn.

In 1935 the lease of the Inn, the Cingalee and the surrounding land was transferred at an annual rental of £200 to Paddy Falloon, who changed the name Cingalee to The Chalet (after the cottage at the front). He remodelled the ballroom and organised Afternoon Tea dances on Wednesdays and Saturdays, Saturday evening dances and light music concerts on Sunday afternoons.

The *County Down Spectator* recorded the official opening of The Chalet in September 1935, with 'myriads of lights in rainbow hues festooning the grounds', and a quaint hanging sign inscribed with its name. The evening's programme provided both music from the orchestra directed by Norman Douglas and cabaret which included 'the three Harmanettes' and 'Hilda and Isobel, the rhythm sisters'. It was Mr Falloon, the paper reported, who had conceived the idea however and 'spared neither time, trouble nor expense'. The *Spectator* added that it was hoped to have admirable car parking arrangements, almost at the club door. The premises were after all 'situated on the main road from Belfast to Bangor'.

He then interested the BBC in broadcasting late night dance music by the Chalet Orchestra directed by Tony Linnell from Leicester. The ballroom was one of the few places with its own electricity generator. If the lights started to fade or flicker during the dancing, there would be loud cries of 'Billy', as Billy Johnston (William's son) had the expertise to keep it going.

Helen White remembers attending dances at the Club before the war. She recalls Paddy Falloon as a glamorous individual who was an excellent dancer. Helen also tells the story of her mother attending dances in Crawfordsburn or Helen's Bay, a generation earlier. She drove over from their house at Ballybeen in Dundonald in a pony and trap. On one occasion the road was so slippery that the pony could not get up the hill. She had to get down and walk alongside; thereafter she travelled in heavier shoes, and carried her dancing slippers safely with her.

Paddy Falloon initially had difficulty in getting the licence for the Inn restored. Indeed his application was refused by Judge Bates three years running. In October 1935, the Judge concluded that his might be an old-fashioned view, but a licence for the Inn would 'create an unhealthy atmosphere and expose young people to temptation'; the dance hall continuing under the auspices of the gentleman who had forfeited his licence. The third time, in 1937, the Judge was faced with a broader spectrum of local support. Speaking on behalf of the application, local resident, Professor James Louis Montrose said that the absence of a licence made it 'impossible for him to get beer', and it had also embarrassed him when he had guests to dinner and found there was no sherry in the house. (Montrose was then the widely renowned Dean of the Faculty of Law at Queen's, and recognised as a generous host.)

George Graham, building contractor (and father of Emma), said in his evidence that he liked a drink a few times a week, and people formerly accustomed to taking refreshments at the Inn found it very inconvenient. Even Constable Kyle said the police could get there from Helen's Bay on their bicycles in a few minutes. Counsel noted there had been a licence

Opposite page: Cingalee Tea Gardens, Lovers' Walk and the Wishing Stone.
Above left: Cingalee Tea Gardens, Crawfordsburn – the rustic chalet. Above right: Cingalee Tea Gardens, the Ballroom.

for 200 years, until 1931. In opposition were Mr Donaghey, the teacher, and Rev Park among others. On this occasion Judge Bates found a new reason for refusal – 'the disastrous effects of road traffic' – seeming to link this with drink being taken.

Paddy Falloon was not beaten yet. After taking fresh legal advice, and with help from Sam McCrudden (a linen merchant who lived at the Water Mill, in the village) and others, he had four tennis courts constructed in the grounds behind the Chalet, together with Squash and Badminton courts which were among the first in Northern Ireland. (Sam McCrudden incidentally had to have his garage specially extended to cater for the size of his Rolls Royce.) Accordingly the Country Club was the first to be established in Northern Ireland for its members only. This created enough of a split with the Inn, which led finally to that licence being regained.

Watched by Mrs Reid who was then 90 years old, the Marchioness of Londonderry (in a fur stole) performed the opening ceremony of the Crawfordsburn Country Club on 20 August 1937. In her speech, she was reported to have said that 'she could not imagine anything more lovely than such a country club as there was now at Crawfordsburn'. In his speech of welcome, as chairman of proceedings, Sam McCrudden said that the name of Londonderry was a household word, not only in Ulster, but throughout the British Empire. Commenting on the facilities, Mrs Reid noted that less had been required in the way of amusement at the Inn in her day, when life was much simpler.

Professor Montrose, who lived at Glendore House, was the Club's first elected President. He had, Kerry Greeves recalls, a superb eye for the ball; after the war he regularly played hard-fought squash matches against Kerry's brother Tony Greeves. During the war, when their father, Colonel Ronnie Greeves, was in a distant post beside the Suez Canal, he was accosted unexpectedly by a large man in uniform who said 'Colonel Greeves, I presume?' Professor Montrose, then serving as an intelligence officer in the RAF, had tracked him down.

According to the official history, in the early months, before the Club was registered and licensed under the Clubs Act in 1938, those in need of refreshment were obliged to bring in refreshments in 'paper parcels to wooden cases, according to taste'.

After an initial avalanche of new membership applications, 1939 brought a fall in membership as many joined the forces. Blackout regulations and petrol rationing further aggravated the situation. In late 1940 Colonel Unsworth negotiated a change in the lease to ease the financial situation. Then activities increased as members of the Forces stationed nearby were invited as guests, many becoming Club Members.

The famous RAF pilot Douglas Bader was one distinguished visitor to the Club during the war. He danced stylishly with Peter Clarke's mother, notwithstanding the handicap of his tin legs. For those in the Services, there was a good value concessional joining fee of one pound, which one contributor to this article happily paid. Another member of the Club recalled seeing a serving officer standing on his head in the corner of the cottage, to prove to a colleague that he could do so without disturbing his monocle. Clearly both the hospitality and entertainment were great. While it may not be in the official history, local war hero Colonel Blair Mayne DSO and three bars, was on one occasion asked to leave, escorted by the local constabulary.

It is interesting to consider the prices in the immediate post-war years. Club subscription was 3 guineas, a meal of Dover Sole with all the trimmings cost 2 shillings and 9 pence (14p today). In the mid-50s the subscription was increased to 6 guineas and a meal in the dining room cost 7 shillings (35p today). The Coronation Ball held on Tuesday 2 June 1953, in the midst of a week's festivities at the Club, was open to members at 11 shillings and 6 pence. Later that decade another fall in membership accompanied a rise in the prices and fees.

A resident orchestra was contracted rather than engage bands on a one night stand basis, and many gifted musicians have played at the Club. One of these was Eddie Pearl, a friendly face smiling above the piano in the days when it was possible to hold one's partner and converse at the same time. Other players were Sam Stewart and Tom McMurtry who played on occasion on the same bill as Joe Loss. Jimmy Savile also visited

Above right: Crawfordsburn Country Club Coronation programme.

to support a disabled children's party. Music and dancing, some in fancy dress, and indeed film shows, were not the Club's only activities. During the popular Sunday evening shows, the waitresses obligingly served drinks throughout the film.

The sports facilities led to success in national and international competitions. As early as 1941, when Tom Cull was Games Secretary, the *Spectator* recorded that the standard in the squash competition fell 'little short of international standard'. In later years, Tom Boyle, a former international badminton player, coached a selected group of youngsters of whom three went on to play for the Irish Senior International Team and two for the Junior Team. Cyril Kemp, an international squash player, promoted the game at Crawfordsburn, and on two occasions the Club 'A' Team were the All Ireland Champions. In 1976 Northern Ireland's first glass-backed squash court with seats for 200 viewers was built. The rally driver Paddy Hopkirk was a not infrequent visitor.

In 1989 an outdoor bowling green was laid and very soon teams were competing in the Private Green Junior and Midweek League and in the Veterans League.

The Club was fortunate in having loyal staff, many of whom were long-serving, notwithstanding rumours that the premises were haunted, with sightings variously of a monk, 'Lord Crawfordsburn' and a hanged maid.

When he was 10 or 11 years old, Gary Graham came in to help his mother, a silver service waitress in the Club in post-war years. He remembers cleaning the glasses, and the fun of going home in a big, old taxi. They would look through his mother's tips, at the end of a good day, hoping to find a silver tanner or a bob, rather than the more usual pennies or threepences. Both her sister and her brother also worked there. The Chalet, as she called it, was a large part of his young life.

Not long after celebrating its 75th anniversary, the Club suffered from what proved to be a terminal decline in membership. Despite plans to update the facilities, related to commercial development in the vicinity, the Club came to a sad end in August 2009. It is to be hoped that future development of the site will in be keeping with the character of the village, and that the memory of the Club may be preserved in some appropriate way.

Above right: Mrs Brown and Mrs Ross, both Ladies Captains at Helen's Bay Golf Club.

Helen's Bay Golf Club

This account draws heavily on Bill Clark's superb history of 'Helen's Bay Golf Club: The First Century'; we are most grateful to him. Other snippets come from a 1954 article in The County Down Spectator.

The Club was founded in 1896 on land leased from the First Marquess of Dufferin and Ava. It is understood to be among the oldest clubs in Ireland. The first meeting to plan the club was held in the Temperance Hall; Samuel Ross and James Pyper were key figures there.

The oldest cup is the Dufferin Medal, which the Marquess presented as the first patron, when he was the British Ambassador in Paris. In the formative years the caddies were the sons of Clandeboye Estate workers, although competition for the role was more widespread in later times. The original Captain was George Herbert Brown of Tordeevra and his wife held the same office for the Ladies. His yacht was moored in the bay while he completed his round of golf.

On the opening day, 16 May 1896, the highest gross score was 168. Fortunately for some players in the early days, handicaps could be as high as 90. Although it cost the founding members a guinea a year, the Club swiftly established itself. It has come a long way since Kathleen Brown signed a card for 282 strokes.

In 1910, members won the Golfing Union of Ireland's Junior cup. At that time the green fees were just one shilling (five pence in today's currency). The 'Goose Club' was established before the war, holding an annual dinner at which the bird was served.

The first war interrupted play, as oats and potatoes were grown on the fairways, and occasioned many lost balls. In 1915 club members ferried 50 wounded soldiers from Belfast hospitals out for a day's entertainment at the Club. At times in the second war, sheep grazed on the course which led to other hazards, though soldiers who were members elsewhere could play for free. There was also an anti-aircraft

emplacement set up on the sixth hole. Grazing sheep were not actually a new phenomenon; in earlier years the Club had no mowing machinery and had to close for periods during the summer when the grass grew too long, until a flock could reduce the sward to a playable condition once more.

In the 1920s a major regatta was successfully held in the Lough, organised by the Club. Two large marquees were erected on the sixth fairway.

Between the wars, Billy Pyper, or 'Mister Helen's Bay' as he was known in golfing circles, held sway. His amateur course record of 68, set in 1929, was not surpassed for 36 years. (This was all the more remarkable given his diminutive stature – the stationmaster at Helen's Bay would bring out a special stool to enable Pyper to enter the railway carriage.) The Ladies who won the prestigious Irish Golf Union Shield for the Bay closely matched his prowess.

Perhaps the course's proudest moment was in July 1946 when it hosted Fred Daly, who went on to win the Open Championship the following year – the last Ulsterman to do so before Darren Clarke in 2011. The Ulster Professional Championship was held at the Club as recently as 1983.

There have been some great characters associated with the Club. Tom McKinstry was – uniquely – professional, captain and then president, having first played in 1933. Kitty Stephens was captain for four years, following in the steps of her mother and her sister, and president for 25. In 1972 Tom Hunter nobly interrupted his round on the 7th hole to rescue a swimmer in difficulty off the beach. It is recorded that his and his opponent's balls had been borne off as 'finds' before they returned to resume their round. Frank Thompson was struck by lightning when sheltering in a corrugated iron hut beside the 8th tee. All the hair on one arm was singed – when he got to hospital he found eight doctors waiting to examine this curiosity. Bob Wightman, steward and greenkeeper, for years went out early in the mornings to sweep the dew off the greens, equipped only with a very long cane. John Prifti was for many years involved with the juvenile players; drawing on contacts from his university days, he established an annual match against the Hermitage Club at Lucan.

For a remarkable 40 years, the course record was held by Robin Longmore who returned a magnificent card of 67 shots – one under par – on a Saturday in July 1965. Robin's memories of his achievement are vague but he does recall,

> 'I played off a seven handicap but can't remember if I'd ever beaten 70 before. But I do remember a very enthusiastic reception in the clubhouse and a little sadness as well.'

The ladies' record at Helen's Bay is really special – set on a day when gales and lashing rain forced quite a number of players to abandon the tournament.

It was actually Rhoda Strain's captain's day – 17 June 1985 – and the atrocious weather became incidental as Jane Allen, another villager, battled round in 70 shots – level par – to win Rhoda's prize and break her own course record established four years earlier. Jane somehow put six threes on her scorecard that memorable day.

It would all have been beyond belief for the ladies who entered the club's very first competition on 14 July 1897. The winner was a Miss Edwards whose round of 137 was too hot for the rest.

The original clubhouse was described as a quaint old cottage, though there were also meetings in The Nest (or Ardeesin) beside the

Above left: A View of Helen's Bay Golf Course, toward Church Road.

third tee, and Point House was used for a while. Leslie Montgomery, or Lynn Doyle, the novelist, first conceived many of the short stories in his book *Lobster Salad* (first published in 1922), while sojourning in the clubhouse.

The present clubhouse dates from 1971. The wooden bar is a particularly fine specimen, having been acquired from the 'SS Bermuda' which was broken up at Harland and Wolff. Until recently there was still a member who could recall standing on the first green watching the Titanic sailing down the Lough.

Uncertainty over the future of the lease on the Course was finally dispelled in August 2004 when the Club reached agreement with the Dufferin and Ava Estate for a further lease until the year 2039. Although the course sits on just over 40 acres of prime land in the middle of the village, less than three acres of this land belongs to the club, with the remainder being retained under a lease agreement.

In 1996 Helen's Bay Golf Club celebrated its centenary. As well as a splendid re-enactment of its beginnings in 1896, to mark the milestone, the Club spent £350,000 remodelling the clubhouse. The millennium was celebrated by the planting of several hundred trees which make the course more attractive – and challenging. The course, although not long, has been considerably improved in recent years, benefitting from the attention of former European Tour professional, David Jones and although still not intimidating for beginners, is a stern test of accuracy for low handicap golfers. These features, along with its renowned restaurant,

make the club a major asset for the village in particular and North Down in general. Its website is www.helensbaygc.com.

Helen's Bay Tennis Club

Tennis has long been a feature of life in the two villages. There were a number of private courts, eg two grass courts at Tordeevra (where a club formed by Mr and Mrs Shuttleworth existed for some 20 years from before the second war) and until recently Rathwyre, both on Kathleen Avenue, as well of course as the facilities at the Crawfordsburn Club.

The Helen's Bay courts have been available in their present site, owned by North Down Borough Council, for just on 50 years. Hugh Moore, then a Councillor, was a key figure in their creation, while Councillor Denise Sawers served the first ball, when the courts were officially opened on Saturday 19 May 1962. (Both Councillors incidentally are remembered in the names of streets off Carolsteen Park.) But, as recorded in the *County Down Spectator*, it was Kitty Stephens who made the main speech, in which she paid tribute to Helen's Bay's Council of Youth – 'this Council saw the need and got something done'. The North Down Rural District Council were, in her words, 'fairy godparents'. Mrs Stephens then unfurled the flag, which flew brightly in the dry but blustery conditions, before Deirdre Rollins presented her with a memento. Responding on behalf of the Club, the men's captain, Terry Eakin said that as there was no caretaker, it was 'our responsibility to make sure the courts are properly used'. Miss Marion Lilburn was the first ladies' captain, while Oscar Rollins was the chairman, and Councillor Sawers President. There was then an exhibition match of mixed doubles, followed by juniors. The cost of the courts was £1,200. The erection of the pavilion (or clubhouse) was approved by North Down Rural District Council at an estimated cost of £2,400 in January 1963.

In the 1950s a cricket team was formed by a retired bank official, Mr Humphrey Worthington. On the grass area adjacent to the tennis courts, he arranged many impromptu cricket sessions; he also collected groups of local boys to play beach cricket for hours.

The Helen's Bay Lawn Tennis Club, (as it came to be called),

Above left: The original clubhouse at Helen's Bay Golf Club. Bottom left: Members of Helen's Bay Golf Club celebrating their centenary on 30 March 1996, traditionally attired in their railway carriage; (Bill Feherty in the foreground).

based on the Council courts, has had varied fortunes over the years in competitive tennis. The 1970s were a time of success at adult level in various Leagues, while the junior section in particular is currently thriving in the summer leagues. Phyllis Strawbridge who joined the Club by the mid-1970s and later became Ladies Captain, recalls the high standard of home-baking that was required, when entertaining visiting teams. Additionally, the Ladies Captain had the unenviable role of not merely emptying but even washing out the rubbish bins. 'You did what you were asked in those days', she reflected, 'it wouldn't happen nowadays'. In the 1970s the social scene was also a significant feature of community life, centred on the clubhouse. With more young families moving into the area this continued into the 1980s, and there were ever ready surrogate parents at the tennis courts, so prams, scooters and tricycles were much in evidence. Many a game was interrupted by the need to rescue a toddler from prickly hedges or the top of a slide – there was no rubberised landing area in those days.

The League team was probably at its strongest in the 1970s and into the early 1980s, when it was occasionally graced by former Ulster inter-provincial players. The Belfast and District Knock-out Cup bears the Helen's Bay name more than once. In June each year the famous HBLTC barbeque was the social highlight of the year, attended by many who never lifted a tennis racquet as well as the regular weekly players. That tradition continues to this day, come sun or – as frequently is the case – rain.

Since 1999 the building has been shared with the Montessori pre-school. The courts were resurfaced by North Down Borough Council in spring 2001 with a porous bitumen macadam. The Club has a strong junior section in particular, and some dedicated coaches; its website is www.helensbaytennisclub.co.uk.

Crawfordsburn and Helen's Bay – Masonic Order

This account draws heavily on a lengthy article in the County Down Spectator in October 1931 when the current Masonic Temple was consecrated by Colonel RG Sharman Crawford, the Provincial Grand Master of Down.

Masonry was first recorded in Crawfordsburn in 1813 when meetings were held in a room 13 feet by 12 feet in a small cottage on the Main Street adjacent to the later Orange Hall. From this birthplace they moved to two houses occupied subsequently by Miss Warnock, and then removed to the house of Langford Megarrell. When additional members came from Bangor, the Lodge determined in 1882 to build their own hall. This later became the Orange Hall when the current premises were acquired, after negotiations with the representatives of the late Richard Wallace. (Alfie Mairs records that Captain Taylor, a far-travelled linen agent, had lived in the Red House previously.)

The *Spectator* noted that 'the new temple is regarded as one of the most beautiful in Ireland'. Naturally the 'live wire' of the new quarters was Colonel Sharman Crawford who in his speech said that the day put the coping stone on his long life as a Mason. He had initially summoned William McNeilly and James Chatfield who were the virtual owners of the former Hall, and they had examined the potential of the Red House, with John Moffatt. A meeting of the Rising Sun Masonic Lodge No 170 at the Terence Memorial Hall had then determined to proceed with the purchase, at a cost of £1,500, with up to a further £500 for alterations.

The opening ceremony was attended by 300 brethren, beginning with a procession from the previous hall. The Colonel said that 'if the world could be governed by masons what a different place it would be'. Noting the Lodge's past, he pointed to the social activities undertaken by the Lodge in former years. He proposed bringing ladies within the

Above left: Helen's Bay Lawn Tennis Club winning team, 1975 (back row Norman Atkinson, Bill Clark, Fergus Barkley, Peter Clarke, Paul Emery; front row (from second left) Margaret Neill, Ann Belford, Sheila Brookes, Phyllis Strawbridge.

scope of such activities in 1931, as the Lodge indeed already had in 1857. He quoted from a circular:

'A Masonic Ball will be held in Mr Robert Crawford's Hall, Crawfordsburn on the evening of 9 January. Dancing to commence at 8 o'clock…. Self and partner 2 shillings.'

The hall was extensively altered and modernised in 1962, the lead being taken by Lodge No 170, with support from two others.

Crawfordsburn and Helen's Bay – Orange Lodge

Helen's Bay and Crawfordsburn were never seen as strong centres of Orangeism in its early years. This would probably be explained by the fact that the landlords of the area, the Crawfords, the Dufferins or the Kennedys were never recognised as strong supporters of the Order.

The first Lodge recorded in the general area was formed in 1869 at Ballyrobert warrant No 1920 under the leadership of John Purvis; it took the name 'Victoria True Blues' and continues at that place until today. It has always been a fairly strong lodge of between 50 and 70 members. In the 1880s the Order seems to have got a boost with the arrival of the Rev JB Crozier to the Vicarage, Holywood, and in 1883 three Lodges in Holywood, LOL 785, LOL 1687, LOL 1906 along with LOL 1920 Ballyrobert, sought permission to form a District Lodge under the leadership of the Rev Crozier. In Crawfordsburn a Lodge No 1091 was formed in the village in 1905 under the leadership of Hugh Brennan of Bangor, but in 1907 the Master was John Ferguson of Carnalea, Crawfordsburn. The Lodge probably met somewhere in the Crawfordsburn area but does not seem to have had a hall of its own until the 1940s. It had a resident caretaker in the period after the war. It became and remains one of the strongest Lodges in the Bangor area.

The *County Down Spectator* recorded, in its 12 July edition in 1963, the unfurling of a new banner for LOL 1091, the Crawfordsburn Chosen Few Temperance Lodge. At Crawfordsburn's own little Twelfth, the parade had been headed by the Fitzsimmons Memorial Band. The Terence Memorial Hall had been the venue for the dedication, while the celebration tea was held in the Orange Hall. Mrs George Graham, widow of the Lodge's past Master, ceremonially unfurled the banner, while Rev Dr Park dedicated it. The Bangor District Master wished the Lodge many happy days walking behind the new banner.

Emma Graham recalls that the previous banner had been unfurled by Mrs Lindsay, the Colonel's wife.

The earliest Orange demonstration held in the area was at Ballyrobert in 1921, most of the Lodges from Bangor, Holywood and Newtownards walked to there that day. The next demonstration was in 1946 and many of the Lodges that day came by train to Craigavad. The last time there was a demonstration at Ballyrobert was in 1971, that day all came by bus.

The Robert Graham Memorial Band was previously the Crawfordsburn Protestant Boys Band which had been formed in 1973.

Helen's Bay Players

Helen's Bay has the War Office to thank for the origins of the Players. When Captain George Hinves was posted Officer Commanding the Fort in the early 1950s, he brought with him an overriding passion for drama. In a short time he had recruited a small and enthusiastic group and in March 1953, Noel Coward's *Hay Fever* went into production in St John's old hall. George was producer, designer and painter, carpenter and lighting expert. He also played David Bliss. Joyce Smiley attended the first production along with most of Helen's Bay. The tale is recorded that the sound effect of rain was made so loudly that when an actor forgot their line, the prompt could not be heard, despite a cry of 'I can't hear you for this blasted rain'. Consternation reigned until someone crawled below

Above right: Mrs George Graham marching at the unfurling of the Orange Lodge banner, 1963.

the sight-lines off stage to silence the rain-maker. It might be said that this set a happy precedent for the level of audience appreciation that still applies to productions today.

The following year *Fools Rush In*, by Kenneth Horne, was produced. Both productions were front-page news in the *County Down Spectator*. After a third one act play in Crawfordsburn Primary School, and a couple of aborted attempts, the short life of the original Helen's Bay Players came to an end when Captain Hinves was transferred in May 1956. Hinves was also an accomplished artist – the painting is of Trevose (on Grey Point) into which George and Joyce Smiley moved in 1951. (Joyce recalls that both of them being dentists then working in Belfast, friends told them they were crazy to move to Helen's Bay – that was too far away for commuting.)

The revival of the Players in 1967 stemmed from concern in the community to involve some of the many newcomers who were arriving at that time. The chief begetters were Trevor Boyd, Brian Waddell, Tony Lindsay and Tony Finigan (who became the Players' second President after the death of the Marquess of Dufferin and Ava). Colonel Harry Garner was vice-president. Trevor Boyd was then chairman, the first of a long line who have brought leadership and new ideas to the eager members.

The first full-length production of the new series in March 1968, was *Pink String and Sealing Wax*, by Ronald Pertwee, again in the old hall. The photograph records the cast : Back row (left to right) - Jonathan Hutchinson, Tony Lindsay, Elizabeth Maxwell, and Gary Gillespie; middle row – Clare Jolley, Doreen Parr, Laurence Lennard and Thelma Armstrong; front row – Felicity Ricketts. Gary Gillespie recalls his frustration in one performance when, as a young actor, he went to turn off the 'gas lamps' at the back of the stage. Peter Ross who was looking after the stage lighting should have switched them off at the relevant

cue. Notwithstanding several loud prompts from Gary, they remained resolutely switched on. Thinking quickly, he ad libbed 'I think I'll leave the gas lamps on after all, tonight, mother'. The biggest laugh from the audience that night occurred when Ross then after all turned them off, several seconds later.

Some thought was given to doing a children's play, drawing up rules and a constitution, and having a library in the Tennis Club's pavilion. Lights were bought and are still used for play readings.

In the spring of 1969 Lawrence Lennard produced *The Crucible* by Arthur Miller. The cast of 19 included the Anglican and Presbyterian clergy of the time and the Players' first life member, John Knipe, himself a patriarch of amateur drama in Northern Ireland.

The players have continued with varying success. Farces, those of John Chapman in particular, have given much entertainment, not only to their cast but also to the large numbers of local people who continue to support each event. Plays for children have included *The Wizard of Oz*,

Above left: Trevose, Grey Point, painted by Captain George Hinves.
Above right: The cast of 'Pink String and Sealing Wax', March 1968.

Alice's Adventures in Wonderland and Through the Looking Glass, and *Dick Whittington and his Wonder Cat*. There has been an average of just under two productions a year, almost all in St John's old and new halls, though the Tucker Hall at Rockport School was gratefully used in 1985/6 while the new hall was being built, and the Presbyterian Hall has generously been made available from time to time for rehearsals. For many years an annual dance was held, initially at Bennet House, then at the Banqueting Hall at Clandeboye and later at several other venues.

For a few years from 1999, the Junior Players, led by Suzanne Johnston, were active for those between 7 and 17; several productions of a high quality were performed, including an ambitious yet excellent *Midsummer Night's Dream*.

The Players aim to promote and foster an interest in the dramatic arts, both for the benefit of members and for those in the wider community. They continue to produce plays (normally biannually) that are open to members of the public, members host play and poetry reading evenings (normally monthly in winter), and there are various other social activities organised by the Committee.

New members are welcome, and one does not have to be a seasoned or even a budding actor to belong. Those with creative talents can assist with the wide range of activities in support of the productions, both behind the scenes and with front of house: these can include set design, building and decorating the scenery, costumes, lighting, music, leafleting and publicity. There is a website at www.helensbayplayers.org.uk.

The local community is fortunate to have a bunch of dedicated thespians in their midst.

The Helen's Bay Police Station

The annual Constabulary List first notes a station in Helen's Bay in 1921, under the charge of Sergeant Hudson, though its location was on the side of Bridge Road nearer the railway line. It is recorded that through the late 1930s the names of the Sergeants changed annually. Indeed prior to that, the first police facility in the two villages was in Crawfordsburn, housed in the two storey building directly opposite the entrance to the Country Club. Until about 25 years ago, there remained a painted sign there.

Chief Superintendent Robin Sinclair served as a young constable based in Helen's Bay before the war. Their beat, which had to be covered on bicycle, extended from Craigavad, to Carnalea and up to Rathgael. Duties up until the 1950s included an obligatory annual visit to all local farmers warning them of the danger of allowing ragwort to grow in their fields. In earlier years the police had also fulfilled a valuable function in posting up notices on public notice boards at post offices and elsewhere about legislation, animal diseases, the coronation of new monarchs and notices in time of war about aliens and the supply of intoxicants to injured members of the Armed Forces. In December 1933 the *County Down Spectator* advised local farmers that forms for the compulsory licensing of boars farrowed before 30 September that year should be obtained from any police barracks.

In the 1950s a ten shilling bounty was paid on production of a fox's tail at a police station. The tale is told of one farmer, returning home late one evening, who bundled a fox lying by the side of the road into his car boot. Later the next morning he remembered his prize, but when he went to open the boot he found not a dead but a very much alive and indignant fox. Thinking quickly the farmer nipped into the house and returned with his gun. The fox was quickly shot but alas the effects on the inside of the car were not what had been intended. The repairs no doubt cost more than the reward.

Lights on bicycles were clearly an issue. Maurice Lindsay recalls that batteries were a high price in the post-war years, and it was for many the custom to switch on the lamp when approaching the police station, and then off again when safely past it. Another resident experienced a style of policing that would not be countenanced nowadays. He had late one evening, with some friends, unfastened the wires securing the punt to the jetty by the sluice gates on the mill pond at Crawfordsburn. The Helen's Bay policeman had spotted the unauthorised expedition from afar, but when he pedalled furiously up the Cootehall Road to the further end of the pond, as he thought to apprehend the culprits, they had cheekily paddled across to the far bank. The chase was given up for that night.

But when the boys returned to the village on the school bus the following afternoon, there was the constable waiting calmly at the bus stop. One miscreant recalls being comprehensively booted up the road all the way to his home. This was deemed a fair punishment – it would have been worse had his father been told. Other stories suggest that while the local police may have been safely evaded in the short term, they usually got their man (or their boy) in the end.

Although plans for a new station had been included in the building programme for 1939, it was not until 1951 that a lease for the land was acquired. Sergeant C Sullivan was in charge in 1955-56 and Sergeant W Johnston in the following year. Up to this point the complement had been a Sergeant and four constables. When the new two-man station at the junction with Golf Road, opened on 16 August 1957, it became a sub-station. This was to 'be a fresh concept in rural policing designed to make the most efficient use of available manpower when the strength of the Force was in the order of 3000 men'.

The new building had no cooking facilities or recreation room but did have one cell and an office. A 250cc motorcycle was based there. The station was linked to married accommodation for the two constables and their families.

A reduction in status occurred in 1967 when the station was converted to limited opening. By the early 1980s the station was only open two hours in the morning and another two hours in the late afternoon. One officer stationed there for six months described it as a pretty boring post. Whether this comment included the then daily evening patrols round the village is not known.

No doubt many tales can be told of past policing, but a few must suffice. Sergeant Griffiths was obliged to use a motorbike after the station's Ford Anglia was removed (no doubt as a cost-cutting measure). One resident had called in for petrol which led to the Sergeant being telephoned to hasten to Crawfordsburn to apprehend a miscreant driver who was displaying no tax disc. The driver in fact met the Sergeant on the sharp bend down to Helen's Bay, later removed when the 'ski slope' was made. However Griffiths was in the hedge, having failed to negotiate the corner on the motorbike which he never mastered. Unknowingly he was given a lift back to the station in the very car that he had been summoned to deal with. He did have other skills that were greatly appreciated. When another resident inadvertently locked herself out of her daughter's house, the Sergeant came to the rescue, opening the door in a trice, with the aid of a metal coat hanger.

Constable Williamson was once out on his bicycle at midnight, doing his rounds. He came across a car, without any lights, at the side of the road. Approaching with his torch, he was surprised to find two stark naked occupants. Courteously he asked them if they would mind turning on the car lights before someone ran into them.

After the station's closure later in the 1980s, there has been no permanent police presence in Helen's Bay.

The Royal British Legion

The local branch is known as the Craigavad and Helen's Bay Branch, which was formed in 1928. The first recorded activities were a concert party and parade to Glencraig Church on Remembrance Day of that year.

Rear Admiral McKeown was an early President and the Secretary for the first eight years was a well-known personality in Helen's Bay called Hunter Tate. (Tate was known for cycling everywhere, often accompanied by his dog, Tester.) He combined this post with that of Poppy Day organiser and welfare representative in addition to enthusiastic recruiting. He succeeded Rear Admiral McKeown as President in 1962 and served in that post until his death in 1966, but not before being awarded the MBE and the Legion Gold Badge. The Branch's standard was dedicated at the Remembrance Day Service in Glencraig Church, the first standard bearer being Edward Beale, postman at Craigavad, who had been wounded while serving with the Royal Irish Rifles. The Standard has represented the Branch on many occasions. It was at Balmoral to celebrate the 50th

Above: Helen's Bay police station, newly-occupied.

anniversary of the Battle of the Somme, and in 1970 it was in the Albert Hall when it was carried by Eddie Beale, son of the first standard-bearer. Several members have attended the Memorial Services at Thiepval and, on at least one occasion, a member has given the Exhortation at the Menin Gate in Ypres.

Until the second war there were usually two parade services on Remembrance Sunday, the larger morning service alternating between Glencraig and Ballygilbert Presbyterian Church, and the smaller evening service between St John's Church, Helen's Bay and Helen's Bay Presbyterian Church. Today parade services are held in each of the four churches in rotation.

The Branch had no permanent accommodation so meetings and activities were held in various locations. Shortly after the second war a British Legion Convalescent Home was opened in Kathleen Avenue, Helen's Bay, called Bennet House, and Branch meetings were held there. (Tordeevra was renamed Bennet House.)

A *County Down Spectator* reporter visited in September 1951, where he was welcomed by Mr Zebedee, the dapper Secretary of Bennet House. He found 'a home from home inside a hotel'. There were 36 beds in 8 bedrooms, with two on the ground floor for disabled servicemen and those requiring isolation. The six acre grounds offered beautiful surroundings and a putting green, while the house provided billiards, darts etc. On that day a choir came from Newtownards, and further endeared themselves by distributing cigarettes and chocolate. Interestingly about half of the residents were from England, with at least one from the Republic of Ireland. The senior resident had begun his military career in the Punjab, before serving in the Boer War and the First World War, and then fire-watching in the second. In 1964, the *Spectator* recorded the unveiling by Lord Carew, chairman of the British Legion, of a portrait of Captain Bennet

and his war medals. He said that Bennet had 'directed all the Northern Ireland Area activities and set it on the many wonderful paths of service which have been carried out'. The five men then resident 'were loud in their praise of Bennet House'.

The Home was independent of the Branch having its own manager and management committee, but there was close liaison between the two and several Branch members served on the committee. On occasions the Branch hosted concert parties for the residents, but the main social event was the Bennet House Ball held after Christmas each year. When Bennet House finally closed and moved to Portrush, the Golf Club became the location for Annual General Meetings, Committee meetings and Dinners. This facility is still enjoyed today.

With the closure of the Convalescent Home the Branch sought other outlets for their efforts on behalf of veterans. Outings were arranged for the patients of the UVF Hospital in Belfast and these included visits to Ballykinler and St Patrick's Barracks, Ballymena. Regrettably dwindling numbers and increasing frailty brought these outings to an end. When several ladies joined there was a suggestion to form a Ladies Branch, but this was not taken forward and today ladies enjoy full membership of the Branch.

There has been a succession of worthy office holders. Sir Francis Evans, after a distinguished diplomatic career, and a period as Ulster Agent in London, succeeded Hunter Tate as President and, like him, was awarded the Legion Gold Badge. Eric Tucker, Headmaster of Rockport School followed Sir Francis.

During Remembrance Day Services, the Act of Remembrance begins with the Branch Chairman reading the names of the fallen from the Roll of Honour. There are names on the Roll from both World Wars, but the last is a soldier of the Ulster Defence Regiment.

Captain Leslie Bennet CBE, after whom Bennet House was named, was a keen Branch member who lived in Seafield on Church Road, but much of his work for the Legion was in the rarefied atmosphere of National Vice President and – before that – for over 30 years Northern Ireland Area chairman. He was in the Royal Irish Fusiliers, served at Gallipoli and was seriously wounded and discharged. He initially led the Ulster contingent of the Comrades of the Great War, joining the British

Above: Captain JL Bennet CBE, Royal British Legion.

Legion when it was formed in 1921. According to his 1963 obituary in the *Spectator*, he commanded the Home Guard motor-boat patrol in Belfast Lough in the second war, and played a prominent part in the acquisition of Bennet House.

Scout Camp at Crawfordsburn Country Park

The Estate, of which the Scout Camp now forms a part, was acquired by William Sharman, (1780-1861) of Moira Castle, on his marriage to Mabel Crawford of Crawfordsburn House. The nearby village of Crawfordsburn commemorates the family name and one of the very first patrols of Scouts was formed there in 1908.

In the late 1940s, the Northern Ireland Scout Association realised they needed a substantial camping ground for the growing membership, both for camping and training purposes. They had been offered, but declined, the site now occupied by the Folk Museum at Cultra, owned in the 1930s, by the Kennedy family. It was considered too big a commitment at that time. Sir Christopher Musgrave was the Chief Commissioner for Northern Ireland in the 1940s, but perhaps the prime mover was Judge William Johnson, who was to succeed Sir Christopher. David Harrison and Robert Brown were also senior Commissioners and assisted in the negotiations and consultations.

A lease for 50 years was obtained from the Tuberculosis Authority. This was signed about 1950, but it seems camping had already commenced a year or two prior to this. Lord Carswell, formerly a distinguished Lord Chief Justice for Northern Ireland, but a young teenage Scout then, can recall camping there in the late 1940s. The lease was renewed in the late 1990s for 99 years, this time from the Department of the Environment. The gate lodge was also acquired for the Warden's living accommodation. Without this renewal it would not have been possible to obtain Government Grant Aid to fund the many new developments required to bring the site up to the modern standards

it commands today, and these are still ongoing.

Since 1950 a huge number of events have taken place, from major International camps to single Scouts enjoying the great outdoors in beautiful surroundings. For many years, Warden Billy Chambers was in charge of allocating campsites and ensuring good standards of camping and discipline prevailed.

Lord Wakehurst, Governor of Northern Ireland, opened the first cabin on the site, in 1953. It was of wooden Scandinavian design. This is awaiting replacement now, but many Scouts over the years will recall a campfire inside on a wet or windy night when the outdoor alternative would have been unpleasant, or a Scouts Own on a Sunday morning with its own special message.

Prior to the campsite opening in October 1948 many Leaders and Rovers volunteered to assist with necessary infrastructure work. One of the shorter straws was drawn by Norman Ling (GSM 54th) and

Bottom left: The gate lodge to the Crawfordsburn Estate on Bridge Road.
Top right: Boy Scout encampment on Crawfordsburn Beach.

Rover G Scott (55th). They were asked to assemble a flat pack latrine kit – corrugated iron, hessian and timber which does not feature in MFI catalogues today.

The job was done and the great day dawned with pouring rain. Norman camping nearby in a small hike tent decided that cooking breakfast in these conditions would be difficult. As there was a big dry shelter close by, he soon had his frying pan sizzling away on his primus stove, while sitting on the 'seat'; his mate sat in the next booth practising his musical turn for the campfire on his bagpipes. It is not recorded who was more shocked or surprised when Judge Johnson and Ernie Moore stumbled on his unusual scene while making an inspection prior to the opening ceremony. The fact that the latrine had neither been opened nor even christened may have been reason to plead clemency. However Norman still reckons that it was fortunate that transportation to Botany Bay was no longer in the judicial repertoire.

Sadly two railway apprentices travelled all the way from Croxley Green in England, but alas they were a week too early for the camp.

The Chief Scout in 1958, Lord Rowallan, visited as part of the half centenary of scouting celebrations. Prince Edward did the honours in 2007 in Centenary year. Many other famous characters have passed that way in between.

Leaders have been trained, and Scouts taught how to light fires or cook almost anything, even on one occasion high in the trees. Cubs and Beavers have added their own dimensions as younger members and sometimes the sun even shines. Occasionally the Warden spots an older man having a wistful look around as he remembers the 'good old days' when he camped there with his friends.

Back at the start, a shilling or two would have been the overnight charge. At £4 today it remains one of life's bargains. The 'lid', a sort of covered open sided barn with a soft-fall floor, was recently added with an integral climbing wall to add some excitement. There is also an assault course and even a Caving complex, and a Beaver trail. The outdoors Heasley Chapel is used when weather permits and there is a Chalet for winter overnights with duvets in bunkrooms and a well-equipped kitchen for cooking. This luxury costs just a little more than camping. The Warden's team, which is mostly volunteers, led by the permanent Chief Warden, now have a substantial home of their own, replacing the rather antiquated quarters used previously.

Sadly the old Lonesome Scots Pine, which used to dominate the central camping, has gone, but a number of commemorative copses have been planted around the site, thus ensuring it remains well wooded. Most of the firewood is brought in now to avoid trees being felled or damaged in the constant hunt for fuel. There is still a flag break and lowering daily, when the site is in use, and the bell tolls to tell everyone on site to respect the flag as it is raised or lowered.

Thousands of Scouts, Cubs, Beavers and now even Squirrels, the newest section for very small young people, use the site throughout the year, and outside organisations may also do so. This helps to provide the necessary fees to run the operation and ensure it remains for generations to come.

St John's Badminton Club

Badminton was originally played in the old wooden church hall, built in the mid-1930s, affectionately referred to as 'the box which the church came in.' The players then, who included youngsters, benefited from the instruction on Saturday afternoons of two Sunday school teachers, Nan McCammon and Cassie Beaney. In general, visitors had to take their boots off, owing to the delicate state of the floor. The building also lacked proper heating and leaked like a sieve on wet nights,

Top left: Scouts preparing for an inspection.
Top right: The Copse dedicated to Campbell College Scouts killed in the Second World War.

but despite these setbacks a junior team of that time won a major local championship.

In the early 1980s, Norman Armstrong and Bill Smiley ran the club. Membership fluctuated between 16 and 20 adult players and more than that number of juniors. The latter had tuition on Saturday mornings, occasionally with the privilege of coaching by the former Irish international, Ron Reddick.

In May 1986, the new church hall was opened. It had been specially designed to accommodate the needs of a badminton court. The new facilities were most luxurious in comparison. Membership increased and modern equipment was purchased, in keeping with the new surroundings.

Paul Armstrong then took on the responsibility of running the club in the early 1990s. Robin and Rosemary Masefield donated a challenge shield, complete with Latin motto, for an annual competition among the junior players. The Club still meets on Monday evenings from September to Easter, with an active junior membership.

Yachting

Whilst there has never been a Yacht Club at Helen's Bay many Helen's Bay and Crawfordsburn residents were keen yachtsmen, as might be expected from the prime location on Belfast Lough. One of the earliest was George Herbert Brown, a founder of the Ulster Reform Club. As set out in his great-grandson's recollections at page 128, he lived initially at Tordeevra in Kathleen Avenue and was a member of the Presbyterian Church, whose Minister, Reverend WJ Archer, was his brother-in-law. Nearly half of the extensive *News Letter* obituary of 14 December 1908 chronicled his prowess as a yachtsman. He was the first Commodore of the North of Ireland Yacht Club from 1899 to 1908, presiding over its gaining the Royal prefix (in part when Thomas Lipton became a member) in 1901. In his career he acquired a yawl built by Workman Clark, but his best known yacht was the 122 ton *Chanticleer*:

'.. one of the finest yachts ever owned in local waters, being a roomy, well-found and beautifully-furnished boat in every respect.'

He had also for some years been treasurer of the Royal Ulster Yacht Club, and indeed an office bearer of the Bangor Corinthian Sailing Club.

The first Commodore of the Royal Ulster Yacht Club was the Marquess of Dufferin and Ava, (he had also been Commodore of the Ulster Canoe Club). He tried, unsuccessfully, to entice the Club to Helen's Bay, offering land and a grant. The Royal North of Ireland Yacht Club was founded by Robert Edward Workman, born in 1868. He was Honorary Secretary of the Club from 1893 until his death 52 years later. (Two other Workman relatives were subsequent Commodores, for a total of 29 years between them.) The Club later considered leaving Cultra for a deeper site near Seapark and Lord Dufferin offered them one of the Coastguard Cottages, but it also came to nothing.

As set out in the chapter on the Sharman Crawfords, the Colonel was a keen yachtsman and crewed for Sir Thomas Lipton in two of his Shamrock challenges for the America's Cup. Tommy Ross, a stalwart of the RUYC since 1930 recalled that while Lipton's challenges may have been unsuccessful, the exercise hugely promoted sales of his tea in America.

Fun was also had with dinghies, at the other end of the spectrum. Toni Cotton recounts a story from wartime. As a member of the Workman family, she visited Craigdarragh House regularly. A lightship was then moored in the Lough opposite Rockport. She and her siblings

Above left: St John's Badminton Club Challenge Shield. Above right: Robert Edward Workman 1868-1945.

conceived the notion that the men from Trinity House on the boat might be suffering from scurvy. One holiday time, they secretly raided the vegetable garden at Rockport School, loaded up their dinghies and sailed out to the lightship. History does not record if the cabbages were ever cooked, but she did recall hugely appreciating the chocolate bars that they were given in return.

Many others from Helen's Bay and Crawfordsburn over the ensuing decades have had their own boats or sailed with others; both Donald Ross and Dr Hector Northey were office-bearers in the RUYC, and Dennis Rebbeck was a keen sailor too. Jim Davis, who served in the Home Guard, kept a sailing boat in the boat-house below the Coastguard Cottages. Once when he took it out with a friend, a gust of wind came before they had got the oars on board. The boat was quickly blown out into mid-Lough, and before the sail could be got in, the boat swamped and capsized. Fortunately a cargo boat passed at the right time, and rescued the bedraggled pair. When they eventually returned on the train, having been taken into Belfast docks, Jim's wife was still unaware of the near disaster. In the 1950s Trevor Boyd campaigned, unsuccessfully, for a slipway to be built at Helen's Bay.

It is not only small boats that can get into trouble; in October 1997, a coaster, the 'Sea Humber', en route from Glasgow to Belfast, ran aground on Grey Point, one foggy night. It was several days before it was refloated.

Above: The Sea Humber aground on Grey Point.

Chapter 9

The Sharman Crawfords of Crawfordsburn House

The following two chapters deal with some of the personalities and characters of Helen's Bay and Crawfordsburn, told either in their own words or, as in the case of this account of the Sharman Crawford family, by local residents who have researched their topics in detail. We are indebted to Peter Stark for this chapter.

William Sharman Crawford

The Sharman Crawford family, while not as aristocratic or ever rising to the great political heights of their land-owning neighbours the Blackwoods, (later the Marquesses of Dufferin and Ava), nevertheless played a significant role in shaping the political landscape of Ireland at the turn of the 20th century. This chapter recounts the life and political contribution of the most eminent family members.

The story began with the birth of William Sharman on 3 September 1780 at Moira Castle, which the family rented from the Earl of Moira. It was considered to be one of the most elegant mansions of the day and its upkeep would have required considerable means. William's father was a gentleman of the period, having inherited estates in Banbridge, Rathfriland and Staleen in County Meath, as well as farming the castle demesne and being the collector of taxes and revenue for the Lisburn district. He played a prominent part in the Volunteer movement and sat in the Irish Parliament from 1783-1790. (The portrait by Thomas Robinson is of William's father against the backdrop of Moira Castle.)

In the introduction to a political pamphlet in 1844, William wrote a brief autobiography of his childhood years:

Above: Portrait by Thomas Robinson of William Sharman, with Moira Castle in the background.

'I spent my infantile years at Moira castle but every year spending the winter in Dublin during the parliamentary session and not withstanding my early years I took as great interest in all the great political questions on which I could hear my father enlarging. I being for so long an only son was thought a jewel of great price. I was inclined as a child to delicacy of health; at least my parents thought it and I was kept under the most annoying superintendence. I was drugged with medicines. It was alleged I would soon die if I went to school and my father had an abhorrence of tutors. So my father determined to teach me to read and write, arithmetic, Latin and some Greek. I instructed myself in history, mechanics, geography and astronomy. And I was anxious to go to college but was prohibited lest my morals should be corrupted.'

But by not going to university William's education clearly was not neglected as we can tell from the quality of his letters and political writings.

In 1805 William married into a family as well established as his own, the Crawfords of Crawfordsburn. As described earlier, the Crawfords came to Ulster from Scotland in the reign of James 1 and settled at Crawfordsburn as tenants of Sir James Hamilton of Bangor. William Crawford later purchased the Crawfordsburn Estate from Lord Clanbrassil around 1670.

It would have been a close liberal affinity that brought the families together. Colonel Sharman and Major John Crawford were equally prominent during the Volunteer period, and in July 1792 when the Volunteers of the outlying districts of Belfast marched to the town to celebrate the fall of the Bastille, Major Crawford, as reviewing general, deputised for Colonel Sharman who through illness was unable to attend.

Following William's marriage to Mabel Crawford the couple lived in Lurgan and Waringstown and in 1819 moved to Dublin living at 11 Fitzwilliam Square East with occasional visits to the family estate at Staleen, County Meath. (The portrait of William is by John Prescott Knight.)

In October 1829 William and Mabel were summoned to Crawfordsburn following the death of her brother in an accident. On arrival they found a grieving father who was determined to have a

successor to whom he could transfer the family name and estates. The following year Major John Crawford died and in compliance with his will, by Royal Licence, William Sharman assumed the Crawford surname in addition to his paternal one and the 'House of Sharman Crawford' was born.

At age 47 William Sharman Crawford found himself the owner of landed estates of such an extent as to make him a richer man than 80% of the titled persons around him.

In addition to the Sharman Estates inherited from his father at Banbridge, Rathfriland and Staleen in County Meath, he now owned the Crawford Estates at Crawfordsburn and Rademon near Crossgar.

Above: Portrait by John Prescott Knight of William Sharman Crawford.

The latter two were the principal residences of the Sharman Crawfords and remained in family ownership until the early 1930s.

Crawford's income from the estates amounted to in excess of £8,000 per annum. He was a liberal protestant and unlike so many of his class, had the conviction that landed property imposed a grave moral responsibility upon its possessor.

His income allowed him to develop his political interests and he stood for Down in the 1831 General Election and for Belfast in 1832, but was unsuccessful on both occasions. On 1 June 1831, he had laid the first stone of the fourth meeting-house of the First Presbyterian Congregation of Bangor – its current location. The event was recorded by the *News Letter* which noted that Rev Hugh Woods, in an address of great length,

> '… next bestowed a very handsome and justly deserved encomium on the Crawford family: that they had always identified the interests of the Presbyterian congregation of Bangor with their own; that they had cast over it the shield of their influence and that by their uniform adherence to the Presbyterian Church amid the defection of others of the same rank, they had secured to their memory the gratitude of posterity.'

However, Crawford's radical views on Land Reform, the securing of legal recognition for the Tenant Right Custom, which he described as 'the darling object of my heart', brought him to the attention of 'the Liberator' Daniel O'Connell who helped him win the seat for Dundalk unopposed in 1834. He eventually fell out with O'Connell over his stance on Tithes and repeal of the Union. Crawford favoured the idea of a federal Ireland based on the Canadian model and wrote extensively on the subject.

Crawford's activities on behalf of the Irish tenant farmers brought him to the attention of English radicals and in 1841 he was elected the MP for Rochdale. He later wrote; 'I stood a contest the electors paying all expenses and I, an Irish landlord was elected for the special purpose of contending for free trade in corn'.

Re-elected again in 1847 at the age of 66, Crawford was the MP for Rochdale for a period of 11 years and throughout his term continued to campaign for Irish tenant farmers.

In 1852 he declined to stand a third time for Rochdale and returned to Crawfordsburn so he could fight the Down seat once again. The 1852 election was one of the most hotly contested of the century. It was also one of the most violent as radicals and conservatives clashed over the issue of tenant right. Because of his unrelenting campaigning on the tenant right issue most of the local press did everything in their power to denounce Crawford. The *Belfast News Letter* in April 1852 described him as:

> '.. the upholder of a desperate democracy, a striker at the roots of property, a secularist in education, a papist in disguise and besides all a man in his dotage.'

The local landlords also did their utmost to prevent Crawford's election by influencing tenants' voting and he again failed to take one of the two Down seats.

In the closing years of his life Crawford became pre-occupied with religion and joined the ranks of the Unitarians.

William Sharman Crawford passed away at Crawfordsburn on 17 October 1861 aged 81, after a short illness. The following day the Irish papers conveyed the sad news to the farmers and people of Ireland that the father of tenant right was no more. However James McKnight, a former editor of the *Belfast News Letter*, made the greatest tribute to Crawford in a speech in 1852 at Raloo near Larne:

> 'When the story of Crawford comes to be written, that story would afford one of the most extraordinary instances of self-denial, devotedness and unswerving rectitude that had ever been known for what was the fact? Crawford a member of the aristocracy, richer a great deal than four fifths of the titled persons around him, came forward nobly to advocate the abolition of the great social grievance which he saw destroying his native country. Men of his own class treated him with the utmost contempt and this might have been tolerable if he had the sympathy of other classes, but they too joined in the ridicule that was heaped upon him and his motives. He persevered however, caring nothing for their sneers until the whole country was aroused in his favour.'

Previous page: Crawfordsburn House, by Proctor and Malloy, 1832.

The Sharman Crawford Children

The marriage of William and Mabel Sharman Crawford resulted in the birth of no less than 11 children, 7 boys and 4 girls, with the majority being born at Crawfordsburn House. As was the custom amongst wealthy families in the 19th century, the heir to the Sharman Crawford estates, John, was sent on a tour of America when he was 24 and his exploits and opinions are recorded in a number of letters he sent to his mother. On 9 November 1835 he wrote from New York:

> 'The ladies demand the most obsequious attention from the gentlemen which they are fools enough to give'. 'There is as much aristocratic feeling and nonsense as with us and it is less excusable because of their pretensions.'

John also visited Baltimore, Quebec and Boston on his travels.

An examination of correspondence between the second son, James, and his father during 1857-1861 highlights a degree of strain over the family's finances caused by a large dependent family, falling rents and crop prices after the Famine. Consideration at this time was given to selling the Crawfordsburn Demesne as a building site and so raising a considerable sum for the settlement of the family's debts. The arrival, in the mid-1860s, of the railway to Bangor, which passed through the Estate, coupled with Lord Dufferin's scheme for the development of Helen's Bay, undoubtedly increased the potential value of the land. In later years the Estate did sell Strickland's Glen to Bangor Council. The photograph of the former Crawfordsburn House, taken just prior to its demolition in 1905, comes from the Welch collection.

Following the death of Major James Sharman in 1884 the family estates passed to the third son, Arthur Johnson Sharman Crawford who, unlike his two elder brothers, had not worked managing the estates, but was a lawyer who had been called to the Bar at King's Inn, Dublin, in 1839. He was also a director of the Belfast Bank for 20 years and the first president of the Belfast Reform Club. Arthur married in 1846 a distant cousin, Louisa Alicia Crawford, the youngest daughter of William Crawford of Lakelands, Co. Cork, a founder of the famous Beamish & Crawford brewery. It was this marriage that largely rejuvenated the finances of the family.

Arthur's obituary from the *Belfast News Letter* in 1891 shows the esteem in which the family was held:

> '.. the deceased was a member of a family long and intimately connected with the County of Down. The name of Sharman Crawford is known and respected in every agricultural household alike for the genial upright character of the family and the interest they have manifested in matters affecting the welfare of the farmer. The deceased, who was of unobtrusive character, was no less sincere than his predecessors for land reform. He quietly but ably advocated the cause, and everything that tended to the improvements of the condition of the tiller of the soil found him a zealous supporter.'

However, of all the Sharman Crawford children the one who most inherited their father's passion for Liberalism and reform was Mabel Sharman Crawford (1820-1912). Educated by a private governess at Crawfordsburn, Mabel travelled extensively throughout Europe and was an accomplished travel author having three books published in both London and New York: *Life in Tuscany* (1859), *Through Algeria* (1863) and *The Wilmot Family* (1864). A great believer in the virtue of travel to woman, Mabel wrote in *Through Algeria*,

> 'If the exploring of foreign lands is not the highest end of the most useful occupation of feminine existence, it is at least more improving, as well as more amusing, than crochet work'.

To this day Mabel's work is quoted in articles on 19th century women's feminism – for example a 2003 article from *Women's Writing* by Maura O'Connor entitled 'Civilizing Southern Italy: British and Italian Woman and the Cultural Politics of European Nation Building' quotes extracts from *Life in Tuscany*.

Letters in the Dufferin Papers in the Public Record Office from Mabel to Lord Dufferin cover a range of women's issues including the eligibility of women to stand as Councillors and Aldermen, and demonstrate her life-long devotion to women's rights. Mabel, who never married, died aged 92 in London.

The later Sharman Crawfords

The family's other great passion was sailing. The architect of the present Crawfordsburn House (1906) was Vincent Craig (elder brother of James, later Viscount Craigavon, the first Prime Minister of Northern Ireland) who was also responsible for the design of the Royal Ulster Yacht Club in Bangor. Both families were avid sailors and an examination of the members of the RUYC for 1867 lists Colonel RG Sharman Crawford's father, Arthur, and uncle, John, as members. Robert Gordon became member 164 on 15 August 1871 aged 18 giving his address as the Glen House, Crawfordsburn, which was then part of the Estate.

The Colonel owned many yachts during his sailing career including *Mollie 1 & 2* named after his daughter, and the famous *Red Lancer* named after the 16th Lancers in which he served. *Red Lancer* in 1893 won 24 flags in 34 starts. The remains of the private quay from which the Colonel sailed can still be seen at low tide on Crawfordsburn beach directly below the house.

The highlight of the Colonel's sailing career came in 1899 when the RUYC consented to take up the challenge for the world's most famous race, the America's Cup. The Club on behalf of one of its members, the millionaire grocer Sir Thomas Lipton, issued the challenge. It was his wish, as he considered himself an Ulsterman, that the RUYC would have the credit of the entry and that the yacht was to be built by Harland & Wolff, designed by the famous William Fife and sailed by an Irish skipper and crew. As it turned out, it was designed by William Fife Senior but neither built in Belfast nor crewed by Irishmen. Colonel Crawford, or Major Crawford as he then was, travelled to New York to undertake the preliminary negotiations for the Club's first entry.

This caused a degree of furore from the Commodore of the RUYC, the Marquess of Dufferin and Ava, who appears from a series of letters in the Dufferin papers held by PRONI, not to have been informed in advance of the Club's challenge. In one particular letter from Mr Hugh Kelly, the Club's Hon. Secretary, to the Marquess, he asks him to consider the great glory the challenge, whether win or lose, will bring to the Club and Ireland. Sir Thomas Lipton went on to challenge for the America's Cup on five occasions in 1889, 1901, 1903, 1920 and 1930 and was runner up on every occasion. All the yachts were named the *Shamrock* and RG Sharman Crawford crewed on *Shamrock 1* (1889) and on *Shamrock 3* (1903) and was on the committee boat for the 1901 race. Considering Lipton's 1901 entry cost in excess of $200,000 the Colonel was moving in fairly lofty circles.

Rathmoyle House on the Craigdarragh Road or Eldon Green, as it was originally named, was built in 1901 also by the prominent Ulster architect Vincent Craig who lived there till 1911. The Sharman Crawford and Craig families were closely connected through both politics and sailing.

Colonel RG Sharman Crawford, who built the current house, was the last of the family to live there. He was born in Dublin in 1853 and educated at Trinity College, where he graduated with both a BSc and MA. He was a career soldier, gazetted to the 15th Hussars and later to the 16th Lancers from which he retired with the rank of Captain. Following his retirement from the regular Army he continued to serve with the voluntary forces and became the Hon Colonel of the 3rd Battalion Royal Irish Rifles, which recruited in County Down. Just prior to his retirement from the regular Army in the late 1890s his elder brother died from typhoid fever in London and left

Above left: Colonel RG Sharman Crawford on board (holding binoculars). Top right: The former Crawfordsburn House just prior to its demolition in 1905. Bottom right: A sketch of Crawfordsburn House, prior to its conversion into apartments.

Sharman Crawford a sum in excess of £100,000. His brother had been a major shareholder in the family's brewery Beamish and Crawford in Cork. It was this inheritance, together with that of the family estates in Crawfordsburn, Rademon, Rathfriland, Banbridge and Staleen, which provided the capital to build the current house (1906) and Estate improvements such as the Home Farm (now Sharman Manor) in 1899. Robert Gordon was a major figure in the emerging unionist movement and, along with James Craig and Edward Carson, a member of the Ulster Unionist Council. He was also appointed to the five-man Commission, which drew up the provisional constitution of Ulster – had Home Rule been implemented. Edward Carson was staying at Crawfordsburn House on 24 July 1913 when a telegram arrived via Helen's Bay railway station bringing the news that Robert Gordon's son, Lieutenant Terence Sharman Crawford serving with his father's old regiment the 15th Hussars, had been fatally injured in a motorcycle accident at Aldershot when an Army horse ran out in front of him. That evening Carson and Sharman Crawford were to have addressed the North Down Division of the Ulster Volunteer Force at Six Road Ends. Before Sharman Crawford left for Aldershot that afternoon, Carson said to him, 'You will bear up as a man'. Sharman Crawford replied, 'Sir, I will certainly try,' and went on to tell Carson,

'Let nothing interfere with your meeting this evening, because we are engaged in a struggle that is so important and so grave, with results so far reaching to each individual of us, that even the greatest sorrows as passing events cannot and ought not to deter us from the path of duty which lies before us.'

At the rally that evening a resolution of sympathy was passed and the Union Flag was lowered to half-mast. Colonel RG Sharman Crawford played a major role in the UVF. As well as being the North Down Battalion Commander he also controlled the UVF finances, which amounted to over £100,000, held in the Belfast Banking Company in 1914, plus sums lodged in London and Paris banks.

In memory of his son he erected in 1914 the Terence Memorial Hall, now recently renamed Sharman Lodge, as a community hall. A plaque in St John's Church, Helen's Bay, also commemorates the life of Lieutenant Terence Sharman Crawford.

It is also recorded that the Colonel was wont to drink at the spring beside a stream flowing down from Skelly Hill (which can still be found) in what is now the Country Park on his way on foot to Helen's Bay station. One local resident who did the same in the 1930s said it tasted better than tap water. It is known that the Colonel, and his wife, had a close interest in spiritualism. A *County Down Spectator* article of 2 December 1933 underlines this. The Colonel chaired a lecture at the Ulster Hall by Mr Shaw Desmond entitled 'You can speak to your dead'. Introducing the speaker, he said that spiritualism was 'the dominant question of the hour' – indeed a future election might be decided on whether one was for or against. He himself had

'had a personal communication with my dead son and since that time he has been in constant communication with me. Last week he spoke to me for an hour in London, and said he would be here tonight. As sure as you are sitting in the hall, he is present with me on the platform'.

He concluded 'I did not come here to make a speech but to testify to the truth of this great religion'.

The Colonel died in 1934. Initially the Independent Unionist MP Mr WJ Stewart leased the house, until his death in May 1946. (In 1938 Stewart had founded the Progressive Unionist Party. The firm of Stewart and Partners in which he had joined his father were builders of Parliament Buildings at Stormont.)

During the War, especially in the run-up to D Day, the grounds were home to large numbers of American troops housed in Nissen huts in the field below the windmill, adjacent to Old Windmill Road. After they left, the accommodation was used for several years as 'Tin Town' – to house returning servicemen and families from Belfast, some who had lost homes in the Blitz, and were waiting for other more permanent housing.

A copy of the catalogue of the items sold on behalf of the Crawford's Estate has been preserved. The sale ran for no less than five days, although it didn't start until 11 am every morning with an hour's break for lunch. Dickie McBride attended the first day and recorded some of the sale prices - £27 for a mahogany three-tier dumb waiter, £115 for a Chippendale mahogany silver table, and £120 for a Sheraton inlaid mahogany display cabinet. Items sold later in proceedings included a croquet set, an 'old gramophone and records', and a strong collection

of historical books on Ireland, including Lyell's *Life of the Marchioness of Dufferin and Ava*. The catalogue contained some photographs of the interior of the House.

The House and 152 acres of the 510 acre Estate were transferred in 1948 to the Northern Ireland Tuberculosis Authority. The official opening of the Hospital and the adjacent nurses' home was performed by Dame Dehra Parker, the Health Minister in March 1950. It was a sanatorium for the treatment of non-infectious children, holding up to 80 invalids. At Crawfordsburn Hospital, 'they could not have anything better for the progress and recovery of children', the Minister said. The nurses' home was reconstructed out of all recognition from the out-offices and stores, to include a dining-room, recreation room, and snackery. The first matron was Miss Ann Porter. Dickie McBride also worked at the hospital, as the caretaker, while his wife Anne was a cook there. Jim McClements recalls going to its walled garden in the 1950s, which by then was run by Lindsay Finney, to buy produce on a Saturday morning. (Wild cherries and sweet crab apples abounded beside the drive down to the garden.)

Grace Darling has supplied the following recollection. Dr WM (Terry) Darling had served in China during the second war, with the Quaker Friends Ambulance Unit. He had developed tuberculosis and was very ill for four years, after his return. As he began to get better, thanks to streptomycin and surgery, he asked God for a small job to do. The ward sister asked him to look after Jimmy Morton, a young lad on a men's TB ward. When Jimmy left to go to the newly-opened hospital for children at Crawfordsburn, Terry went to visit. He helped to get a Sunday School going, with Dr Bill Godden and Grace Beattie running it. A range of activities was provided for the children, including a visiting ornithologist, as well as walks in the beautiful grounds. When extra help was needed, Terry Darling came along. Romance blossomed, and he and Grace were married, in India. The photograph shows Dr Philip Elwood, who assisted after Bill Godden left, with the Sunday School at Christmas.

Top left: American soldiers newly arrived in 1942 marching beside Nissen huts adjacent to The Square, on the exit from the Crawfordsburn Estate.
Bottom left: The Dining Room in Crawfordsburn House. Large Drawing Room, Crawfordsburn House.
Top right: Staff at the TB hospital, with Dickie McBride on the left. Bottom right: Christmas at the children's TB Hospital.

When the scourge of TB had been virtually removed, the children's hospital was extensively altered, in 1961, to cater for senile geriatric patients, under the management of Purdysburn Hospital. The first patients arrived on 15 January 1962. Two and a half years later, its role was changed again, by the North Down Hospitals Management Committee, to accommodate geriatric and post-operative patients. It is recorded, though the date is not known, that a disconcerting headline was carried in the *County Down Spectator*, when the hospital pioneered a new form of mobility for those in its care: 'At Crawfordsburn Hospital – electric chair for patients'. This was honoured by a mention in *Private Eye*.

The Sharman Crawford Estate in the meantime sought to continue its influence in the locality. The *County Down Spectator* reported in January 1956 the Estate's opposition to the Rural District Council's proposal to buy two acres on the Cootehall Road for 16 three-bedroomed bungalows. Representatives of the Estate argued that that would reduce the scope for it to develop land nearby with larger houses, and be prejudicial to the general development of the area. Alexander Kinnaird, the Estate agent, said he would not be able to let a site for a good type house adjoining a council site. Mr HSL Knight, the Council Surveyor who lived off the far end of the Ballymullan Road, had no hesitation in recommending the site for this development.

The current Crawfordsburn House development was carried out in 1998.

Previous page and top: Two watercolour reproductions by Philip Armstrong of Crawfordsburn House, showing the walled garden around 1900 and the desmesne in 1838.
Bottom right: Aerial photograph of Crawfordsburn Hospital. Crawfordsburn House as a nursing home.

Chapter 10

Personal Perspectives and other Notables

People from this small locality have influenced and in turn themselves been influenced by local, national and worldwide events. While many have been mentioned elsewhere in this book, this chapter contains other recollections, researches and experiences that do not fit neatly into the other chapters.

The Brown Family of Helen's Bay
by John Shaw Brown III

'My Grandfather, George Herbert Brown (1855-1908), was a son of Mr and Mrs John Shaw Brown of Edenderry House, Shaw's Bridge, Belfast. John Shaw Brown (1822-1889) was a wealthy linen manufacturer, and Chairman of the well-known weaving company that bore his name.

Completing his education at 'Inst', George Herbert Brown joined John Shaw Brown & Sons Ltd, and on 20 April 1888 he married Miss Kathleen Kertland, from North Wales, and they made their home at Tordeevra (now called Bennet House), in Kathleen Avenue, Helen's Bay. On the death of his father in 1889, George Herbert became Chairman of John Shaw Brown & Sons Ltd. He was also a Justice of the Peace and was appointed High Sheriff of County Down in 1904. He was also the first Captain of Helen's Bay Golf Club, whilst my Grandmother Kathleen was Lady Captain for six successive years. She was also President of the Helen's Bay Tennis Club and allowed the Club to use two courts and the summerhouse at Tordeevra. My Grandfather was a keen yachtsman and the first Commodore of the Royal North of Ireland Yacht Club and also ex Rear-Commodore of the Royal Ulster Yacht Club. He seems to have enjoyed a friendly relationship with Lord Dufferin, who directed that the road be renamed Kathleen Avenue, after my grandmother.

My father, Herbert Brown (1883-1961) joined John Shaw Brown and Sons after leaving school and on 20 April 1906 he married Miss Dorothy Alan Rogers at Glencraig Parish Church. They took up residence at Rathwyre, adjoining Tordeevra, but in 1911 he bought Rathmoyle House on Craigdarragh Road. The whole property then comprised some 120 acres, including the home farm. By 1915, the Brown family consisted of my parents, six daughters (Barbara, Peggy, Dorothy, twins Betty and Nancy, and Kathleen) and one son (myself); to look after us we had a retinue of 18 staff. In the summer we learned to swim at Craigdarragh beach, and from that beginning emerged 'The Five Brown Sisters' who

in the late 1920s and early 1930s between them won the Irish Diving Championship twice (Peggy and Nancy), the Irish Breast Stroke Championship (Nancy), the Irish 100 yards (Kathleen), the Ulster High Diving Championship (Dorothy) and the Whitehead to Bangor Race, twice (Nancy and Betty). Rathmoyle House with its gardens and farm was an idyllic playground and I have very happy memories of my boyhood spent there'.

Given the local connections, it is worth adding to the above account. A passage on George Herbert Brown's yachting prowess is recorded separately. His father had been largely responsible for building up the huge John Shaw Brown linen mills and associated village at Edenderry. When news of George Herbert Brown's untimely death at the age of 48 reached Bangor in December 1908, the *County Down Spectator* recorded 'a thick cloud of sorrow seemed to settle down on the whole township'. He is buried in the

Top right: Five Brown sisters, a swimming sensation. Bottom right: George Herbert Brown, when Commodore of the Royal North of Ireland Yacht Club.

family plot at Bangor Abbey, the grave being marked with a huge boulder which his indomitable widow, known to the family as 'Dan Dan', had brought from the Mournes – to ensure he didn't get out, as one family member put it.

His son Bertie was then a Director of the firm, but appears to have mixed his duties with social activities, including following his father's love of sailing, owning several yachts, including the River class *Shimna*. Bertie had been born at Tordeevra and grew up there. In the first war, he joined the Royal Naval Volunteer Reserve. As the family account puts it, 'at the end of hostilities, Bertie Brown returned to the good life'. He was both generous and well connected, attending Cowes in the presence of King George V whom he is said to have described to his face – without ending up in the Tower of London – as a 'hairy wee admiral'.

He also saved the lives of two children in trouble in the sea off the local shore. On the following day, a service was held to mark the extension of the church to which he had contributed handsomely. The Bishop paid tribute, noting that the previous day Bertie had saved lives, today he was saving souls. At this point, an aunt was heard to comment, not sotto voce, 'he couldn't save his own soul, let alone anyone else's.'

In 1914, Bertie renamed Eldon Green, Rathmoyle which he felt more distinguished. The house was run on military lines, with the children numbered off before meals, but they could canoe on the small 'lake', ride ponies and play bicycle polo in the grounds. But in 1921, he was asked to leave the Board of the company, so the family had to move out of Rathmoyle, with his daughters giving up their schooling, and the family moving for a couple of years to Pontoon in County Mayo, before they returned to live in Bangor. This was when the daughters achieved their remarkable swimming feats, which included synchronized diving from all the boards at Pickie Pool, although they each went to work to support the family. In 1928, Nancy completed the swim from Whitehead to Bangor in 3 hours, 24 minutes, followed closely by her two sisters. Male competitors struggled in a long way behind. Bertie went off to Canada, on his own, for some years, before remarrying and settling in Newtownards. When he died, the *Belfast News Letter* commented,

> 'He spoke ill of no-one and was the staunchest and most loyal of friends…. throughout the tempestuous race of life, he sailed with every stitch of canvas set.'

It was a fitting epitaph.

In the second war, Nikko Duffin and his family spent several years at Rathmoyle, which they rented from the Mitchells, as their own home had been taken over as emergency accommodation after Gallahers' offices were bombed. This allowed his sister, Peggy, to keep a look-out for the naval officer who was then courting her. A sheet was waved from Rathmoyle's tower when his frigate passed up the Lough. Nikko remembers finding a large model steamboat and yacht in one of the Rathmoyle ponds, probably a legacy of the Brown era. In his book, *Buildings of North County Down*, Brett describes the house as quite exceptionally handsome and well-furnished.

Down our Way
by 'Rene Shuttleworth

These are reminiscences written over 20 years ago by 'Rene Shuttleworth, who lived for many years with her husband Joe in Lowood on Fort Road until their deaths in the last decade of the 20th century.

When they first came to the village, they had a flat adjacent to the station – she recalled the smoke and steam made it impossible to keep their clothes or their rooms clean. She watched out for Mr Downey who was always late for his train and would throw down his bicycle on the platform for the stationmaster to rescue and return to him after his day's work.

'As we have lived in our present home (Lowood) in Helen's Bay for over 50 years we have seen many changes 'down our way'.

In those early days there was a typical Irish Cottage at the bottom of the road (Fort Road). It was thatched and had an earthen floor. In

Above: Rathmoyle, the home of Bertie Brown and his family from 1911 to 1921.

Point Cottage, lived Sergeant Green (locally known as 'Honey'); he was Water Bailiff to Lord Dufferin. His duty was to keep an eye on the shore to see that there was no further storm damage. (His cat was known affectionately as 'Greedy guts', while his goat grazed the green below the Gilmer's bungalow.) Opposite the cottage was 'The Drive'. This led to Clandeboye House and Helen's Tower. One of our favourite walks was to Helen's Tower and to climb the steps to the top room where there were some mementoes of 'Helen' Lady Dufferin including a plaque – still on the wall – containing Lord Tennyson's poem on Helen's Tower, especially written by him at Lord Dufferin's request.

Sergeant 'Honey' Green's duty also was to look after the Drive, there was a wooden gate at the Helen's Bay end, which he had to open each morning and close at night to prevent the Drive becoming 'a right of way'. He had to make sure that there were no overhanging trees or other obstructions as the family used the Drive to access the station.

If needed there was transport in a jaunting car run by Billy Hutchinson. If it so happened that he had 'drink taken', the horse could always find its own way home. On one occasion Billy fell off and broke his nose. The doctor attending him asked him; 'Am I hurting you?' 'What the Devil else could you be doing?' said Billy.

In addition to the jaunting car there was a trap run by Hugh McCorry. If the children of those days went to a party, the trap or the jaunting car was the only form of transport. This meant that on occasions some children would arrive at almost the end of the party as they all had to wait their turn to be transported.

'Honey' also supplied water to the day visitors. If, as sometimes happened he was 'thawn', they used to come to the local householders to supply them. The water at this time came from the Clandeboye lakes and if the filter were not working well, queer things such as small worms or fish would come through the taps with plenty of brown sediment.

However if newcomers sent a sample to the 'Ministry' it always came back labelled 'a pure sample'.

At the top of the hill, on the other side from Honey's cottage, was Tordeevra - a house standing in its own extensive grounds, here lived Mrs Brown and her family. She was the typical 'Lady of the Manor'; she always dressed in black and had a marvellous presence. Although in those days there were very few cosmetics, she had a really beautiful complexion

When I came to Helen's Bay as a bride, Mrs Brown came to visit me, bringing a present of beautiful used linen – she said that no bride ever had anything old. I did appreciate such a kind thought.

Later Mrs Brown became President of the Tennis Club. Every year she had the members to tea when her staff served a luxurious tea of homemade cakes etc – it was always appreciated. My maid and her cook were cousins and the cook passed on the recipe for a special chocolate cake. Once Mrs Brown came to tea and I had made this cake, she said that she had never tasted anything so delicious and would I give her the recipe. Naturally I did not confess that the recipe was from her cook.

Adjacent to Tordeevra is Ballygrot House. Mr and Mrs Trelford and family lived there. Mrs Trelford was Brown Owl and also County Secretary to the Girl Guides. She lent the coachman's upstairs room as a Clubroom. The Guides had to climb up a kind of a ladder and then mostly sat on the floor. However, it was a wonderful company and we had great fun for many years.'

Mrs Trelford took a great interest in the church. At that time there was already a Presbyterian Church in Helen's Bay but the Church of Ireland congregation met in a hall behind the only shop. The wall was covered with sporting prints and Mr Trelford did not think that this was an atmosphere conducive to worship. He and two other residents (Mr Close and Mr Ewing) got together to have a church built. Lord Dufferin gave the beautiful site and the foundation stone was laid by Lady Dufferin in 1909. Mr Trelford's daughter Kathleen (now Mrs Stephens) was the first child to be baptised there.

'Rene also recorded that there was still bleaching in the fields round Helen's Bay when she came to the area in 1922.

Above: Point Cottage – previously home to Sergeant 'Honey' Green, no longer thatched, with Point House behind (both now demolished).

Helen's Bay Remembered
by Jim Page

Early in the 20th century, a stone, red sandstone topped wall, 16 feet high (with round hardwood stumps sunk in the sand about 10 feet from the bottom of the wall as protection from the breakers) ran the entire length of the beach. In 1925, part of the centre of this wall was still standing, but today only a very small portion at each end of the beach remains. A slated boat-house (at Quarry Port – the old quarry is still visible nearby) and Horse Rock, with its barbed wire entanglements, topped by its tall white War Department pole were at opposite ends of the bay. A much *mis*-used wooden 'ladies' bathing box was near the Bangor end of the beach.

In the 1920s and 1930s, the social life of Helen's Bay centred round the railway station, the few shops, the two churches, the Parochial Hall, the halls at Buckler's and Miss Thompson's Hotel, around the 9 hole golf links with its red corrugated roofed clubhouse, the Masonic Hall at Crawfordsburn and of course, the much visited beach which frequently had 12,000 trippers for whom no toilet facilities whatever existed.

The railway station had a staff of four over the years. These were the greatly respected and popular stationmaster George Rooney, his assistant Arthur Sloan, the ever-present Harry Parkhurst, and tall Reggie, plus signalman Billy McKee of Carnalea. Over 30 trains daily passed through Helen's Bay. The excursion return fare from Belfast was 10 pence (4p today) and a family of seven paid £40 yearly for 2nd class unrestricted travel between Belfast and Bangor. Jim Robinson's boot repair hut occupied the Bangor corner of the Square.

A permanent RUC barrack (opposite the later one built in the 1950s) was permanently manned by a Sergeant and five Constables in those law-abiding days. A Dublin family, the Bolands, occupied the 'Sunbeam Stores' and two sisters, the Miss Creaneys, staffed the 'Sweetie Shop'. Boland sold out to George Buckler Senior, father of the more recent proprietor. He and his family returned to Dublin about 1930. Other smaller shops were owned by the McKnights, the Foleys (adjacent to the Drive) and by an ex-RIC Sergeant Thomas ('Honey') Green, who sold lemonade and buns in his cottage on Bell's Hill. Two milkmen delivered milk, at this time. One was a Mr McEwen, he delivered

it by van from Crawfordsburn and the other Sam Bradley delivered it initially by horse, 'Sally', and cart from Ballygilbert. The only garage was built and run for 25 years by Tommy Shiels. There was controversy, when in 1927, petrol rose to 1 shilling (5p) per gallon.

From 1915 to 1948 Canon George Capsey was rector of Glencraig and St John's Church, (being driven to the latter by his maid Amy in his pony and trap, accompanied by his poodle). Harry Page, of Bangor played the organ till he was 86 years of age. The sexton was Mr Neill, who lived at the top of the Crawfordsburn Glen. The Rev Leslie Martin (from Armagh) came to the Presbyterian Church around 1930. His organist was a blind ex-Shankill Road lady, Miss Lottie Millar, who travelled twice on Sundays from Bangor, with her lady chaperone Miss Agnew. Three youths Jim McAllister, Jim McIlwaine and Jim Page shared the task of 'blowing the organ'. Lottie's morning repertoire invariably included McDowell's *To a Wild Rose*. The sexton was the tall, erect George McCorry of Coastguard Avenue. (Jim's sister Joan remembers that Mr McCorry had a long neck; he was a popular Father Christmas for the Sunday schoolchildren but any sense of mystery about his identity was removed by this aspect of his appearance.)

Above left: Painting by FT Walker of Helen's Bay Beach showing the remnant of the Clandeboye Estate wall.
Above right: Bolands in Station Square, Helen's Bay, with Mr and Mrs McDowell, with their daughter Rae, 1929.

The Sunday school Christmas parties were held in Thompson's Hotel or Buckler's Hall. The annual Sunday school picnics were local outings to Major Workman's home on Craigdarragh Road. In later years this progressed into a bus outing to Helen's Tower at Clandeboye. Major Workman's brother in law who was Margaret Garner's father, Mr James Yeames, had posed, when he was a young boy, for the famous Civil War painting *'And when did you last see your father?'*, by his uncle William Yeames.

It was largely on the instigation of the Rev Leslie Martin that a 24-strong Boy Scout Troop was formed in 1933. The Scout Master was Mr Ian Alderdice, a dental student from Bangor. Simultaneously, a Girl Guide Company was formed, led by Miss Maureen McCleery from Bangor. Virtually every local boy and girl belonged to these organisations. There were two annual highlights. Summer Camps in Great Britain and the Annual Armistice Day Parades with the Helen's Bay and Craigavad Branch of the British Legion. These were carried out under the control of Hunter Tate and Sammy Thompson and the parades were to one of the local churches.

In my time a small number of General Practitioners have faithfully served Helen's Bay. Dr Archie Lennon, Dr Hector Northey and Dr Douglas Blair (along with Dr Berney and Dr Edwards both more briefly) fulfilled the role for some 60 years. 5 Church Road was for many years home to one of them, and provided accommodation for the RAMC in the second war.

In the late 1920s and 1930s membership of Helen's Bay Golf Club was £2 per annum for adults. For juveniles it was seven shillings and sixpence for girls and ten shillings for boys. The Steward and green keeper was George Thompson and the caddy master was a Crawfordsburn 'character', known for his left lower handgrip, named Jimmy Moffett. His assistants were Pat McWha and John Charters. A dozen caddies regularly carried the heavy golf bags for a fee of seven pence for nine holes. One penny of this fee went to the caddy master. The low handicap men, those below seven, were Billy Pyper, Albert Bothwell, Sydney Morton, Dick Ross, Edwin Morrow, John McCallum, Arnold McKnight and Ernest Page.

There was a pronounced improvement in standards when, shortly before the war, a young, handsome, debonair golf professional called Tom McKinstry was appointed.

Against a background of high national unemployment, during the summers of 1933 to 1936, work camps were set up based at the Coastguard boat-house. These were organised by the Belfast YMCA for about 50 unemployed men. Mr Haughton and Mr Norman McNeilly organised the outdoor work at the back of the shore and also tended to the men's welfare. Locally the organisation of bonfire sing songs (including the Cornish floral dance), concerts in the Parochial Hall and Church Parades were part of this most valuable project.

Helen's Bay between the wars had a large number of English, Scottish and Southern Irish 'settlers'. Many of these entered the employment of the new Northern Ireland. There was also a large quota of ex-service officers, such as Colonel Sharman Crawford. There was also Brigadier Oswald, Colonel Morse, Major Workman, Captain Morrison and Sea Captains Jermyn and Harper.

There was no threat of war's return when the first Territorials trained and held sports days, concerts and drumhead services at Grey Point. Grey Point had been famous, for many years, as the setting of the popular annual Horse Show. Many magnificent mounts were on display in various events.

However, by 1938, war clouds were again looming over Europe, and many of the local young men and women enlisted in Reserve Units. Air Raid Precaution lectures were held in Thompson's Hotel and Buckler's Hall. These were organised by Mr Carlisle of Newtownards. It should be recorded that during one demonstration, just prior to the outbreak of war, Mrs 'Rene Shuttleworth had the misfortune to lose a beautiful Brittany souvenir ring while assembling a gas mask. Mr Churchill's victorious government never reimbursed the value of this ring.

After the war, Helen's Bay expanded with post-war buildings. Much of its character and charm was lost under the expanse of brick, concrete, asphalt, cars and people which engulfed its lovely hedgerows, glens, thickets, meadows and farms. Farewell forever to 'bosky woods and slumberous streams'.

Craigdarragh House and the Workman Family

Craigdarragh House (latterly St Columbanus nursing home) was built in about 1850 for Francis Gordon, to a design by Charles Lanyon. As an impressive local house, with very historic connections to the Workman family, it certainly deserves inclusion in this book. Brett's book notes that it was built in Lanyon's most ornate style, almost as grand as Ballywalter Park (although some of the window ornamentation may owe its origin to Thomas Turner who was Lanyon's senior assistant until he set up on his own in 1852). It seems that Gordon ran short of funds for he never occupied the House. The gate lodge which stands today was built by Thomas Workman when he acquired the property. According to the Valuation records, the House had a number of owners or occupants prior to him, including apparently for two very short periods, Lord Dufferin.

The two storied house stands at the top of the grassy slope running down to a sandy bay, with the drawing room and the dining room (which remains intact) looking out over the Lough. The square front hall has six elaborate doorcases and a series of niches. There was an associated courtyard and stable block. It is unfortunate that this comparative architectural gem is so little known about. The parkland surrounding the house, which includes an attractive wooded glen, stretches across to Seahill and down to the shore. The glen contains many different species of trees, some of which are over 100 years old, and is clearly now enjoyed by many badgers and other wildlife.

Thomas Workman was the son of linen merchants, who then prospered through his association with the founders (one being his younger brother Frank), in 1880 of Workman Clark and Co Ltd, shipbuilders of Belfast, known affectionately as the 'Wee Yard'. In several years before the first war, this yard's output exceeded that of Harland and Wolff. As well as serving as vice-chairman of Workman Clark, Thomas was himself a linen merchant which took him all over the world, (with the chance to acquire his collection of spiders, four species of which are named after him).

Thomas bought the freehold of Craigdarragh House from the Dufferin Estate in 1883. Margaret Garner recorded that on one occasion Thomas, who was her grandfather, had a falling out with Lord Dufferin whose agent claimed that one of his men had encroached on Dufferin land when he was ploughing. The correspondence ended with Dufferin writing from Rome where he was then the British Ambassador. He did however write later to Thomas's widow offering her any help when Thomas died.

Thomas Workman was a keen member of the Bangor Corinthian Sailing Club formed in 1881, which thrived for about 15 years. Many of its members then joined the Ballyholme Sailing Club before it became the Ballyholme Yacht Club when it was renamed after the first war. The records for the Corinthian Sailing Club in 1886, contained in Charles Milligan's book, show that Thomas Workman then had a 26 feet lugger named the '*Walrus*'. (Interestingly the rules of the prestigious Buenos Aires Club were modelled on those of the Corinthian Club.) He was also a member of the 'Canoe Club', subsequently the Royal North of Ireland Yacht Club at Cultra.

His second son, Major Robert Workman of the Royal Irish Rifles, (1878-1949), who was wounded at Ypres, was later Commodore of the Royal North of Ireland Yacht Club for 18 years. His uncle, Robert E Workman, had played a very central part in its establishment, being described as the founder of the Club. He served as Honorary Secretary from 1893 until his death, over 50 years later. In 1941 Major Robert stood unsuccessfully for Parliament, in the North Down constituency.

Charlie Brett, in his book on the *Buildings of North County Down*, recalls from his youth living on the Craigdarragh Road that the Major was a 'kindly old boy, good to his neighbours', who let the Brett family walk down to the shore through the glen. Mr Edgar, the grandfather of Alfie

Above: Craigdarragh House at the marriage of Thomas Workman's eldest daughter Jane to James Yeames, 1900.

Beaney's wife was a gardener at Craigdarragh, living initially in the row of cottages (now ruined) behind Fairholme, When he was promoted to be the head gardener, the family moved to the gate lodge. Alfie recalls the lovely ponds just beside the approach to the big house.

After the Major's death, and following that of his sister, the house was sold to the Sisters of Mercy, and converted into a nursing home specialising in the care of the elderly. In 2003 the house was again sold; its future has remained in doubt while the planning process has been underway; the proposed development is located within Green Belt. In the meantime this historic house is shut away from public sight but is visibly decaying. It will soon be too late to save it.

Sir Crawford McCullagh of Rust Hall

We are indebted to Susan Cunningham who is preparing a book on her relative Sir Crawford, for some of this material.

Another of Helen's Bay's distinguished early residents was Sir Crawford McCullagh. His story was described by one newspaper as 'the culmination of one of the romances of the commercial world'. Born in County Armagh, having been apprenticed to a Belfast draper, he opened his first shop in High Street, Belfast in 1894. Three years later he had made enough money for the family to move to Helen's Bay where they lived at Rust Hall in what is now Bridge Road. In 1900 he was elected Treasurer of the Helen's Bay Presbyterian Church, and was ordained as an Elder in 1911. In 1905 he had been elected to Belfast City Council as Councillor for Cromac Ward – in the same year he built Castle Buildings Department Store in Donegal Place. In 1914, he moved his family to Whiteabbey. He was elected Lord Mayor in 1914, 1915 and in 1916. (In that year, he proclaimed a 'five-minute silence' at 12 noon on 12 July as a tribute to the sacrifices by the 36th Ulster Division in the battle of the Somme. This is considered a precursor to the Armistice two-minute silence.)

In 1921 Sir Crawford was elected to represent South Belfast in the first Northern Ireland Parliament, and then he again held the position of Belfast Lord Mayor for a further 15 years from 1931 – the longest serving Lord Mayor in these islands. His was described in his obituary as an example in service to the community 'which is probably unequalled in municipal history'. His son became a well-known ornithologist who achieved celebrity for successfully breeding eider ducks in captivity.

Rust Hall continues as an imposing family dwelling on Bridge Road – later occupants included a Director of the Belfast Bank, and Councillor Denise Sawers with her husband John.

Coastguards and Customs

This section draws heavily on the work of Denis Mayne in describing both the initial Customs post at Grey Point (which may come as a surprise to many residents) and then the Coastguard Station where the Coastguard Cottages now are.

As many writers have noted, Grey Point has a commanding view overlooking practically the whole of Belfast Lough. It is known that Grey Point was listed as a Customs Post in 1730 with one (tide) waiter in charge. It was taken over as a Coastguard Station in May 1823, under the command of a chief officer in charge of nine men. The name of the station was changed to Crawfordsburn shortly thereafter. (In 1822 Customs had acquired responsibility for the Coastguard operation, following a major survey by Sir James Dombrain who was appointed Inspector General of Coastguards, Ireland in 1819.)

It now seems clear that the initial Coastguard Station stood on Fort Road, west of the modern junction with Grey Point. It is designated as a Coastguard Station on an Admiralty chart of Belfast Lough prepared by Captain Beechy in 1841. It is also known that in 1834 John Bell was subletting the property to the Admiralty at an annual rental of 15 guineas, and there is reference to a seven year lease. (It could well be after him that 'Bell's Hill' is so named.) It appears that the premises are

Above: Sir Crawford and Lady McCullagh.

shown on the first *Ordnance Survey map*, although without any designation. On a subsequent *Ordnance Survey map*, there is a mark for 'Annabel Cottages'. The last cottage was demolished over 20 years ago, though several sections of wall and two gable ends still exist (in the garden of private houses on Grey Point). One of the walls in particular appears old, containing a number of very large stones, and is of a thickness to suggest the original building was stronger than a traditional cottage would have been. It was in this cluster of buildings that 'Wee' or 'Old Mary' (see page 39 above) lived; the other two cottages housed the Beaneys and the Crothers. This location would fit the Beechy chart and

before all the more recent houses were built, it would have afforded good views in most directions, being at the crest of Bell's Hill. There is nothing in the records to provide any succour to the theory that the house on Golf Road, Ardseein, was an official customs dwelling.

In 1858 the 'Clandeboye' Coastguard Station was built, two years after the Admiralty took over the Coastguard, from Customs. A lease for the premises was agreed with Lord Dufferin, and it appears that he influenced the somewhat unique, ornate design of the Coastguard building, and perhaps also the form of the boat-house on the shore below. The brick terrace is a series of nine gable bays; at the west end is a two-bay officer's house and tower house, while there are slightly smaller gabled houses of uniform height for members of the crew and their families, see picture on page 49. The structure is embellished with variegated courses and bands including a bold chevron course of black and cream bricks; there are black pointed arches over the doors, windows and niches. The tower contains a two-storey canted-bay below an attic sandstone-dressed slit window. In a valuation around 1860 it is recorded as sitting in three acres leased from Lord Dufferin with an annual rent of 15 guineas.

Although the 1858 map designates the boat-house on the present site, the Board of Works annual report for 1891 states 'boat-house for Clandeboye completed'. The barrel-roofed building is partly built with large stones. It was used to house a Coastguard cutter.

Some form of self-defence was usually provided – it is recorded that the Coastguard station at Cultra, built just two years later, had no less than 23 gun-loops.

Entry to the Coastguard Service was initially restricted to ex-Naval men, and they were regularly moved between stations. There was a deliberate policy, for understandable reasons, of posting men away from their home areas. The *Ulster Directory* of 1892 names the six men at what is called 'Clandeboye Coastguard Station' then under the leadership of Chief Officer Richard

Kane. Six years later Alfred Beaney was the Chief Coastguard and a subscriber to the Presbyterian Church. He was born in Croydon and joined the Royal Navy in 1877, serving in such wonderfully named ships as *Impregnable* and *Implacable*. On his retirement from the Coastguard, he moved with his family to a cottage on Bell's Hill, at an annual rental from the Marquess of £8, notice to be given from any 'gale day'. He remained in the Reserve however and was mobilised during the First World War. The photograph shows Alfred, his wife Agnes, and their children. Alfie Beaney's father, Charles, is standing in the back row. Charles worked at Tordeevra as a young man, as did his brother Albert.

Top left: Grey Point Coastguard, from the Beechy Admiralty Chart, 1841. Above left: A section of the old wall that may have formed part of the original Grey Point Coastguard station. Gable ends of the cottage lived in by either Mary Megarrell or Cassie Beaney. Above right: The family of Alfred Beaney, taken just after 1900; from left to right, back row – Charles, unknown, unknown; middle row – Harry, Agnes with Cassie on her lap, Nellie, unknown, Albert, Alfred, Billy; front – Lizzie.

Two of Charles' sisters married soldiers in the Royal Artillery at the Fort, one the grandfather of Gunner Curtis. Cassie is the baby on her mother's lap. Alfie recalls that after she was widowed, his grandmother Agnes took in washing for some of the local big houses that did not have their own laundry maid; there were out-houses across the lane from the cottage on Bell's Hill, with boilers and an open fire where the flat irons that she used were heated.

In the 1901 census, Walter Pring is recorded as the Station Officer with seven colleagues, all from England; each was married and a total of 40 persons lived in the cottages then. The Cornishman Walter Squance, who features in the 1911 census, along with now only four colleagues, one of whom was from Waterford, was probably the officer in charge until his retirement the following year. Although only eight were still at home by then, he and his wife had 16 children in all. It is possible he was the last to hold the post, as by 1919 the Station was closed.

When they had to leave their cottage in the garden of Carrig Gorm in 1952, Alfie Jess moved his family into one of the Coastguard cottages. His son Denis recalls that the accommodation was still pretty basic then with no running water and only an earth closet. The terrace is now B1 listed, and the cottages have all mod cons.

George Best in Helen's Bay

Few people in the two villages know that George Best spent at least two weeks living in the locality, shortly before he went to Manchester United.

The story starts with Bob Bishop, who was the club's long-serving talent scout in Northern Ireland from 1932 to 1986, and whose protégés vastly contributed to its success.

For many seasons, Bishop brought his young charges to hone their skills on the beach

during the Twelfth Fortnight and at weekends, based in the bothy or so-called 'Manse' hidden away at the back of Glenholme farmstead, off Bridge Road. Ignatius Geddis recalls seeing Bishop escorting groups of Belfast lads along the road from the station on a Friday afternoon. These would have been boys from the inner city who had never experienced the countryside, yet between them Bob, with Bessie McCormick in the wings, ensured they were well behaved.

Bishop had first spotted young George Best playing for Cregagh Boys Club, the week after he qualified to become a printer's apprentice. It is said that he sent a telegram to Matt Busby saying simply 'I have found a genius'. Indeed he had.

Not only had George been a regular attender at Bishop's training sessions in the Manse, but also he had returned to visit on a number of occasions.

On a visit by the editor to the Manse in January 1990, it was an ivy-clad small single storey building with a main room and an open fire, and off it a smaller cooking area with an ancient stove and sink. It had been completely undisturbed since Bishop had left, for the last time three and a half years previously, as the dates on the newspapers strewn around and the generous cobwebs mutely testified. There were three bunks in a tier (still with blankets), a table and five chairs, and some very basic furnishings.

There were many posters of football teams of the day, and two press cuttings about Bishop himself. The bunks had boys' names carved on them, including Norman and Sammy, which could well have been Messrs Whiteside and McIlroy. There was also a deflated black and white leather football, a pair of well-used (if unmatching) football socks, and incongruously a six-inch model of a Tyrannosaurus Rex.

It was easy to sense (and even scent) the boys' presence. A number of photographs were taken that day in case the building was not preserved. Sadly, even before the rest of the farmstead was demolished, the Manse had gone, with, one must assume, all its contents.

Bottom left: The bothy (also known as the Manse) at Glenholme Farm. Above right: Inside the 'Manse'.

Chapter 11

The Ratepayers (or Residents) Association

While at first glance an account of the history of the Helen's Bay Ratepayers Association might appear to be of limited interest, it does however provide a unique insight into not just the development of our local area, but also the issues that concerned local residents. This chapter, taken mainly from the minutes of the Association since its birth in 1945, covers the period up to the late 1980s. It should be noted that the body broadened out into the Helen's Bay and Crawfordsburn Residents Association many years ago.

Planning concerns and public conveniences have been the leitmotifs of the Helen's Bay Ratepayers Association since its foundation. A meeting of at least 60 residents in October 1945 was convened in Buckler's Hall following 'a considerable amount of inspection and measuring taking place' on the shore – 'a rumour was rife that public lavatory accommodation was to be erected'. The Clerk of Newtownards Rural District Council (RDC) had confirmed it. The Trustees of Lord Dufferin would fight it unless a man and a woman would be in constant attendance. James Ewing took the chair.

The first motion that a public convenience was unnecessary and should be abandoned was narrowly defeated, but a second opposing the location chosen by the RDC (at the near end of the beach) was passed unanimously. The meeting favoured the far, boat-house end.

It was then proposed that a committee be formed to liaise between the residents and the Council on the matter and thus was born the Ratepayers Association. Those elected were: Mrs Henderson and Mrs Neilly and Messrs Ewing, McKeown, Jackson, Trelford and Irvine with J Hunter Tate as Secretary. The Committee reaffirmed their choice of location (notwithstanding 'the isolated position lending itself to abuse' and the great expense of getting water there). They also set an annual subscription for the Association of 2/6d.

An early example of the use of media spin is contained in the report of the Council's discussion in the *Newtownards Chronicle* of 17 November. The Council Engineer stated the sea was making serious inroads at that end. (The boat-house stood undamaged for another 34 years). One Councillor sagely noted that 'the proper place for a public convenience was where it would be most convenient.' Indeed in the homes of those objecting they would find lavatories 'perhaps next to the parlour'. The Committee met in its turn and noted that the public 'is actually using this particular area as a convenience'.

A second flank of attack on the Council was opened up in relation to bins. The Treasurer was mandated to draw up rules for 'our Residents Association'. The secretary in his next letter referred to 3-5,000 people thronging down at summer weekends. The Council concluded they could not proceed on a site to which the residents were unanimously opposed and offered a meeting in spring 1946.

The Council chairman agreed then to abandon the plans by the 6th hole of the golf course and revisit the boat-house option if the Golf Club would agree access. The reply from the Club's secretary was that 'in no circumstances could they agree to having cartage over the course'.

The bins issue was also coming to the fore. For some years Robin Lindsay had been calling with his horse and cart and emptying the bins of the older residents. However, Cotton, the Clandeboye Estate manager, had banned Mr Lindsay from using the dump. The Council was equal to the challenge and the Association heard with relief that the Dufferin dump had been reopened to Mr Lindsay. No such joy on the public convenience site, which was reaffirmed on the portion of the golf links at the bottom of Church Road.

The Committee met on 20 May and could not understand the Council's intransigence after what had seemed a positive meeting. The Committee unanimously decided to tender their resignations, albeit having sent a protest to the Council in the strongest terms. In June the Council backed down to the extent of deferring a decision for six months.

The first AGM of the Residents Association was held in 1947 on 13 January; 77 residents paid their 2/6d. The meeting began with remembrance of Messrs Trelford and Irvine who had passed on since their election. The Secretary tried to resign but was not allowed to do so.

A new committee was elected to carry on the work. A constitution was approved. However at the following Committee meeting, one member claimed the procedure had been flawed – not that he had any criticism of the contents. It was agreed the police sergeant should be summoned for an interrogation. (This he prudently escaped by leaving the RUC and going abroad the day after the scheduled meeting.) Issues about parking in Church Road and behaviour by visitors were therefore put to the District Inspector.

Mr Maurice Jackson (clearly a direct action member of the Committee, who had of course commanded the local Home Guard contingent) proposed that since the County Council had no authority to erect No Parking signs, 'before someone was killed, we should erect these ourselves'. Mr Robson undertook to have some made. The Committee protested to the Council at the ice-cream seller's hut. It was noted the police were powerless to take action against street trading. August was clearly hot and fine – the September meeting was full of concern over the beach – 'energetic measures should be taken to avoid a recurrence'. The No Parking issue was 'clarified' in a newspaper cutting in late 1947 on the Council debate where it was recorded that 'there is no common law or statutory right of parking on the highways… we share the view of the 1933 committee that it should be assumed that parking on the highway is prohibited in the absence of a sign to the contrary.'

The 1948 AGM was held in Miss Thompson's Hall. Apart from Mrs Kitty Stephens winning a contested election for the last Committee place, the main interest was in the change of ownership of the Belfast and County Down Railway and the effect on both the station area and the timetable. Only 59 subscriptions were paid. Tribute was paid graciously to Harry Gilmer for clearing up the broken glass etc on the beach. It is of interest that the terms Residents' and Ratepayers' Association seemed to have been used interchangeably.

The new Committee again decided to invite one member on the Rural District Council, Mr Henderson, to raise their concerns. Perhaps wisely he did not show up until later, but the No Parking signs were reportedly nearly ready as was one requesting visitors not to break bottles. Other new issues were the provision of the new water supply and the question of a bus service through Helen's Bay. The chairman made clear on the latter that 'the thought appalled him', as it did all the Committee. By June 1948 the No Parking signs were reported as having a good effect, though the Assistant County surveyor objected to them.

And then we had the first residential planning issue – a letter of protest is sent about the number of bungalows being built on Taylor and Crawford's farms.

The 1949 AGM, attended by 40, noted the debt arising from the No Parking signs. The annual report from the Committee expressed concern at the Taylor's field 'bungalows, huts and caravans' but went on to acknowledge the 'present shortage of accommodation', still after the War.

Mr Cotton, on behalf of the Dufferin Estate, was a regular contact. Re the issue of refreshment sellers, he replied that the Estate had the Crown rights of the shore and this was profitable business they meant to continue.

A new issue was a report about the sewer at Grey Point, which was raised with the Garrison Engineer who had promised to attend to it. The February 1950 AGM received a splendidly sardonic report:

'In dealing with some local committees and Government Departments one comes to the conclusion that a five yearly annual or general meeting would be sufficient to report progress … a thousand ages are but an evening gone.'

Station Square was very vexing. The hope had been that the Estate would pay the lion's share of the work required to improve it (only £120), and then get the Transport Board to persuade the County Council to take it on thereafter. But the contractors did other work in the village and then left. One item of good news was the new post box in Fort Road.

There was only one Committee meeting that year and just 35 residents attended the 1951 AGM. By the Association's own rules Mr Robson, as Chair, was not eligible for re-election and the Secretary, Mr Hunter Tate, said he did not wish to go forward for that post again. A postscript to the minutes records that, 'the final arrangement was the Association should remain in more or less a state of suspension…'

In September 1955, 'at the request of residents', a meeting was held in St John's Hall – about 100 were present. Mr JP Robson took the chair and spoke of the principal concern – the awful state of the beach.

'A lengthened' (sic) discussion followed, with a mandate to write to North Down Rural District Council asking them to take over control of the beach (from the Clandeboye Estate), and – once again – before a public convenience is erected, the residents should be consulted.

The performance of the Ratepayers Association hitherto was challenged and Mr Joe Nelson proposed a further trial period. On Leap Year day in 1956 no fewer than 150 concerned residents filled the hall to hear the ensuing correspondence with the Council and the Estate. At an interview in Clandeboye, representatives had been told of definite arrangements by the Estate to close and fence off the beach, erect turnstiles, charge admission fees and use the proceeds to clean and police the beach. Joe Nelson and Harry Parkhurst proposed the Association be reformed. Mr Agar replaced Mr Tate as secretary. In debate, most speakers were against the Estate's plan; it was pointed out that a right of way along the beach had existed for over 50 years. Only two present dissented from rejection of the Estate's plan. The Association was authorized to take legal advice on the right of way – up to a sum of £50. A total of £6.13s.9d was collected.

The *County Down Spectator* contained a musing article by Malcolm McKee in April 1956 entitled 'Who owns the foreshore?' Was the attempt by the Clandeboye Estate Company to protect Helen's Bay beach by erecting a fence an infringement of a right of way? The people of Belfast had as much right to the foreshore at Helen's Bay as the residents of Helen's Bay. Something must be done to keep the foreshore clean – 'in this land of the free, it would appear that children are not taught how to behave'. He went on to propose that the issue be taught as a lesson in governance in schools; children like beaches, they don't like Governments, he concluded.

Three months later a similar meeting included the solicitor. He reported that their QC had given two opinions, but could not be sure without access to the Clandeboye title deeds. It would cost up to £150 to compel disclosure in court. Several speakers noted that the Estate's actions (which it was not prepared to alter) were resulting in a cleaner beach, albeit at a cost to residents. In real controversy, resulting in a 'secret ballot', alternative proposals were advanced: (a) proceeding with court action or (b) asking the Estate nicely after the summer to reduce the charges. The good burghers of Helen's Bay favoured the latter course by at least 2 to 1, though clearly a fair number present were unable to decide.

And there the first minute book of the Association tantalisingly closes, with only blank pages thereafter. We do know, however, from copies of correspondence that the Estate declined in autumn 1956, after the first closure of the beach, to reduce the £1 season ticket and the 1/- and 6d admission charges (for adults and children). We also know of Hunter Tate's resignation as Treasurer due to the division in the Association and the minutes of that fateful meeting were never signed.

The next minute book begins with the record of a meeting in May 1962, again, attended by over 100, but this time held 'to inquire into caravan sites in Helen's Bay'. Mr Robson reported on action taken

Top left: Crowds on Helen's Bay Beach – still with no public toilets.
Bottom right: Aerial view of the caravans on Skelly Hill, Helen's Bay in the late-1970s.

since the matter first came up in 1960 – so we know the Association had remained in being in some form. Concern was expressed to the Estate about access to the Skelly Hill site (now Chimera Wood) from Golf Road and a proposed site at McCormick's farm (lately Glenholme) recently bought by Mr Wardle. Captain Ker of Portavo was also involved in correspondence. The residents of Blackwood Crescent were vociferous in their protest. The upshot was that planning permission was granted for 160 caravans on Skelly Hill, screened by trees, but the caravans on McCormick's field were to be removed.

Dr Nixon MP, no less, attended and gave his support though was not hopeful much could be done, though he had raised planning appeals in the House of Commons. The Chairman, Mr Robson, though not opposed to caravans (elsewhere), felt it would turn the area 'into a shanty town'.

So, not for the first time in its turbulent little history, the Ratepayers Association was then reformed. Again Brigadier Calwell was nominated ex officio by Colonel Carew. (The Colonel was then living at 11 Bridge Road, while the Brigadier, who lived at the recently-demolished white house at the Bridge Road end of Kathleen Avenue, was Black Rod at Stormont.) Mr Robson declined the chair. Criticism of Mr Wardle and the lack of sanitation continued – 'lavatory buckets were being thrown over the hedges'. Did the sites not 'constitute a public nuisance?' On the other hand, it was noted that the Government favoured provision of caravan sites. The meeting decided a letter of protest should be sent to Down County Council, with a copy to the Minister of Home Affairs, so strongly did feelings run.

The Committee, meeting at the Golf Club, appointed Dr Blair as Chair and Mrs Neely as Secretary. Its first meeting gives us more potential insights into local history – the field behind Blackwood Crescent had been full of huts before it was built, and it was thought the McCormick's farm was held in Trust.

A trenchant letter from Mrs McCormick was read, pointing out that the Queen Mother and Dr Nixon, as well as Mr Robson, all owned caravans; in short 'caravan owners are not all confined to the working class.' She also noted that Mr Robson had opposed the building of Blackwood Crescent. Moreover she pointed out that close to St John's Hall were nine or ten houses without sanitation or water.

Two weeks later, the Committee had received 'not at all satisfactory' replies to their letters. A further flurry of letters was authorized and Mr Walker undertook to speak personally to Brian Faulkner MP about the opening from McCormick's site onto Bridge Road.

Subsequently the Down Council seems to have concluded in a putative Prohibition Order that no more caravans be permitted on McCormick's field.

At the first meeting of 1963, caravans were the main issue once more. The state of Blackwood Crescent's upkeep was also raised – had the road been adopted? Dr Blair proposed sending a detailed description of Bridge Road including the hairpin bend (remember that?) to a long list of recipients including the RUC Inspector General. It was reported that Clandeboye hadn't answered on getting the Crescent into good order to be taken over by the County Council.

In May there was reference to the Clandeboye injunction proceedings, and the Association stood down their legal adviser. But Lady Dufferin was to be written to along with a complaint about increased charges for access to the beach. Related issues included unauthorised access to the beach across the golf course to which the Club objected. It looked from planning discussions that Mr Wardle planned to replace the caravans in McCormick's field with houses …

In June 1963, the Annual General Meeting was recorded on the front page of the *Spectator*, its pugilistic proceedings occurring on the same evening as the Wembley clash between Henry Cooper and the then Cassius Clay – 'Helen's Bay Residents are Up-in-Arms'. The 150 attendees were given a standard letter to submit requesting a reduction in rates, owing to the proximity of the caravans. The future of the beach and the Matthew Report pointing to a role for the National Trust was another big issue.

Above: A postcard of the caravan park, Helen's Bay.

The following month, Dr Blair courageously tackled the original 20 year old issue and now carried the Committee in proposing that the (Fort Road) car park was a good place for a toilet for the beach. Mrs Neely took a bottle of dirty mains water to the Commissioners for testing. (It was found to be bitter tasting, but not poisonous.) That autumn a long list of issues were identified for tackling with Mr Chelmick, the Estate's agent. Local residents were canvassed on the public convenience site. On 15 October Dr Blair reported the only outcome of the meeting at Clandeboye – the removal of the turnstile to the beach the day before. Immediate residents having objected to the tickets, the idea was shelved. Councillor Sawers reported that the Planning Officer had promised her 'there would be no further building in Helen's Bay' beyond the current permissions. (If only…) She also enquired about building at Grey Point once the present huts were demolished.

In spring 1964 a formal complaint was made to Clandeboye Directors about Mr Chelmick's failure to reply to the Association. By summer the North Down Council were taking court orders against Clandeboye about the state of the road in Blackwood Crescent and the sanitation in Coastguard Cottages, although this had spurred Mr Chelmick into fresh promises of action. By September he had done nothing on either.

In March 1965 Mrs Sawers 'reported that under the new Act both Blackwood Crescent and Rushfield would be completed and that nothing further could be done at the moment.' The National Trust was to be written to about the houses at Grey Point and damage to the trees there.

Plans for a children's playground at the back of the old dam behind the Country Club in Crawfordsburn (now Glen Park) were noted.

For the first time the issue of traffic from Craigdarragh Road joining the A2 was raised and a roundabout suggested. The County Surveyor said a dual carriageway was the only solution.

Next month saw alarm concerning a restaurant planned for the Battery at Grey Point. Dr Blair was inspecting the cleanliness of the beach regularly by now and the sanitary inspector had been brought out to inspect rubbish dumped in the Carriage Drive. The Committee agreed to write to Professor Muskett, the Adviser to the Minister of Development on the closing of beaches in Northern Ireland. They also requested a second roadman for Helen's Bay, due to the growing quantities of litter. Mrs Sawers reported on Grey Point again – compensation of £30,000 was required by Clandeboye if planning permission was withdrawn, and the National Trust could not finance a coastal walk from Holywood to Bangor – it must be undertaken by the Government.

The mains water supply had still not reached one of the Coastguard Cottages. The October meeting was updated on the coastal walk and a proposed 'amenity area' at Crawfordsburn Hospital. While the Ministry of Development would establish rights of way to provide a coastal walk, the Rural District Council must acquire 27 acres for this. Professor Muskett had spoken of taking 20 yards off the Golf Club but Mrs Sawers said there would be very strong protests. Dr Blair 'was against the coastal walk' on the grounds that if access was open to the beach any cleaning by the Council would be no better than that by Clandeboye. It was noted that Harry Parkhurst was retiring at Christmas 1966 and a collection was raised.

The next meeting recorded is not till February 1968 when Mr Moore's land on Bridge Road is up for development – it was felt 'most undesirable'. A rare event was a positive proposal put to the Association for a squash court in Helen's Bay and a slipway on the beach, from Mr Trevor Boyd. Mrs Sawers noted however that the Council was not really getting a sufficient return for creating the tennis courts and doubted the viability of a squash court. An AGM was proposed for April 1968 – the first for several years; alas no record remains, though Dr Blair was returned as chair. Mr Shaw became secretary. At last Clandeboye did up Blackwood Crescent's roadway. The Committee mourned the loss of trees for housing between the tennis courts and Coastguard Avenue. A sub-committee was formed to request Helen's Bay's designation as an amenity area from the Ministry of Development.

Above: Helen's Bay police station, during construction of Blackwood Crescent.

Mrs Sawers undertook to mention to the Council having a lamp placed in the lane between Kathleen Avenue and Rushfield. (40 years on there still isn't one.)

By December 1968 concern was expressed about youths setting fire to trees at the new car park at Crawfordsburn beach.

In early 1969 refusal of planning permission for flats at Rockmount on Bridge Road was greeted with acclaim. Officials from the Ministry of Development were met for discussions on – yes – the siting of the public conveniences. It was noted that the Clandeboye Estate planned a licensed hotel and restaurant on the Grey Point parade ground; the view was that only a Grade 'A' facility would be acceptable. An appeal against the decision on the flats was also noted. Finally, letters indicating that the public convenience would be erected in the car park at Fort Road were 'not opposed'.

The formal records of the Association in the early 1970s are skimpy – just one Committee meeting in Dr Blair's house in 1970 and 1971 and then silence until 1975. There was however a public meeting which opposed by 74 votes to 20 the plans for an off licence in Station Square. Contributions were made to the legal fees to contest it. (Mr Desmond Boal kindly agreed to cancel his fees subsequently.)

One issue in 1975 was the plan for houses on the parade ground at Grey Point. However the Committee did conclude an AGM was required in 1976, with the first elections for eight years. There were complaints about the footpaths but 'labourers could not be obtained even in times of high unemployment'. As the 'new trains were causing great vibrations', Colonel Garner wrote about fitting silencers. The Committee referred to 'Coyle's Lane' between 52 Craigdarragh Road and Maryfield. Road Safety was a continuing theme, and the Ratepayers wrote to join forces with the Crawfordsburn Road Safety Committee. The new Committee included Mrs McCullough, Mrs Bushell and Mrs Pilling.

Councillor Rollins reported that Mr Donaldson and the local Youth Club had said they would help keep the station tidy (though the Trade Union later objected).

In 1978 the graffiti on the station had got so 'monstrous' that the Association wrote to Sir Myles Humphries (then NIR Chairman) at his home address. There was dismay at the newspaper article about Helen's Bay receiving the lowest marks in the Best Kept Village competition. Dr Blair said local school children, some from Sullivan Upper, were responsible and appealed for responsible parenting. Dr Dewar was told the Police had looked for young people sleeping rough on the station. There was, however, a limit to fraternisation: Councillor Rollins suggested broadening the Association to include Crawfordsburn; this was unanimously rejected by the Committee. A proposal by David Marshall for a grant-aided Community Hall was thought not to be a popular idea.

Dr Blair told the 1978 AGM that the Committee met irregularly and Messrs Robson and Shuttleworth were the oldest members. He encouraged residents to notify Constable Griffiths at the Police Station about misbehaviour, and thanked him for his help. He referred to 'a large roundabout scheme' in hand for the Bridge Road and Crawfordsburn Road intersection.

The wider security situation did impinge in one suggestion, which 'caused considerable hilarity', that the confidential telephone be used to say a bomb had been planted in an unsightly furniture van to which the Association objected.

The new Committee met a year later to endorse the Golf Club's proposals for a fence and hedge along Church Road. The records then skip to late 1983 when the Association was told by Dr Blair there had seemed no point in meeting unless something worthwhile was to be discussed. The AGM was addressed by Councillor Mrs Bradford about the state of Mr Geddis' property. There was a long discussion with Mrs Bradford suggesting corporate action – 'civil servants dislike loud complaints raised against them', it was noted.

In 1984 a lengthy letter about the site was received from the Minister for the Environment, Chris Patten. The Committee opposed a planning application for 10 acres on the site and wrote to Mr Kilfedder MP. At the same meeting, another proposal to join up with a proposed Crawfordsburn Ratepayers Association was this time, six years later, endorsed.

Over 100 people attended an AGM to hear three officials from Planning and Public Health; 'searching questions were asked without gaining further information'. An employee of Mr Geddis outlined his plans. With one dissent, the meeting opposed the breaching of the Green

Belt. A new Committee was elected with Messrs Rogers, Boyd and Sir A Kennedy joining.

A further planning application was considered at a public inquiry in June 1986 and an AGM held in May. Dr Blair welcomed those from Crawfordsburn. He mentioned that Dufferin Avenue was to be preserved as part of the Ulster Way. A 'vociferous' discussion followed, leading to unanimous opposition. Curiously, given the intensity of the issue, the next minuted Committee meeting was not until November 1988. This concerned another planning application – for 9 flats at 18 Grey Point replacing the former house on the sea front, overlooking Horse Rock. The Committee was opposed and arranged a general meeting which was addressed by the architect. Some present feared a 'monstrous carbuncle', only one spoke in favour while another recalled the original house had had to be camouflaged in the War and feared the proposed building would have to be demolished in a future war. Resolutions were passed opposing the plan but recognising the scope for a smaller building.

The Association took on a new lease of life in subsequent years, energetically spurred on by John Rogers who took a huge interest in planning and local amenity matters. Voluminous records remain. Although this era will no doubt be of interest to future local historians, it is felt not necessary to include any further account in this book.

Above: Horse Rock, Helen's Bay beach.

Chapter 12

Natural History and Other Aspects of Local Interest

Crawfordsburn Country Park

On the southern shores of Belfast Lough, the Country Park features 3.5 km of coastline and the two best beaches in the Belfast area. The Country Park was opened in 1971 and soon became a popular venue both for local residents and visitors. While the Seapark which is reached off Coastguard Avenue has much of interest, including of course its own stretch of the coastal path, the main Park area consists of the wooded Crawfordsburn Glen and the coastal area.

Above: Crawfordsburn Lower Glen.

The Crawford's burn enters the Park below the Old Inn. One of the two signs erected by North Down Borough Council depicting the historic four mile Bayburn Trail is beside the pedestrian entrance to the park between the Inn and Crawfordsburn SPAR, (the other is at the Fort Road car park). As noted earlier, much of the planting in the Glen was carried out by William Sharman Crawford and his family. In the Victorian era sight-seeing tours from Bangor came to Crawfordsburn where 'a Glen, Cascade and tastefully planted grounds' were among the attractions. Some of the trees are specimens, with just on 50 different species, and at one point the burn skirts the roots of a Western red Cedar and a Monterey Cypress. Much of the higher part of the Glen is given over to beech trees, under-planted with a covering of laurel which was maintained as short-clipped cover for pheasant shooting. The burn above the viaduct provides a home for dippers – birds which feed by waiting submerged in the water searching for insect larvae and other aquatic food. Higher up, there is a giant Redwood with dark green foliage and a round, stunted top – probably the result of an old lightning-strike. The rock face at the side of the path has been colonised by mosses, ferns and liverworts that thrive in shady, damp conditions. Enchanter's nightshade, one of the willow herb family, also thrives here; the introduced Alaskan snowberry, that is also prolific around the path at Smelt Mill Bay, grows in profusion. Raspberries are another ornamental introduction growing at the side of the path leading up to the viewpoint at the top of the steps. Needless to say, the waterfall is at its most impressive after heavy rain. Around 1850 the energy of the fall was assessed at 40 horsepower.

The *Downpatrick Recorder* for 20 July 1850 has an article headed 'Disgraceful outrage at Crawfordsburn':

'The beautiful grounds and gardens at Crawfordsburn, the property of W Sharman Crawford, Esq, MP, are open to the public with the utmost liberality, and neither trouble nor expense is spared the accommodation of visitors. A new Gothic bridge, for example, has this year been thrown across the river, so as to form a public passage from the gardens to the shore, and many other improvements have been effected for the advantage of visiting parties. Some time ago, however, certain persons, who, from their social position, ought to have been respectable, took advantage of the

indulgence shown to them to tear up and wantonly scatter about the grounds a number of the richest and most valuable flowers in the garden. Again conduct of this kind cannot be too severely censured, and the name of the offenders ought to be forthwith published of the world, in order that their real character may be generally known.'

Even then, vandalism was an issue.

But the most ingenious use of the burn came in 1886, as GH Bassett writing in the *County Down Guide and Directory* records,

'.. *this year Mr A Sharman Crawford made use of the water of the burn to generate electricity for lighting purposes. Lamps are erected in the Glen, and one beside the Cascade, on dark nights produces a beautiful effect.*'

By this time the original corn mill had been converted and no less than three saw-mills were powered by the burn.

In the 1920s concerts were still being held in the Glen, in the amphitheatre near the waterfall. Pat Nickels remembers her mother being taken by train to her aunts at Carnalea, before they would come to attend the concert.

Margaret Garner noted that the area was sometimes known locally as 'Grace's Glen', after a lady of that name who lived in the farm at Glenside.

The spread of the gorse in season – and it is rarely out of bloom entirely – is both a visual and an olfactory delight; sea pinks provide contrasting colour, while bluebells are increasingly colonising both the woodland to the west of the Fort and on both sides of the coastal path where it rises up the steps below Craigdarragh House. Ragwort is also becoming more common and the case for and against it was vigorously debated in the letter columns of the *BayBurn Life*. However the full variety of flowers that grow, across the year, both in the Glen and nearer the shore, is too numerous to detail. Helpfully, some, as well as examples of sea-birds on view, are depicted on the various information boards erected by the NIEA.

No information is provided about possible gun-running before the first war. Gus Drew, an early Head Warden at the Park, was of the view that guns had been dropped a little way off Crawfordsburn beach, where the burn debouches, weighted with salt. They were brought in when the salt dissolved and stored locally. There is no proof now, but he did say that he had found old .303 cartridges when preparing the Country Park for public visiting.

Outside the Country Park is the area around Crawfordsburn Dam, between Glen Park and Main Street. This was worked on in the 1990s by the Crawfordsburn Conservation Group, led by Heather and Bruce Crawford (who also constructed two coracles), which won a Shell Environmental award. The main project was reinstating the old mill pond as a wildfowl pond and nature reserve, and constructing a small weir across the river at the site of the old sluice gates. Native trees like bird cherry, whitebeam, wayfaring tree and dogwood were planted. The Group constructed two islands in the form of crannogs by hammering posts into the base of the pond. While regrettably it has not been maintained in recent years, there is an initiative under consideration to restore the pond to the state it was in nearly 20 years ago, if not on quite the scale it once had. The pond originally provided the water for the Crawfordsburn saw-mill which the earlier corn mill had been converted into. It was in former days, also a source of trout and eels. Two punts were kept on it at that time too. (It is known that Emily Jess, aged some three years, sadly drowned in the pond, over eighty years ago. It is also suggested a boy may have too, in a separate incident. Bobby Mairs said that a crane had toppled into the pond, but no trace has been found, yet.)

Opposite the entrance to the Country Park, between Bridge Road and the Carriage Drive is an attractive, varied wood planted in 1991 by the Woodland Trust and the Townswomen's Guild in the nation-wide Rooting for the Future Campaign.

Above: A sketch of the waterfall at the head of Crawfordsburn Glen.

Flora and Fauna

Many of the gardens of the two villages are of note, and gardening has been a keen interest for many over the past hundred years; for example, the Shuttleworths' at Lowood was entered in the Ulster Garden competition in 1980, and the recording of the BBC team's visit pays tribute to the wide variety of shrubs, soft fruit and vegetables, as well as to the splendid eucalyptus tree which remains prominent today. Trevor Edwards highlights two of the more historically significant gardens, below.

'I believe that **Guincho Garden** was named after a beach, lying at the foot of the Sintra hills in Portugal. The garden on the Craigdarragh Road was started in 1948 when Mr and Mrs Frazer Mackie bought Guincho, a property of 16 acres. At that time the garden contained mostly herbaceous and bedding plants – this was not all to Mrs Mackie's taste. Over the years she set about creating a garden in her own style. Thanks to the extraordinary dedication of the head gardener, the late William Harrison, who tended the garden even after Mrs Mackie had left the house, we are fortunate to be able to see and witness that she made a true plantsman's garden. With an emphasis on rarity and careful selection she produced a result that is both decorative and interesting. Sadly I never met Mrs Mackie but I was most fortunate to meet 'Harrison' on a number of occasions. The garden has been immortalised by virtue of the fact that to this day we can obtain, from nurseries nationwide, *Sambucus 'Guincho purple'*. It is interesting to note that people will travel great distances to see the parent plant still growing well. Today the gardens are in the custody of Mr Eric Cairns and are maintained and developed by his enthusiastic and knowledgeable gardener – Nick Burrows.

Old Mill House was for many years the home of Colonel Harry and Margaret Garner. Old Mill and its garden have experienced many changes. Originally there was a scutch mill on the site. To scutch is to break the outer skin of the flax stalk. Long ago the stalk was beaten by hand, but by the time the mill was built, probably more than two hundred years ago, wooden beaters driven by waterpower scutched it. The mill was burnt down in 1850, leaving the barn, stables and manager's house. The mill itself stood where the garden is now. When Mrs Garner's parents married they came to live here, in what used to be the manager's house. It was at this time that Margaret's mother started her garden. It was long and narrow, running the length of the house and barn, with a path down the middle flagged with Scrabo stone taken from the house. Margaret was an artist. She trained at the Glasgow School of Art. Her bold, colourful oil paintings were mainly of flowers and foliage. She said that her garden was her canvas too, calling it a 'Robinsonian' or natural garden. (This is after the Irishman, William Robinson, who advocated a system of planting in groups, on a less formal basis.) She planned that her garden would evolve as she aged and this it did most successfully and became low maintenance shrubs, trees and ground cover. Nick Burrows for a period also cared expertly for this garden. Over the years Margaret Garner generously opened the garden in support of the Ulster Gardens Scheme.'

Old Mill House itself then contained some fascinating historical artefacts. These included a spinning wheel belonging to Margaret Dixon whose family had come over from Scotland with the Hamiltons, and a quern stone, albeit from outside the local area, which had been used illicitly in the 17th century when tenants were legally required to take their corn to the landlord's mill to be ground.

After the Old Mill House was sold, the historic walled garden has been leased to John McCormick of Helen's Bay Organic Gardens who plans to restore a number of aspects of its former splendour.

The Butterflies of Helen's Bay and Crawfordsburn
by Trevor Boyd

Thirty different species may be encountered in the whole of Ireland, and 21 or 22 may be or have been seen in our area, although a few are non-breeding visitors from places further afield, such as continental Europe or North Africa. Some are regular visitors such as the Red Admiral and Painted Lady; others are very rare vagrants such as the Camberwell Beauty and the Monarch, a visitor from North America. Neither of these two have yet been seen in Helen's Bay or Crawfordsburn, but have been in nearby areas such as Marino and are therefore potentially on our list. (The Monarch is usually seen in October following hurricanes in the Caribbean, which blow them off their regular southward migration to Mexico.)

2006 was a great season for migrants, both butterflies and moths, with Clouded Yellow butterflies being fairly numerous on the coast and Humming-bird Hawk-moths and Silver Y moths being particularly numerous. Both these hover around red valerian or buddleia, sucking nectar through their long proboscis. The Humming-bird Hawk is particularly striking with its proboscis (longer than the moth itself), white tail markings and rapid wing movements that cause the characteristic audible 'hum'. It is a regular migrant from the Mediterranean area.

It was also a remarkable year for Peacock butterflies with as many as 25 on a single buddleia bush in early September. We have had most of the other species, Cabbage Whites, Green-veined Whites (our most numerous butterfly - no danger to cabbages), Meadow Browns, Ringlets, Speckled Woods, Small Tortoiseshells, Small Coppers, Common Blues etc, and Real's Wood White, a rare colony of which is to be found in the equestrian area of the Country Park, known as 'the common'. Real's Wood White is the only butterfly found in Ireland which does not occur in Britain. It was only discovered here a few years ago, is small and has a weak flappy flight, but in May or June is usually the most frequently seen 'white' on the common. The caterpillars feed on vetches.

The best areas for butterfly watching, apart from bloom-filled gardens, are along the coastal path to Grey Point and in Dufferin Drive. Clandeboye woods themselves contain Ireland's largest butterfly, the Silver-washed Fritillary, and both this and the Dark Green Fritillary have been recorded from Helen's Bay. All these butterflies are to be found in this corner of North Down and, who knows, others might remain to be discovered, especially with a warming climate. The Green Hairstreak was seen here in the 1940s and the Holly Blue could spread up from mid-Down. Good hunting.

The best butterfly-attracting plants in the gardens are: Spring – aubrietia; early summer – red valerian; late summer – buddleia (the butterfly bush); autumn – ice plant and Michaelmas daisy.

The Crawfordsburn Fern

During the research for this book, one of the most intriguing issues has been the existence of the 'Crawfordsburn Fern'.

It is known that a plant, which came to be called the Crawfordsburn Fern, was discovered on the Estate in 1861 by one of the Sharman Crawford workers. It is understood that only a single plant was ever found. Miss Crawford however succeeded in getting her name attached to the discovery. The Latin name is *Polystichum Setiferum*

Above: A real Crawfordsburn Fern frond.

Divisilobum Crawfordiae (or *Crawfordianum*). This means it is a variety of the Soft Shield-Fern. Margaret Garner told the author of this chapter over 20 years ago that the find had been registered in the 1860s with William Hooker Ferguson, then at Belfast Botanical Gardens, and also with Kew.

The 19th century has been described as the era of the fern craze – pteridomania. This social phenomenon included not just the identification of new species in the wild and then the development of cultivars, but also the creation of ferneries (like the one in Belfast's Botanic Gardens), and even pottery and sugar containers in fern shape.

One expert commentator has said that the find of the Crawfordsburn Fern was very significant, and paved the way for others. Certainly there was much interest in and knowledge of ferns at that time. The work *The Ferns of Ulster* lists about 50 varieties of *Polystichum Setiferum*; 'the most famous is the Crawfordsburn Fern', according to Paul Hackney's edition of the *Flora of the North-East of Ireland*. This book goes on to note that

> 'the plants usually sold as Crawfordsburn Ferns in the market are a far commoner form, viz Divisilobum Alchinii. This fake Crawfordsburn Fern is in fact very different in appearance to the genuine article which is recognisable by the very broad and overlapping character of the pinnae and the extreme breadth of the fronds, according to The Ferns of Ulster'.

(This analysis was written by two distinguished Holywood residents, William Henry Phillips of Lemonfield and Robert Lloyd Praeger, and published in the *Proceedings of the Belfast Naturalists Field Club volume 2, appendix 1*, in 1887.)

Above left: Polystichum Setiferum Divisilobum 'Crawfordiae' – the real thing.
Above right: Polystichum Setiferum Divisilobum Alchinii – not the real thing.

The survival of what a number of local residents believed to be a Crawfordsburn Fern was reputedly due to the Sharman Crawford's last head gardener and another Estate worker, who rescued examples after Colonel Sharman Crawford had died. Another resident has a variety, the provenance of which can be vouched for from her grandmother in 1904.

Contact has been made with a range of fern experts, not just in Ulster, but also in Britain. The identification of *Divisilobum Alchinii* for the specimens seen locally so far has been consistently made, with the exception of a further different variety, also seen in a Crawfordsburn garden, which – although a pretty fern – is *Athyrium filix-femina cristatum*, with the pinnae being crested or forked.

Does this mean the Crawfordsburn Fern is extinct? No, because at least one specimen is known still to be alive, albeit in County Antrim rather than County Down. The illustrations show, for comparison, the 'fake' Crawfordsburn fern (*Divisilobum Alchinii*) and the real *Divisilobum Crawfordiae*. Let the search continue, but regrettably it must be accepted that the fern – pretty as it is – masquerading in some of our gardens as the Crawfordsburn Fern is only an imitation of that elusive and very special item.

Local Weather
by Trevor Boyd

Trevor was awarded the MBE in 2003 for services to meteorology. For just on 50 years, he kept meticulous records of rainfall, temperature and sunshine hours in Helen's Bay. The daily information was passed on to the Met Office. This item is drawn from an early edition of the BayBurn Life Newsletter.

Our climate is determined by our geographical position on the east coast of Northern Ireland, close to Belfast Lough. Ireland as a whole is strongly influenced by Atlantic weather brought to these shores by the Gulf Stream and its northwards extension, the North Atlantic Drift. This ensures a mild maritime climate with regular rainfall. Being on the east coast we benefit from the shelter afforded by the Irish land mass and are thus drier and sunnier than areas further west. Winter temperatures are particularly mild as wind from almost any direction has crossed relatively warm water to arrive here, and the effects of Belfast's urban heat island are also felt. Sunshine is enhanced by the proximity of stable air over Belfast Lough and the North Channel, also by the warming effect of descending air near the east coast (fohn effect).

The result is that while summer temperatures are generally as warm as those further inland, winter temperatures are mild enough to allow tender plants to remain outside all year round. Nowhere does Griselinia (New Zealand privet) grow more lushly and mimosa flowers profusely from late January where it has shelter from the wind. Begonia and dahlia tubers can stay in the ground all winter and tender fuchsias don't need to be in a greenhouse. Air frosts occur on no more than 14 nights during an average year, and hardly ever persist through the day. Damp rather than cold is the enemy.

While rainfall totals around 900 mm in an average year, this falls during an annual average of 787 hours, which means that it rains for only 9% of the available hours, and that 22 hours of the 24 are dry. May is the sunniest month and July the warmest, with January the coldest and wettest.

Averages of the main parameters (up to the end of 2004) were as follows:

	Temp. deg. C	Rain mm	Sun hours	Seawater deg. C
Jan	5.0	98.5	49.7	6.9
Feb	5.1	67.2	69.1	6.8
Mar	6.6	70.8	105.8	7.2
Apr	8.3	57.8	161.6	8.1
May	10.8	57.0	188.3	10.0
Jun	13.3	61.0	184.7	12.8
Jul	15.3	56.4	161.1	14.1
Aug	15.1	75.6	159.5	14.7
Sep	13.2	79.5	119.8	13.8
Oct	10.5	91.2	94.3	11.8
Nov	7.3	89.5	63.6	9.0
Dec	5.8	96.8	40.8	7.7
Year	9.7	901.3	1398.3	10.2

The highest temperature recorded was 28.8 degrees Centigrade on 29 June 1995. The lowest temperature recorded at that time was –5.4 deg. C on 30 December 1985. The wettest day recorded was 96 mm on 15 August 1970.

There has been a noticeable warming of air temperature during the period amounting to 0.1 deg. C per decade.

The seawater temperatures are those which would be experienced by a bather a few yards off the beach, and were taken from the Horse Rock.

Postscript – it may be worth adding to the above analysis, a flavour of the impact of the great blizzard of early 1963, which many will still recall. The *County Down Spectator* recorded

'a scarcity of bread and milk. Worst hit were the households with young children but the generosity of neighbours alleviated the position in many cases…Many households were left without light or heat… For practically all Wednesday, telephone communications were cut…residents also had to suffer the inconvenience of having their water supply affected – the pumps at Whitespots were unable to operate…Conditions were so bad at one time that Council workmen were nearly lost, so deep were the drifts they had to negotiate in trying to restore supplies.'

The snows of December 2010, which still sufficed to maroon Helen's Bay for a day or two for most vehicles, were a mere bagatelle in comparison.

Bibliography and Further Reading

- Evans EE *Prehistoric and Early Christian Ireland*, Batsford, 1966
- Hanna WA *Celtic Migrations*, Pretani Press 1985
- Hannan RJ & Hughes AJ *Place-Names of Northern Ireland vol. 2, The Ards)* The Institute of Irish Studies, Queens University of Belfast 1992
- Herity M & Eogan G *Ireland, in Prehistory* Routledge & Kegan Paul 1977
- Macalister RAS, *Ancient Ireland* Methuen 1935
- Mark Thompson and William Roulston, *Ulster-Scots Biographies: The Ards and North Down,*
- Kenneth Robinson, *North Down and Ards in 1798*
- Angelique Day and Patrick McWilliams, *Ordnance Survey Memoirs of Ireland, Parishes of County Down II*, The Institute of Irish Studies, Queen's University Belfast, 1991
- Con Auld, *Holywood, Then and Now*, 2002
- Harold Nicolson, *Helen's Tower*, 1937
- Margaret AK Garner, *North Down as displayed in the Clanbrassil Lease and Rent Book*
- DB McNeill, *Irish Sea Passenger Steamship Services, Volume 1*, 1969
- Edward Patterson, *The Belfast and County Down Railway*, 1978
- William Seyers, *Reminiscences of Old Bangor*
- CEB Brett, *Buildings of North County Down*, 2002
- Margaret AK Garner, *A History of Helen's Bay Presbyterian Church 1896–1958*
- Margaret AK Garner, *A History of the Parish of St John's Helen's Bay*
- Dr John W McConaghy, Mrs Eleanor M McConaghy, *A Light For The Road; Ballygilbert Presbyterian Church, 1841-1991*
- Mr Alex Boal, Miss Mollie Miscampbell, Mrs Doreen Gilmore and The Very Rev Professor Finlay Holmes, *Helen's Bay Presbyterian Church 1895–1997*
- *A Guide to Grey Point Booklet*, Environment and Heritage Service
- Charles Milligan, *My Bangor from the 1890s*
- Bill Clements, *Defending the North, The Fortifications of Ulster 1796-1956*; published by Colourpoint in 2003
- *Rockport School 1906-1986*
- *Crawfordsburn Country Club Diamond Anniversary, 1937 – 1997*
- Bill Clark, Editor, *Helen's Bay Golf Club, The First Century*
- Frederick E Harte, *The Road I have Travelled*
- WH Phillips and Robert Lloyd Praeger, *The Ferns of Ulster, Proceedings of the Belfast Naturalists Field Club, volume 2, appendix 1, 1887*
- Stewart and Corry's *Flora of the North-East of Ireland*, third edition, edited by Paul Hackney, Queen's University of Belfast, 1992

Above right: Margaret Garner outside Old Mill House, 1960.

Acknowledgements

Grateful thanks are acknowledged to all of the following, who have helped so much in a variety of ways, especially through sharing their memories and also in many cases illustrative material:

Colleagues in the Bayburn Historical Society, in particular Councillor Marion Smith, Barry Spence, Pat and George Henderson, Lesley and Johnny Dowds, and Carol Dickinson.

The Marchioness of Dufferin and Ava for her support, including the use of photographs by kind permission of the Dufferin and Ava archive.

Ian Wilson, (former Curator) and Leanne Briggs and colleagues at the North Down Museum.

The Linen Hall Library

National Museums Northern Ireland

The National Trust, Castleward

The Deputy Keeper of the Records, the Public Record Office of Northern Ireland.

The Northern Ireland Environment Agency

Mike Rendle, without whose patient expertise in collating the illustrations this book would not have been possible.

Peter Stark, both for his expertise on the Sharman Crawford family and for his professional advice.

Brian McCourt, for his exemplary assistance in all aspects of design.

Joan Bushell, for her comprehensive knowledge of Helen's Bay, and
Emma Graham for her particular guidance on Crawfordsburn.

Evelyn Aickin
Lola Armstrong
Philip Armstrong
Jane Badcock
Alfie Beaney
Adam Bell
Jean Blair
Heather Boyd
Sam and Angeline Bradley
Paddy Buckler
Lionel Carew
Tom Cave
Anne Cheatley
Lyn Cheatley-Robbins
Bill Clark
Peter and Pauline Clarke
John Cochrane
Alan Cook
Jennifer Corbett
Colonel Bertram and Toni Cotton
Susie Cunningham
Grace Darling

Ashley Davis
Osmond and Ellen Dixon
James Douglas
Nikko Duffin
Trevor Edwards
Dennis and Jo Farrell
Peter and Andy Galbraith
Ignatius Geddis
James Getty
Gary Gillespie
Pam Gilmer
Gary Graham
Iris Graham
Kerry and Anna Greeves
Gertie Gribben
Clive Henderson
Belinda Hill
Fred Hoare
Jim Holden
Ruth Houston
David and Ann Irwin
Denis Jess
Mabel Jess
Gill Johnston
Nigel Kelso
Brian Kennedy
Edythe Kennedy
Rev Canon Tim Kinahan
Allenby and Olive Leech
Derek Lindsay
Maurice Lindsay
Betty Lowry
John Lyons
Ann McCabe

151

Jean McCadden
Betty McCartney
Carol McCartney
Jim McClements
Margot McClements
Helen McCormick
Linda and John McCormick
Joe and John McEwen
Chris McFerran
Etta McGucken
Lawrence McKeag
Terence McKeag
Roy McKinty
Richard McMinn
Alfie Mairs
Lily and Colin Mairs
Jean and Leslie Mann
Alfie Martin
Rosemary and Anna Masefield
Rev Colin Megaw
Billy Mercer
John Murphy
Michael Murray
Jeanette Neary
Pat Nickels
Jim Page
Rev Roy Patton
Wendy and Kevin Quinn
Garvan Rice
John Rice
Doreen Ricketts
John Ritchie
John Shaw Brown III

Anthony Shillingford
Patricia Skelly
Joyce Smiley
Bertie and Jean Spence
Mary and Bill Strahan
Phyllis Strawbridge
Don Sykes
Meredith Thompson
Shaun Welles
Patrick and Terry Wells
Campbell White
Helen White

North Down Borough Council Mayor, James McKerrow

Sammy Baird, ex-Royal Engineers, Guide at Grey Point Fort

The Belfast Natural History and Philosophical Society

Charles Hurst Limited

Melanie Truss, Royal British Legion, Bennet House, Portrush

Hugh Forrester, Curator of the RUC Museum

Denis Mayne

The National Archive of the United States

Thanks are due also to many others, not individually recorded here, who have opened doors and provided guidance, encouragement and sustenance, and without whose help the project would never have been completed.